Scientific Realism
in Studies of Reading

Scientific Realism in Studies of Reading

Edited by

**Alan D. Flurkey • Eric J. Paulson
Kenneth S. Goodman**

Lawrence Erlbaum Associates
Taylor & Francis Group

New York   London

Figure 5.1 from *I Saw a Dinosaur*, written by Joy Cowley and illustrated by Philip Webb, Rigby Literacy, 2000, is reprinted with permission.

Lawrence Erlbaum Associates
Taylor & Francis Group
270 Madison Avenue
New York, NY 10016

Lawrence Erlbaum Associates
Taylor & Francis Group
2 Park Square
Milton Park, Abingdon
Oxon OX14 4RN

© 2008 by Taylor & Francis Group, LLC
Lawrence Erlbaum Associates is an imprint of Taylor & Francis Group, an Informa business

Printed in the United States of America on acid-free paper
10 9 8 7 6 5 4 3 2 1

International Standard Book Number-13: 978-0-8058-4990-5 (Softcover) 978-0-8058-4989-9 (Hardcover)

Library of Congress Cataloging-in-Publication Data

Scientific realism in studies of reading / editors Alan D. Flurkey, Eric J. Paulson, Kenneth S. Goodman.
    p. cm.
Includes bibliographical references and index.
ISBN-13: 978-0-8058-4989-9 (alk. paper)
ISBN-10: 0-8058-4989-0 (alk. paper)
ISBN-13: 978-0-8058-4990-5 (alk. paper)
ISBN-10: 0-8058-4990-4 (alk. paper)
    1. Reading. 2. Miscue analysis. I. Flurkey, Alan D., 1955- II. Paulson, Eric J. III. Goodman, Kenneth S.

LB1050.S367 2008
372.21'8--dc22   2007015027

Visit the Taylor & Francis Web site at
http://www.taylorandfrancis.com

and the LEA and Routledge Web site at
http://www.routledge.com

CONTENTS

Section Six ∾ STUDIES OF READING THAT
RECONCEPTUALIZE "ERRORS" AND "FLUENCY"

FOREWORD
Border Crossings: The Theoretical and Conceptual Frameworks of Scientific Realism

*I*F YOU ASKED ME TO NAME the reading theoretician who has had the most influence in the 20th century and whose influence will last long into the 21st, then without a moment of hesitation I would say Ken Goodman. I would then tell you that Ken Goodman is a remarkable scientist, realist, and humanist. I would add that Ken's sense of the social, his understandings of the importance of community, and his support of young scholars is exemplary within the academy and within public schools. If you asked me to name some of the young scholars who Ken has mentored who have themselves gone on to become major researchers and theoreticians in the field of literacy, then I would tell you that Alan Flurkey and Eric Paulson are at the top of the list. I would add that Alan Flurkey's research on flow is in itself revolutionary, that Eric Paulson has pioneered eye movement/miscue analysis, and then I would then tell you that many of those who are on that list are in *Scientific Realism in Studies of Reading* and would encourage you to read the book.

If you said to me that the research conducted by Ken Goodman and his colleagues has been rejected and that the pedagogical practices that have emerged from his work have been rejected, then I would again tell you to read *Scientific Realism in Studies of Reading*. I would encourage you to question what you have been told and what you have read in academic journals and in the popular media.

"We are at the most dangerous point in the history of American education," Ken Goodman says. "Teachers are being forced to teach absurd programs labeled as 'evidence-based,' schools are threatened with being closed down, and thousands of kids are being pushed out of schools." (Scholar's Forum: Language, Literacy, Politics and Public Education. Hofstra University, Hempstead, NY. November 2001)

Ask the questions behind the questions, I would urge. Do not reject unpopular ideas unless you have a clear understanding of why they are unpopular. In my own work, I am continuously engaged in such contemplation; in the car, on a plane, at the grocery store I play with the social and the scientific, and in the next couple of paragraphs I share some of that thinking to make visible why I am so enthusiastic about this book and why I think those in the field of literacy should read it, discuss it, and use it to inform their own research and pedagogical practices. What follows is my take on "science."

In social, medical, and physical sciences, there are complementary and contradictory interpretations of human life, behavior, language, and thought. Scientists work within frameworks of different laws that have different principles, and often their scientific explanations exclude other interpretations. There are turf battles and paradigm wars. Within the field of literacy research, ethnographic interpretations often do not include detailed and systematic analysis of language processes, and language process explanations often exclude the ethnographic, while the cognitive research of mainstream behavioral science is stuck within Cartesian ways of thinking that exclude just about everything that does not fit within their own narrow, distorted definitions of science.

Often, the dominant or "received" paradigm is accepted without question. Researchers stick within their own theoretical frameworks, talk to each other, write for each other, and reject any ideas that do not adhere to the conceptual frameworks that they have developed for scientific study. Rarely are there border crossings; psychologists who study informational processing approaches to cognition do not include social explanations of the cognitive and more often than not do not consider linguistic appreciations of the phenomenon under study. In my own lifetime as a teacher and researcher, I have made many border crossings, beginning with the study of human behavior, early childhood education, and art, next the psychology of reading, followed by an interdisciplinary doctoral degree that engaged me in anthropological and sociological research. Later, I added the study of socio- and psycholinguistics, and most recently my theoretical studies have focused on the psychiatric and psychoanalytic, especially in relationship to language, literacy, and trauma.

If you were now to ask me what scientific idea I think is most destructive, then I would say the idea that in science we have to test to explain is hugely problematic. This narrow view of what counts as science is particularly destructive because the results of the tests are so often presented as "facts," that over time the facts become accepted as universal truths, and that grand theories are then constructed that nobody questions. Based on my own research and continual border crossings, I consider the idea that you have to test to explain to be unacceptable, and that the contention that research is only reliable if it is replicable to be nonsensical.

The double whammy within the field of reading is that not only is the underlying principle of reliable and replicable fundamentally flawed, but also the problem is compounded by the loose and sloppy way in which reading experimentalists interpret "the scientific method" within their own paradigm. Much of the research that is conducted and used as the basis for educational policy and enforced in classroom practice does not adhere to the tight parameters of what counts as "experimental" within the confines of Cartesian science. In my own work as a social scientist and social activist, I subscribe to no grand theories that seem so often to lead to great catastrophes, such as No Child Left Behind (NCLB) at the present time. NCLB is a social disaster that will affect the lives of children for an entire generation.

It is important to note here that this strong criticism of the interpretations of *the* scientific method does not mean that I regard all experimental research to be fundamentally flawed, and I do not consider ethnographic approaches to observation, documentation, and explanation to hold a unique position or the high ground. If you asked me how you should proceed given such fragmentation of ideas and the inherent complexities of doing and interpreting science, then I would respond that it is absolutely essential that each study is considered on its own merit, within the requirements of the paradigm in which the research is conducted, and that it should then be critiqued within the larger frameworks of science. If we take such a position, then the usefulness of the ideas in advancing our understandings of the phenomena can be weighed against the drawbacks of the conceptual framework that has been used in the research. This is what I am attempting to do in my own research. By using both complementary and contradictory paradigms to inform my thinking, as I focus on complexity and fragmentation, I begin with the social and use literacy as an organizing principle and try to be aware at all times that if I had begun with literacy and used the social as an organizing principle, then I would develop very different interpretations, some complementary, some contradictory, but useful all the same.

It is through these "eyes," these positionalities, sensibilities, and dispositions, that I have read the research studies in *Scientific Realism in Studies of Reading*, and I regard it as one of the most important collections of reading research studies that have been published. The research of Ken Goodman and his colleagues disrupts our thinking about reading, about pedagogy, and about science. When the studies are combined and viewed within the theoretical and conceptual frameworks of scientific realism, which can be traced back to the biological and physical sciences, the research studies presented here are seismic in their capacity to shake the foundations of the dominant theories of reading research.

I have heard it said that the visionaries are the true realists. Ken Goodman's research is not only visionary but also scientific. In the late 1960s, his research began with observations of children reading real texts. He developed disciplined and systematic ways of documenting their readings, and then he constructed explanations of the reading process based on his observations and documentation. He then invited others to participate in the research. Yetta Goodman, of course, participated from the very beginning. Alan Flurkey has been engaged in miscue research since the late 1980s, Eric Paulson since the 1990s. Peter Fries is a second-generation collaborator in Ken's research on the reading process; his father, linguist Charles Fries, had a major influence on Ken's early research. Andrea García Obregón, Peter Duckett, Ann Freeman, Jassem Mohammad Al-Fahid, Shaomei Wang, Koomi Kim, Jingguo Xu, and Fredrick Gollasch, who also have a long history of collaboration, all expand on the research and ask the questions behind the questions. They push our understandings of the phenomenon we call reading beyond the accepted and the taken-for-granted views that we might have.

The many research collaborations of Ken Goodman that have taken place in the last 50 years have resulted in the largest body of scientific studies on the reading process that are currently in existence. Perhaps what is most remarkable is that not only the research papers but also all the documentation are readily available for review, including the audio recordings of children reading, on which many of the research studies are based. Thus, it is possible for researchers to continue to reanalyze and reconceptualize, from multiple perspectives, both qualitative and quantitative, and to construct new and alternative interpretations and explanations of the research. In *Scientific Realism in Studies of Reading*, there are research studies in multiple languages using multiple writing systems as the researchers make many border crossings—conceptual, theoretical, cultural, social and linguistic. Ken Goodman, who has spent his life making border crossings, both metaphoric and literal, has made an inestimable contribution to our understandings of the reading process and of science.

Denny Taylor

PREFACE

Facts are stubborn things; and whatever may be our wishes, our inclinations, or the dictates of our passions, they cannot alter the state of facts and evidence.

John Adams (1735–1826)

We must have strong minds, ready to accept facts as they are.

Harry S. Truman (1884–1972)

*A*LTHOUGH JOHN ADAMS AND Harry Truman were not referring to reading models in these quotations, their sentiments concerning facts go to the heart of what this book is about. *Scientific Realism in Studies of Reading* is concerned with how facts are discovered, developed, and used in the construction of knowledge about reading—a data-driven and theory-driven construction that results from observing the reading process with a variety of tools, methods, disciplines, and conceptual frameworks. And, observation is, of course, the cornerstone of scientific inquiry. This principle has wide-ranging implications. If we observe a phenomenon during reading, then we must respond to it in terms of how it might inform or contradict a model of the reading process. We are not free to ignore an observation if it provides evidence that contradicts our understanding of how reading works. For example, if miscues occur during reading, such an observation should inform our model of reading. The model must be constructed in a way that explains the production of miscues. Likewise, if eye movement analysis demonstrates that readers never look at every word in a text, then that observation should also inform, and should be explained by, our reading model. The challenge we face as reading researchers is to consider and interpret facts when we find them—and work toward assimilating them into a model of reading or accommodating the model to be consistent with the facts—so that our understanding of the reading process reflects how reading does work instead of merely how we think it should work. In this way, observations and theoretical explanations continually inform one another as our understanding of a phenomenon continues to be refined.

How This Book Is Organized

The twelve chapters in this book are grouped into five different sections or conceptual areas: The Study of Reading: From Data to Theory; Sociolinguistic and Systemic Functional Linguistic Studies of Reading; Studies of Beginning Reading; Studies of Reading in Nonalphabetic, Orthographies; and Studies of Reading That Reconceptualize "Errors" and "Fluency." This organizational scheme is not meant to draw boundaries that would separate the contents in each section; rather, it is simply one way to view key approaches, content, or perspectives of the chapters. Because the links and interconnections between chapters—both within and between conceptual areas—are extensive, one should view these groupings as merely one of many ways to organize the information in this book. The following outlines the progression of the book through each conceptual area.

Part I: The Study of Reading: From Data to Theory

This first conceptual area includes two chapters, Miscue Analysis as Scientific Realism by Kenneth S. Goodman and Re-reading Eye-Movement Research: Support for Transactional Models of Reading by Eric J. Paulson and Kenneth S. Goodman. The first frames the volume with an explanation of scientific realism and sets the stage for the book itself; the second chapter in this area serves as an exemplar of a scientific realism approach to understanding data en route to constructing a reality-based understanding of what eye-movement data reveal about reading processes.

Part II: Sociolinguistic and Systemic Functional Linguistic Studies of Reading

This conceptual area consists of two chapters that approach literacy research from novel directions. In chapter 3, Words, Context, and Meaning in Reading, author Peter H. Fries uses corpus linguistics to investigate whether a word-centered or a meaning-centered view of literacy more accurately represents the reality of written texts. Andrea García Obregón, in the chapter Reimagining Literacy Competence: A Sociopsycholinguistic View of Reading in Aphasia, explores a sociolinguistic model of reading through the lens of an aphasic reader.

Part III: Studies of Beginning Reading

This conceptual area includes two chapters that focus on beginning reading and use eye movement/miscue analysis as the research tool. Seeing the Story for the Words: The Eye Movements of Beginning Readers, by Peter Duckett, examines the relationship between illustrations and text in beginning reading. Ann Ebe, in What Eye Movement and Miscue Analysis Reveals About the Reading Process of Young Bilinguals, looks at the reading processes of fourth-grade Spanish-English bilingual readers.

Part IV: Studies of Reading in Nonalphabetic Orthographies

This conceptual area includes four chapters that focus on reading processes with texts written in a syllabic or ideographic orthography. Chapter 7, The Reading Process in Arabic: Making Sense of Arabic Print by Jassem Mohammad Al-Fahid and Kenneth S. Goodman, reports the results of a research project that used an experimental paradigm to investigate Arabic reading. The next chapter, Ideographic Orthography: A Linguistic Description of Written Chinese and Its Cueing Systems by Shaomei Wang and Yetta Goodman, provides a foundation for understanding and investigating reading processes in Chinese. Koomi Kim, Yetta Goodman, Jingguo Xu, and Frederick Gollasch authored the chapter Chinese and English Readings of Embedded Anomalies in Written Texts, which explores the results of experiments with Chinese and English texts with embedded errors. The final chapter in this conceptual area is Making Sense of Written Chinese: A Study of L2 Chinese Readers' Miscues, by Shaomei Wang and Yetta Goodman; it explores native English speakers' miscues while reading in Chinese.

Part V: Studies of Reading That Reconceptualize "Errors" and "Fluency"

In this final conceptual area, two chapters are presented that provide new ways to view some classic issues in literacy. Miscues and Eye Movements: Functions of Comprehension, by Eric J. Paulson, uses eye movement/miscue analysis to examine what actually happens when readers make an oral reading miscue. In Reading Flow, Alan D. Flurkey approaches the concept of fluency in oral reading from a perspective that offers new breadth and depth to our understandings of how readers read.

Final Thoughts

Readers who are familiar with current controversies connected with research in the field of reading will be familiar with the distillation of reading research studies that claim to be evidence based and scientifically reliable and replicable. An important example given much prestige because it was federally funded and controlled was the *Report of the National Reading*

Panel, in which the National Institute of Child Health and Human Development (2000) brought together a carefully chosen panel and instructed them to look only at experimental or quasi-experimental research that met narrow criteria. They could only include studies that were hypothecated studies of reading instruction, that had control groups, that were published in peer-reviewed journals in English, and that dealt with predetermined topics. No studies of the reading process or of reading development were included, and there was no requirement that studies relate their findings to a theory of the reading process. The panel members included a narrow spectrum of reading researchers with a common, though largely unexamined, view of reading and what constitutes scientific evidence. It is not surprising that the small number of included studies are consistent with each other and the principles of the view of reading that informs and guides them. But, the research findings that are offered in the panel report are based on a narrow definition of *scientific research*, in terms of both scope of content and methodology, even excluding a wide range of experimental research. This narrowness causes some facts to be ignored, devalued, or misunderstood, facts that—as we pointed out in the beginning of this preface—need to inform and be informed by an examined and defensible model of reading.

The studies reported in this book also share a common paradigm, but it is an examined one that has been built utilizing the principles of scientific realism. Each of the studies are informed by and inform this evolving theoretical framework as it has been applied to the study of reading. The theoretical framework is a transactional sociopsycholinguistic model of the reading process described in "Reading, Writing, and Written Texts: A Transactional Sociopsycholinguistic View" (Goodman, 2003). These studies, underpinned by this common theoretical foundation, are drawn from such diverse fields as psycholinguistics, sociolinguistics, systemic functional linguistics, and anthropology and use methodologies that range from experimentation, to miscue analysis, to ethnography and include some wholly new methodologies, such as eye movement miscue analysis and the study of reading flow.

The principle of Occam's razor suggests that the most elegant and parsimonious explanations turn out to be the best descriptions of observations of reality. Scientific realism in the study of reading—an approach to inquiry that incorporates and values a wide variety of methods of observation—seeks to do just that: to find the most inclusive, ecologically valid description of the reading process as it is observed in a variety of contexts from a wide range of perspectives. It is our belief that this selection of theoretically congruent, yet widely diverse set of studies makes definitive progress toward this goal. It moves beyond simplistic highly constrained cause-effect research to research that provides an explanation of the nature of the reality of reading.

References

Goodman, K. (2003). Reading, writing, and written texts: A transactional sociopsycholinguistic view. In A. Flurkey & J. Xu (Eds.), *On the revolution of reading: The selected writings of Kenneth S. Goodman.* (pp. 3–45). Portsmouth, NH: Heinemann.

National Institute of Child Health and Human Development, NIH, DHHS. (2000). *Report of the National Reading Panel: Teaching children to read* (00-4769). Washington, DC: U.S. Government Printing Office.

Alan D. Flurkey

Eric J. Paulson

Kenneth S. Goodman

Section One

THE STUDY OF READING
From Data To Theory

INTRODUCTION TO CHAPTER 1

S EVERAL EXPERIENCES I HAD, up to and including my experiences as a doctoral student, laid the foundation for the research I would later call miscue analysis. I suspect there are few examples, if any, of a scientist who first adopted a philosophy of science and then carefully laid out a line of research based consistently on that philosophy. Rather, I think, researchers are socialized into a research community and in the process inducted into its research methodologies, its criteria for formulating research questions, and its view of what constitutes evidence. Gradually, they accommodate themselves to the philosophy that underlies all these. This is not different from other pursuits. Artists are socialized into a community of artists, and their paintings have much in common with that community while differing markedly from those of other communities. Breaking from the norms of that community is risky, as the impressionists learned; their paintings are still not found in the Louvre.

Researchers learn to do research that will be acceptable to a particular research community. Their view of research is shaped by the rewards the research community gives to those who do "good" (that is acceptable within the paradigm) research. Those rewards are degrees, jobs, funding, and acceptance for publication and presentations. Only much later, if at all, do these researchers consider the view of truth, reality, values, knowing, goals, and other philosophical concerns to which they have committed themselves.

In one sense, I am not different. I am only now realizing that there is a name for the philosophy of science that underlies my research: scientific realism. What is different for me is that I did not reach this point by joining a community of researchers doing research based on scientific realism. I was not socialized into my research paradigm, my scientific philosophy. I got to this point by some experiences that caused me to reject the research community dominating the study of reading in the time period I began my research. Perhaps one could argue that what shaped my research paradigm was my awareness that I could not accept the conditions that joining the dominant paradigm would have imposed on me.

In retrospect, I believe that these are the experiences that contributed to my decision not to join the dominant research community and instead to move in my own direction.

1. Born in 1927, I was a child of the Depression, aware at an early age of class and ethnic differences. Even in high school, I was already involved in radical political activities. My personal experiences with anti-Semitism led me to have concern for racism and elitism. I picketed restaurants that refused to serve minorities and the baseball stadium in Detroit because the Tigers had no black players. In college, I joined groups who shared my progressive beliefs; read widely in political, historical, and social literature; and built a personal philosophy of concern for civil rights, social justice, and antifascism. My decision to become a teacher grew out of my growing concern for social justice for the poor and oppressed minorities. I wanted to do something "socially significant."

2. In my teacher education program, I found progressive education fitted well with the strong value system and personal philosophy I had built. That led me to strive to conduct myself as a teacher in a manner consistent with a growing professional and personal philosophy rooted in another era just ending as I became a teacher in 1949. At first, progressive education was an abstract and attractive humanistic and learner-centered pedagogy, but it was actually through my teaching, although I was unaware at the time, that I had actually socialized myself into a community of social realists who I had read and who had left their marks on the California schools where I began my teaching. As a teacher, I tested my beliefs against the reality of real learners in a real classroom. Although success was not instantaneous, and the eighth-grade adolescents I taught tested me, teaching convinced me that my progressive beliefs were sound and framed the only way that I could teach while remaining honest with myself and my pupils. I needed to start where my students were, understand where they came from and where they were going, respect the students as learners, and accept the experiences, language, and culture the students brought to their schooling. As a teacher, I would later discover, I acted as a social reconstructionist—not only preparing my pupils for the world around them but also helping them to become able to improve that world.

3. I found I had personal and professional values that caused me to reject the view of research that was the focus of some graduate courses in my doctoral program. I rejected the behaviorism that dominated the educational psychology courses I started and dropped. I came to realize that I had a strong social view of reality and how we come to know it. I could not accept the narrow deterministic, deficit view

of human learning that I found pervading research on learning, particularly the learning of reading and writing.

4. I participated as a research assistant in experiments in programmed learning. Rather than inducting me into the paradigm, this research caused me to reject the premises, design, and conclusions of the research and strengthened my need to search for alternatives.

5. My graduate courses helped me realize I had a consistent educational philosophy, and they helped me understand why I could not accept, as a researcher, views that were inconsistent with my views as an educator. My desire to do research came not from some abstract search for truth or need to be accepted into a dominant paradigm but from a pragmatic desire to provide teachers with useful answers to their questions and understanding that would make them more effective teachers of literacy.

6. Just as I was finishing my doctoral program in the early 1960s, a bitter controversy was erupting in the field of language arts and English education. Linguists were questioning the value and validity of traditional school grammar. They were questioning the prescriptive view of language and calling for the use of a more descriptive approach, and English educators were calling for more focus on the functional use of language rather than teaching rules that were under questioning by contemporary grammarians.

As I read the linguists, I found a body of knowledge and a methodology for the study of language that I could use in the study of reading. Further, I had a way of dealing with language as a dynamic, living whole rather than the isolated bits and pieces with which the experimentalist researchers had concerned themselves. But, there was no community of researchers applying linguistics to the study of reading to which I could apprentice myself. In fact, my search of the professional literature revealed that there was little interest in the study of written language among linguists up to that time. Most of the linguists interested in teaching and learning had adopted a behaviorist language learning theory and focused primarily on teaching English as a second language.

So, I had to strike out on my own. I saw positive research alternatives in treating reading as language and using linguistic, psycholinguistic, and sociolinguistic concepts and methodology. That put me in a scary and lonely position and one fraught with academic danger because my research proposals, publications, and presentations usually violated the "standards" of the researchers who judged them. But, I also gained an advantage. Freed from the constraints of experimental, behavioristic research, I could ask broader and more basic questions that moved away from hypothecated cause-effect and correlational studies to a broad study of reading as it was happening. Instead of testing hypotheses, my research generated hypotheses. What I learned caught the imagination of the reading education community and of teachers sufficiently that I was able to get funding for my research and a forum in print and at conferences for my findings.

Furthermore, my research led me, I now perceive, into two major requirements of scientific realism:

1. The need to keep my study of reading in its real-world social context. I wanted to study real reading—not responses to letters, words, and short contrived sentences.
2. The need to develop a coherent theory of the reading process I was studying.

In studying real reading, my findings helped me to develop a theory, which in turn helped me to integrate my research methodology and better understand my findings.

Ken Goodman

1

MISCUE ANALYSIS AS SCIENTIFIC REALISM

Kenneth S. Goodman

There is no logical way to the discovery of these elemental laws. There is only the way of intuition, which is helped by a feeling for the order lying behind the appearance.

Albert Einstein

Scientific Realism: Studying Reality

I WILL START BY LAYING OUT the principles of scientific realism and then show how miscue analysis is an example of scientific realism. I am indebted to Ernest House's (1991) succinct summary of scientific realism for much of the information that follows.

In an old example, used in philosophy to differentiate idealism and realism, the question is asked, If a tree falls in the forest but no one was there to see or hear it, did anything really happen? From an idealist's view, all evidence is experiential; therefore, if there was no experience, then there was no event. We can only know the world through our senses and the ideas of the world our minds make of our sensory input. A realist would answer that events occur whether they are experienced or not. The world exists independent of our knowing it. The event of the tree falling is real. It follows that events have characteristics that go beyond anyone's experience with them, and they may **be** experienced differently by different people.

In philosophy, there are many variants within idealism and realism. Scientific realism shares the view that reality exists apart from the fact that it is known, but it is particularly concerned with the nature of that reality and how it can be known through scientific study. So, it offers a third answer to the question of trees falling: Events must be considered in relation to nonevents to understand reality. Why do some events occur while others do not in the same context and under similar conditions? In this case, when do trees stand, that is not fall, and under what conditions do they fall? A scientific realist does not just seek cause-effect relationships (What caused this tree to fall at this time?). The question is, What are the structures and processes in the underlying reality of trees standing and falling? Scientific realists have a view of reality that sees events and our experiences with them as part of a multilayered reality that we are striving to understand.

Let me move this discussion out of the philosophy class and into the real world. Many years ago, my wife, Yetta Goodman, and I took a group of young teens on a camping trip in Kings Canyon National Park in California. One morning, some of the kids told me that a very tall, very large incense cedar tree near our campsite was creaking. They took me to the tree, and I verified that this massive tree was making creaking noises as it swayed in the wind.

Not knowing much about when such trees continue to stand and when they fall, I felt obligated to report the event. So, I went with the kids to the park ranger station. To my embarrassment, the young ranger snickered and said, "That tree's been there for 200 years, and it's likely to be there another hundred years from now." Feeling diminished in the eyes of my young charges, I returned to our campsite.

Half an hour later, a park truck pulled up near the tree, and half a dozen park rangers got out, led by one who looked older and wiser than the one to whom I had reported the tree.

"Is there a problem with the tree?" I asked the senior ranger.

"Maybe, maybe not," he said. "Chances are it could stay here another hundred years. Then again, it might fall down in the next stiff wind. We're going to bring it down." And they did, so deftly that it did not take down a single sapling as it fell.

The difference between my real-world cedar in a crowded public campground and a hypothetical tree falling in a hypothetical place so remote no one knows or cares whether it stands, falls, or even exists, points up the scientific realist's view that events take place in an exceedingly complex world. They are constrained by many forces, processes, and structures at the same time. Only in the unreal world of the laboratory experiment can we come close to finding reliable, replicable events in which single causes have single effects. In the real world, with a lot of knowledge of the complex circumstances under which standing trees fall we may be able to develop a theory of falling trees. We may interpret the creaking of the tree within such a theory and relate that to multiple causes of trees falling and standing. But, it is much more difficult to be sure that a particular tree will fall at a precise moment or as the result of a single causative event. Conditions leading toward falling could be counterinfluenced by other forces acting on the tree.

Table 1.1 Studying Reality

	Real	Actual	Empirical
Structures and processes	X		
Events	X	X	
Experiences	X	X	X

Note: From Bhaskar, R. (1978, p.13) cited in E. House, *Educational Researcher,* August–September 1991.

Scientific realists dig deeply beneath events to the underlying reality to understand the structure and processes that influence and determine the events. So, the purpose of scientific research is not to find replicable cause-effect relationships under highly constrained laboratory conditions but to investigate reality sufficiently well that it may be explained and understood. Science has learned a lot about the structures and processes that produce earthquakes or volcanic eruptions, and they can observe with scientific instruments the events that are commonly associated with them so that the public may be warned of possible occurrences, but no theory yet exists for predicting such an event at a precise time before it takes place.

Through miscue analysis, I have been able to build a theory of which factors are involved in miscues that occur during the reader's transaction with a written text. I can explain why 17 of 32 readers would produce the same or similar miscues at the same point in the reading of the text or why a single reader produces a pattern of related miscues across the reading of a text. My theory cannot predict that any given reader will produce a particular miscue at a particular point in the text.

Reading, my theory tells me, is a complex transaction between a reader and a text. Characteristics of the text and the reader are involved in miscues as the reading progresses, and they also influence what the reader comprehends from the text.

Table 1.1 shows a scientific realist's view of the nature of reality. Reality includes structures and processes that are necessary to but may or may not produce events that may or may not be experienced. All three are real: The underlying structures and processes exist whether they produce events or not. The events exist whether they are experienced or not. The experiences represent someone's processing of the events.

House argues the following:

> Equating what was experienced (the empirical) with actual events (the actual) with the real (the causal entities) led in the wrong direction. Things

> got turned around so that what was real was mistaken to be limited to only to what we directly experienced. Reality came to be defined as equivalent to the empirical—that is, what we experience—and anything beyond was discredited as metaphysics. This double error, of equating experience with events and events with reality must be corrected. (House, p. 4)

Although there is no experience without events, an experience of an event is not the event itself. What happened is always transformed by our experience with the event. In any case, knowing what happened does not mean that we have understood the nature of things involved in the event and the structures and processes involved in their interactions that must be understood to understand fully the reality that results in such events. The purpose of science, then, is not to seek cause-effect relationships but to build a theory of the nature of reality itself. Only then can we understand events and why they do and do not occur.

Before the time of Copernicus, and later Galileo, people experienced the event of the movement of sun, moon, and stars. What they thought they saw was based not only on the events of these movements that they observed but also on a common belief reinforced by law and religious doctrine that Earth was the center point of a system of heavenly bodies moving around it. When Copernicus and Galileo observed the same events, they concluded in their more scientific investigations that the Sun was the center of a system of planets, one of which was the Earth. That led them to offer a different theory of the reality of the universe than that commonly held. Of course, it led to many new questions about that reality that had not been considered before.

I will use miscue analysis now not only to illustrate the concepts of scientific realism but also to demonstrate why I believe miscue analysis is in fact an example of research employing scientific realism.

In deciding to study reading, I made an early decision to get as close to the reality of reading as I could. I was convinced that carefully contrived experiments that utilized isolated events created to reduce variables so that cause-effect relationships could be measured statistically had several faults:

1. The controlled events (e.g., learning words from several exposures, learning words in isolation or in short sentences, learning and applying phonics rules, etc.) were not the naturally occurring events that happened in the course of actual reading. (Here, I use *actual* not only as House does but also to apply to what happens in an act of reading — it is actual reality.)

2. Much experimental research in reading confused the reading process with learning and teaching reading. The National Reading

Panel directed by the U.S. Congress to study reading, for example, confined its scope to include only experimental studies of reading instruction.

3. A theory was lacking that was necessary for both the design of reading research and the interpretation of the findings. Much experimental research produced results that misrepresented the reality of reading.

To get as close as possible to natural reading, I should have studied silent reading, but silent reading does not provide easily observable events. I chose instead to use oral reading of the type of texts pupils might be asked to read during reading instruction. It became clear that this afforded me a rare opportunity in the study of language to go beyond events to get at the underlying structures and processes of reading. Comparing the oral reading with an expected "correct reading" provides a continuous series of events and nonevents.

I discovered early in the research that all readers, regardless of proficiency, produce miscues. A *miscue* is, by definition, an event in oral reading in which the observed response (OR) is unequal to the expected response (ER). My assumption in miscue analysis is that the structures and processes that produce ERs are the same as those that produce miscues, and that by comparing ER and OR I can build a theory of the process and understand how people make sense of written language. This knowledge could inform understanding of reading development.

I have put this into the diagram of scientific realism in Table 1.2. The reality that miscue analysis is seeking to understand is *reading*, which is itself the receptive aspect of written language, which is a parallel language system to oral language, and language is a major aspect of human communication. This definition of reading is a real-world view, not one tailored to fit a research paradigm. I once heard a computer scientist at the Massachusetts Institute of Technology in Cambridge say that computers can read—as long as you define reading as something computers can do.

The procedures of miscue analysis elicit oral literacy events. The components of these literacy events are the written texts and the transactions of the readers with those texts in acts of oral reading. In miscue analysis, there are also speech acts before and after the literacy events. There is conversation and an interview before the actual reading. During that interview, some demographic data are collected, instructions for the reading are given, the purpose of the reading is explained, readers are assured that the reading will not be graded or judged, and a rapport is established between reader and researcher. An oral language sample also results. Following the reading, the reader is asked to retell the story. Following

Table 1.2   Structures/Processes, Events, and Experiences

	Real	Actual	Empirical
Structures and processes	Language Human communication Written language Reading Real contexts in which events occur		
Events	Literacy events Written texts Transactions between readers and texts Oral reading of the texts Speech acts Transactions between readers and researchers Prereading interviews and instructions Retellings Unassisted and probed Other events	Tape recordings of the oral reading Oral miscues Omissions/insertions Substitutions/reversals Complex miscues Corrections/partials Retellings Responses to probes Behaviors and comments of readers during event	
Experiences	Taxonomy of oral reading miscues Theory and model of the reading process	Compilation of raw data Marked transcripts Computer coding sheets Text analyses Grammatical coding Statistical analysis of the data Qualitative analysis of the data	Findings and conclusions Interpretations of the analyses Applications to the theory and the taxonomy Hypotheses about the structures and processes

this retelling, the researcher asks open-ended questions to elicit a fuller representation of what the reader has understood from the reading. The researcher is careful to use the information from the free retelling and to supply only information provided by the reader. These speech acts are additional events available for analysis.

In addition, other events may occur during the research session, such as oral comments on the text, the illustrations, or the experience: "I think I'll skip that word," "That goat's not so fat," "Do you want me to read the next page?" "Can I read another story?" Bells or phones may ring, interruptions may occur, or the reader may do things physically, such as slouching, laying the head on the table, or holding the book at an odd angle.

The readers are told in advance that they are to do the best they can, and no help will be offered during the reading. Indeed, the reading is uninterrupted. and if the reader asks for help overtly or by beseeching looks, the researcher reminds the reader to do the best he or she can. If there are long pauses, then readers are encouraged just to keep reading.

These literacy events are as close to those occurring in self-initiated "real" reading as possible, but there some constraints from the research design:

- The reading is oral (not silent).
- The text is a complete one not written for instructional purposes, but it is usually selected by the researcher to be relevant to the reader but somewhat difficult. In some studies of adults, they have chosen their own texts to read.
- The researcher is present, the reading is tape recorded, and the researcher is marking a typescript of the text, noting miscues and other occurrences.

These are not part of usual literacy events, but they are necessary for the events to be studied.

In the column in Table 1.2 that deals with actual events, I list those aspects of the events that are the subject of analysis. Two things need to be understood about the selective attention to the events represented here. The first is that although the features of the events listed here are actual (naturally occurring in the events), any selection of features of the events to analyze is itself theory driven. In the course of many miscue studies, our definitions of miscues themselves became more sophisticated, so that we had a better idea of the nature of the events and which features of the events offered the richest insights for analysis. Second, constraints of the research questions could be broad, looking at as many aspects as possible or focused. In certain studies, for instance, we looked at specific types of miscues, such as omissions or miscues on pronouns or determiners. Our basic analysis produced a database of many readers reading many texts, which made it possible to "mine" the database by asking general or specific questions.

We learned early that we needed to create a high-quality tape recording of the oral reading, and that we could not rely solely on a typescript marked by a researcher during the reading. Too much was happening too fast to be sure our on-the-spot marking of the typescript was as complete a representation of the literacy event as possible.

Under experiences, I have separated how we experienced the events through the analysis of the reading into the three columns. The taxonomy of oral reading miscues and the theory and the model of the reading process are in the Real column because they represent our developing attempt to relate our interpreted data to the underlying process and structures of reading. These are thus both the product of the research and the guiding concepts that frame the research and the analysis of the data. In the Actual column, the experiences are the procedures that we used in the analysis, moving from raw quantitative miscue data (what happened when and how frequently) to qualitative analysis: How shall we organize the data in terms of their relationship to the theoretical frame? For example, we could count the number of self-corrections and express those as a percentage of miscues corrected. But, we also needed to know which types of miscues were and were not corrected. Furthermore, we needed to look at patterns within the entire reading of the story. If a reader had a number of omissions, then when did they occur? How did they affect the meaning and syntax? When were they corrected and when not?

Because the events in miscue analysis involve whole texts of several hundred words, they produced a wealth of data in which usual significance considerations are irrelevant because there are so many degrees of freedom.

Under the Empirical column, I put the findings and conclusion of the study, where we bring our experiences with the analyzed miscue data to produce findings and conclusions to bear on our underlying questions: How do people make sense of print? What are the underlying structures and processes of reading?

Let us put this now back into House's (1991) view of aspects of a realist's view of science and how miscue analysis is an exemplar.

The Task of Science Is to Invent Theory

It is not enough for science to describe some bit of reality. Science invents theories to explain the real world. Darwin, Newton, Galileo, and Einstein provided the theories that could explain the real world and provide the theoretical base for studying reality. I started my research looking at the reality of what readers do when they read. I used their oral reading to provide evidence of the underlying process they used. Immediately, I was launched into constructing a theory of the reading process.

Science Determines Structures and Processes to Explain How Entities Act, Which Is Always in Terms of Tendencies and Probabilities

In miscue analysis, I found a unique language case: I had the written text with which the reader was transacting as well as an audio recording of a continuous oral response to that text. In a single reading of a 10- to 12-page story, there might be 100 or more miscues of varying complexity. The patterns within the miscues provided ample and detailed evidence of the tendencies and probabilities in the reading process. These patterns were not simple correlations between a few measures. They provided many comparisons at many levels over many events, all related to the overall reader's objective of making sense of the text. Miscue analysis produces what ethnographers might call a *thick description* of the reading process.

The same database, using the miscues of several readers of a single text, could be used to study how the structures of texts influence readers' miscues. An example of such an analysis follows.

Events Are the Outcomes of Complex Causal Configurations That Sometimes Cancel Each Other Out

Figure 1.1 shows a view of miscues as a series of events in the reading of a text. I have taken one sentence out of the reading of *Little Brown Hen* by a fourth-grade African American 9-year-old in rural Mississippi. She made three miscues.

Event: Reader says Mr. where text says Mrs.
Event: Reader says his where text says the.
Event: Reader says $axt where text says asked.

The first miscue is her substitution of Mr. for Mrs. In miscue analysis, we look at three levels of texts: graphophonic, syntactic, and semantic. Mr.

```
Mr.                 his
Mrs. Johnson opened the screen door, smoothing

                                        $axt
her blue apron, "How are you? Willie" she asked.
```

Figure 1.1
Miscues as events: outcomes of causal configurations.

and Mrs. have letters in common. An unusual language convention has resulted in the written forms becoming an abbreviation of the oral forms, Mister and Missus, so they violate spelling conventions, but the two do have sounds in common. Both are titles of respect to be used in proper names of people, so they fit both the syntax of the sentence and the semantic requirement of using such a title before a last name. Furthermore, in the Southern community of this reader, Willie, a child character in the story, would be quite likely to use such a polite form in addressing an adult. Such social constraints are part of the pragmatics of language. To summarize, Mr. and Mrs. look similar, sound similar, share semantic features, and have the same syntactic function.

However, substituting Mr. for Mrs. does change the meaning of the text. Mr. Johnson has already appeared in the story, and Mrs. Johnson has not, so it is likely that the miscue is influenced by what the reader is expecting. That hunch is supported by the miscue that follows. Having read Mr. Johnson, the reader substitutes *his* for *the.* What the reader has done is to attribute the door to Mr. Johnson. This substitution of the possessive pronoun is a common miscue. In English, definite nouns require the determiner *the,* but possessives subsume that function. However, the shift to *his* creates an inconsistency because the possessive in the next noun phrase, *her blue apron,* is feminine. This is a point at which the reader might have corrected, but she did not, at least not overtly.

The final miscue, $axt for *asked,* is marked with a dollar sign, indicating we are spelling it the way the reader said it. This not really a miscue. She read the word *asked* the way she and other members of her dialect community say the word. Our research involved many groups of readers speaking different American dialects, with each showing their own dialect's phonology in their reading.

Several aspects of miscue analysis as scientific realism are illustrated in this short sequence. We start from the premise that the reader is transacting with the text. Miscues, like ERs, result from that transaction. Each miscue is not random but is the result of complex causal configurations in the text, in the reader, and in the transactions of the reader with the text. We cannot know exactly why a single miscue occurs, but we can consider the tendencies and probabilities that are revealed in the patterns of such miscues and come up with probable explanations for the miscues. At the same time, what we have learned from miscue analysis entitles us to reject alternative explanations: Any of these miscues are random or the result of careless reading, saying $axt for *asked* affects the comprehension of the story, and miscues indicate ineffective reading. All these miscues show a reader busily engaged in meaning construction.

Facts Are Theory Laden

It is a fact that readers make miscues as they read, but I chose to call these ORs in oral reading that differed from ERs, miscues based on my theoretical assumption that unexpected responses are produced through the same causal configurations as ERs, and that they therefore provide windows on the reading process. To the extent that the phenomena of mismatches in reading had been noted in earlier research, they were called *errors*, and treated as indications of reading problems. That is because, in the theory of the researchers, reading is a process of saying the words exactly as they appear on the page. Furthermore, because they were errors to be eliminated to be a successful reader (i.e., to read exactly what is on the page), they did not need to be explained. In many informal reading inventories, a passage is judged too difficult if there are more than 7 errors, and a regression to correct an error is counted as a second error. I chose the word *miscue* rather than error to better represent my theoretical understanding of this phenomenon. But, it is not just a matter of terminology. My facts and those with exact word theories are very different.

Knowledge Is a Social and Historical Product

The world exists independent of our knowing it, but our knowledge of the real world is constructed socially, and much of what we "know" is what our culture has constructed over its history. New knowledge is often in conflict with this conventional wisdom. Viewing a miscue as evidence of strength in making sense of texts and viewing reading as a process of meaning construction rather than word recognition violates conventional wisdom. In an era when the U.S. Congress passes laws requiring that reading instruction be "evidence based," differences over what constitutes scientific knowledge, evidence, become matters of great concern.

The Real World Is Complex and Stratified: Explorations at One Level Lead to Discovery of Deeper Levels to Be Explained

Michael Halliday (1985), the linguist, provided me with a stratified view of the reality of reading as a language system. His strata are the signal level, the lexico-grammar where wording and language structure come together, and the semantic, meaning level. I could look at miscues and their effect on texts in terms of these linguistic strata.

Furthermore, I could look at language units: phonemes, morphemes, words, phrases, clauses, sentences, and texts. In my early research, I thought I could assign miscues to single levels or at least a dominant cause for each miscue: This is a word substitution, that is a phoneme shift, this other results from dialect, and still another changes a whole phrase. I soon realized that each miscue involved all strata, and change at one level produced change at all levels.

Reading is language, and I needed a sophisticated language theory to deal with the complexity I was discovering in miscue patterns. I moved from the descriptive theory of C. C. Fries (1963) to the transformational-generative theories of Chomsky (1972) to get at the processes miscues revealed and then on to the functional-systemic theory to put miscues into text and social context. I moved from studying reading as a linguist to the stance of a psycholinguist, and finally I had a transactional sociopsycholinguistic theory. Gradually, it became clear to me that reading is a transaction between text and reader. Miscues involve as much what readers bring to the text as what the writer brought to it. Every reading is a complex literacy event, and each miscue reflects the complexities of the literacy event in which it occurs.

Beyond language theory, understanding reading involves theories of culture, human societies, and the place of written language in both.

How Different Readers Transact with the Same Text

In a major miscue study that contributed to our database (Goodman, 1978), we had analyzed the miscues of 4 readers in each of 8 language groups reading the same sixth-grade story ("My Brother Is a Genius," Betts & Welch, 1963). So, we had a total of 32 diverse sixth graders reading the one text. We used these data to look at the relative difficulty of each sentence in the text and explicitly where multiple miscues occurred at particular points in the text. This provided evidence of how the text itself entered into the readers' construction of meaning.

In the story, a boy is babysitting his baby brother, who begins to cry. The text reads as follows:

> "Go ahead and cry. Cry all you want to. It won't disturb me!" (Betts & Welch, 1963)

We assigned a difficulty score to each text word reflecting the quantity and quality of the miscues that occurred on it. We based our scoring on a rubric developed by Desmond Ryan (1985) in a study he did in Melbourne, Australia. The higher the score is, the more difficult the text is. I selected the following short, four-word sentence to illustrate how text features show structures and processes in reading.

6.82	1.89	1.78	0.40
It	won't	disturb	me!

It has a high score because 17 of the 32 readers substituted *I* for *It*. The group included readers from Hawaii to Maine. Just more than half of all the readers made this identical miscue. Fewer read *It* correctly than produced miscues here. One reader substituted *He* for *It*. Eight readers corrected their substitution, and 4 tried to correct but were unsuccessful. That is a very high rate of correction. Our theory helps us understand this event. *It* occurs many times in this story with few or no miscues, so there must be something about the text and the readers' expectations that produce this unusual event. *It* is used here as a pronoun, but it has no explicit antecedent. The reader must infer that the antecedent is implicit: the baby's crying.

There are 9 miscues on *won't*: don't (5), wasn't, wanted (2), what. Five of these are corrected, and 3 are unsuccessful corrections. Again, that is an unusually high rate of correction.

Although *disturb* would seem to be a difficult word, there are only 5 miscues on it. All 3 miscues on *me* are substitutions of *you*. One is corrected. The other 2 result in *"I won't disturb you,"* which fits the text meaning that the babysitter is going to let the baby brother cry.

The miscue patterns show how readers are transacting with the text in the miscues they produce and their ability to recover and correct as it is necessary to make sense. *It* is not a difficult word, and *I* occurs often in this first-person story. The readers showed a strong tendency to assume the subject of the sentence would be the first-person narrator *I* because the referent, crying, was not explicit. Most corrected or tried to correct. Two readers actually adjusted the text to read *"I won't disturb you"* and saw no reason to correct. Of course, the readers' prediction that the next sentence would begin with *I* was supported by the similar-looking *It*. The miscues on *won't* not only reflect grammar (with 5 as shifts to *don't*) but also show the influence of the orthography because all the words substituted have letter patterns in common with *won't*.

Even though the miscues on this sentence vary in quality, judged by the extent to which they disrupt meaning making, they all show readers actively constructing meaning using the three kinds of information available to them: signal, lexico-grammatical, and semantic. As well, they show how context is used in producing both successful and unsuccessful reading and in recovering when meaning is lost.

In this sentence, we have an example of how scientific realism can explain the multiple occurrences of the same or similar causal events and yet not predict what any given reader will do at any point in the text. There is a strong tendency among sixth-grade readers of this text to make these miscues, and that is how we can use these tendencies to build a theory to understand the structures and processes in the reality of reading.

Scientific Realism Produces a Cycle

Because a major product of research from the perspective of scientific realism is to produce an explanatory theory of the processes and structures of reality, there is a continuing cycle within such research. In the case of miscue analysis, we started with a research perspective: We would use the actual events of oral reading of real texts by real readers to develop a theory of the reading process. Our first analyses of oral reading miscues required us to develop a taxonomy to organize our data. That in turn led to a beginning theory that we used to refine the taxonomy to use in further miscue studies. With new data from analysis of other readings, we further improved the taxonomy and the analysis that resulted from its use and the theory we were building from the research. There is no end to this cycle because the more refined and useful our theory is in explaining our data, the more we see further layers of reality to be understood.

Experimental studies by contrast are self-limiting. The research starts with a hypothesis. The study is designed to test the hypothesis in controlled conditions so that a clear cause-effect relationship can be tested. The hypothesis itself is a statement of belief. It is based on what the researcher believes about the reality under study. Nothing new is learned unless the study does not support the hypothesis. The hypothesis itself is based in a microtheory of some small aspect of the reality assumed to be part of the whole, for example, word identification or response to a set of instructional materials.

On the other hand, because scientific realism produces increasingly productive theories, it can generate high-quality hypotheses for experimental research as well as illuminate the questions that need answers, which can best be studied in a variety of research methodologies. The chapters in this book show the results of research that is informed in strong theory. It includes some experimental studies that use hypotheses based in the theory. Other chapters test aspects of reading or reading in different languages and orthographies. They not only test the strength of the theory but also help in refining the theory. That is the essence of scientific realism.

References

Betts, E. & C. Welch (1963) "My Brother is a Genius". *Adventures now and then.* New York: American Book Co. pp. 246-256.

Bhaskar, R. (1978). *A realist theory of science.* Sussex: Harvester Press. p. 13.

Chomsky N. (1972). *Language and mind.* New York: Harcourt, Brace, Jovanovich.

Fries, C. (1963). *Linguistics and reading.* New York: Holt, Rinehart and Winston.

Goodman K. (1978). Reading of American children whose reading is a stable, rural dialect of English or language other than English, Grant No. NIE-C-00-3-0087, National Institute of Education, U.S. Department of Health Education and Welfare.

Halliday, M. (1985). *An introduction to functional grammar.* London: E. Arnold.

House, R. (1991). Realism in research. *Educational Researcher.* August–September 1991, pp. 2-9.

Ryan, D. (1985). Personal communication.

INTRODUCTION TO CHAPTER 2

*F*OR MORE THAN A CENTURY, the study of eye movements has been of interest to researchers from various perspectives and fields of study. It is one of the earliest interests of reading researchers. But, like every kind of research, it is not simply that researchers know what they see. What the researchers see depends on what they know.

Research paradigms differ in major and minor ways and lead to different understandings of the phenomena under study. How eye-movement researchers design their research, what they treat as data, and how they interpret the data strongly depends on their beginning theory and stance. If the researchers believe that reading is a process of rapid sequential identification of words that are then understood, then they will design studies designed to show how the eye moves in the identification of words. Their data will focus on word identification, and they will interpret their data to support their theoretical perspective and reject alternate theories.

A common belief among researchers is that "facts" exist independent of paradigms. Scientific realists believe that all scientific facts are theory laden. That is, what you believe causes you to fit your observations into the examined or unexamined theory of the processes and structures you are studying.

Consider these facts from eye-movement research. The eye is an optical instrument that supplies the brain with visual sensory input. As such it has a lens that must focus—fixate—at a point in front of the eyes to provide clear input. The area of clear input around each fixation is limited. The eye moves at a variable rate from fixation to fixation. Early research showed that the brain receives no useful visual input while the eye is moving.

To support word-centered theories, it would be necessary for the eye to move from word to word with areas of sharp focus on each word. Fixations would need to be relatively consistent in duration. But, from the earliest eye-movement research, it has been shown that the eye only focuses on about 70% of the words. The points where it fixates seem to involve predictions the reader is making because function words are much less likely to be fixated than content words, even short content words.

If reading is considered to be a process of meaning construction rather than a process of word identification, then the question becomes not how the eyes move as words are identified but how the brain uses visual input in the construction of meaning. As Paulson and Goodman show, the eye-movement research is much more consistent with a view of reading as construction of meaning than it is with a view of reading as rapid accurate word identification. Particularly important is the distinction that eye-tracking studies have shown between vision and perception. The brain uses the eye to provide visual input, but it forms perceptions on the basis of what it expects given the experiential and linguistic knowledge it draws on during reading. The facts of eye movements actually support a theory of reading developed through the study of reading miscues and make it possible to refine the understanding the theory provides of the relationships between vision and perception in the construction of meaning during reading.

As Paulson and Goodman point out, ultimately the problem is not with the research but with the interpretations by third parties of the findings of the research. What eye-movement researchers report is much different from the conclusions drawn by others seeking to support a word recognition view of reading and reject a meaning construction view. In this chapter, Paulson and Goodman look at the findings and conclusions of original eye-movement research reports and demonstrate that eye-movement research actually supports a meaning construction view of reading processes.

Ken Goodman

2

RE-READING EYE-MOVEMENT RESEARCH
Support for Transactional Models of Reading

Eric J. Paulson and Kenneth S. Goodman

Eye-Movement Research

*I*T WAS MORE THAN a century ago when Emile Javal discovered that our eyes do not flow smoothly across a line of print but instead make a series of pauses called *fixations* and when psychologist Raymond Dodge invented a technique that could record those fixations. Soon after that, the implications of eye-movement data for reading research were seen as highly significant to understanding reading (Huey, 1908/1968).

The basic principle underlying Dodge's technique—a harmless beam of infrared light directed at the reader's cornea and reflected onto photographic film (Taylor & Taylor, 1983)—is still in use today, although computers have replaced film, and the level of comfort, authenticity, accuracy, and general robustness of eye-tracking data have made substantial strides. Data collected with an eye tracker provide a record of where in a text a reader looks and for how long the reader looks there. Such a record enables the researcher to construct a map of how the reader navigates the text.

After groundbreaking eye-movement studies in the 1920s and 1930s, particularly by Guy Buswell and Charles Judd, there was not another surge of research until the 1970s, when work by Patricia Carpenter and Marcel Just, George McConkie and Keith Rayner, Ariane Levy-Schoen, and Kevin O'Regan appeared (Kennedy, 1987). The number and type of eye movement studies that have been undertaken since then is considerable, and the research has furthered our understanding of how the eye functions in the reading process.

Theoretical Frameworks for the Interpretation of Eye-Movement Studies

During reading, the eyes scan a visual display and send a continuous signal to the brain. The eye, like a camera, has a lens that must be at rest and in focus to provide a useful visual signal. So, as the eye moves across the text it stops and fixates at points in the text. The movements of the eye during reading have been studied by researchers seeking evidence of how visual acuity and perception are used in the process of reading. Although a theory of the reading process is not always made explicit by the researchers, the design of eye-movement studies and interpretation of the results are both rooted in the theory of the reading process the researcher has accepted or is testing (see Krashen, 1999). This phenomenon has not gone unnoticed, of course; Rayner and Carroll (1984, p. 133) raise concerns about some eye-movement researchers' instructions given to subjects that cause unnatural reading situations. Regardless of the benefits or drawbacks of the research approach, eye-movement studies have often been used to support or reject particular models of how vision is used in reading.

In this chapter, we use eye-movement research to show support for a transactional model of reading. At first blush, this may seem counterintuitive because recent articles that argue against such a transactional model also include in their literature reviews some summaries of eye-movement research. In fact, interpretations of eye movements that are used to refute transactional theories of reading can readily be found in the reading literature. However, if the actual eye-movement studies—instead of only third-party summaries of the research—are examined, a different picture emerges. This discrepancy between what is reported about eye movement findings in research reviews written by researchers not involved in studies of eye movement and what is actually in the eye-movement research reports prompts the question: Does eye-movement research support or refute transactional theories of reading?

The purpose of this chapter is to demonstrate that eye-movement research supports a transactional view of reading, and we begin by addressing discrepancies in eye-movement findings in recent articles concerned with reading theory. It becomes important to see whether past and current eye-movement studies are consistent with those interpretations. That is particularly important because, in the field of reading education, eye-movement interpretations by reading theorists seem to be much more frequently cited than evidence provided by the actual eye-movement researchers.

In this chapter, we pursue questions about the interpretations of eye-movement literature by writers other than those who did the research and review eye-movement studies that inform the discussion. We contrast conclusions from reading theorists with the conclusions of the eye-movement research-ers to illustrate how widely reported interpretations of the research are mis-conceived; further, we recommend that when interpreting eye-movement research, reading the actual research reports in addition to (or instead of) summaries of that research is crucial to understanding the research. This is somewhat an ironic suggestion as this chapter constitutes a research sum-mary; however, where possible we have quoted directly from eye-movement research in order to better preserve the findings of the original studies. After examining eye-movement research interpretations in the first half of the chapter, we move into eye-movement research that supports each of the three cueing systems—semantic, syntactic, and graphophonic—that consti-tute a core part of a transactional model of reading (e.g., Goodman, 1994).

As a note about our view of the reading process, in a transactional, con-structivist view (e.g., Goodman, 1994; Smith, 1994) the focus is not on words or letters but on a situation in which the text's graphic information com-bines with readers' syntactic, semantic, and phonic knowledge to enable them to efficiently anticipate, construct, and confirm meanings, not specific words. Note that this is not a word-centered hypothesis-testing model that, as Gough (1984) asserts, views "reading as beginning with the reader's gen-eration of expectancies, hypotheses, or predictions about the next printed word and the subsequent testing of these hypotheses against the visual data" (p. 244).[1] Instead, we view reading as a linguistic and perceptual transaction between the published text and the reader in which meaning and a parallel reader's text (Goodman, 1994) are constructed.

The Physiological Limitations of the Eye

To understand visual processes in reading, it is necessary to understand the eye's limitations as a data source during reading. There are three regions of viewing information to which the eye has access during a fixation: the foveal, parafoveal, and peripheral regions. The foveal region is the area of vision that is in focus and subsumes 1–2° of visual angle or about 3–6 let-ter spaces around the point of fixation. The parafoveal region extends about 24–30 letters around the point of fixation, and the peripheral region includes everything in the visual field beyond the parafoveal region (Just & Carpen-ter, 1987). The fovea is concerned with processing detail, and the farther away from the fovea an object is viewed, the more difficult it is to identify it. In terms of reading, when letters are viewed within the fovea, they are distinguishable. When a random string of letters is viewed outside the fovea but within the parafovea, the reader can see gross shapes, but they are not distinguishable. Note that this is a physiological limitation, not a perceptual one. When letters are presented in context, as they are in a normal reading situation, they can be distinguished sufficiently to be useful under certain conditions, as is discussed in this section.

In addition to a small in-focus viewing area, the eye is also limited as an information source by the fact that it must be stationary to deliver usable data to the brain. That is why readers' eyes make fixations instead of simply gliding over the text: No usable information is gained during the movement of the eyes, an early finding in the eye-movement field that has been replicated many times (e.g., Dodge, 1900; Rayner, 1997; Wolverton & Zola, 1983). The combination of the eye having a small in-focus viewing area with the fact that the eye must fixate to retrieve usable information means that, physiologically, to "see" a word, it is necessary to pause and look right at what is in foveal view.

Intuitively, it seems that readers must look at every word if they are to successfully read a text. But, physiology is not the only factor in reading; perception plays a crucial role as well. As we discuss, perceptions are mental constructs, and it is possible and necessary to comprehend texts and perceive not-looked-at words.

Before examining the actual research that theorists use to inform views of reading, an example of what eye movements can demonstrate is presented in Figure 2.1; as a reference example for various aspects of this chapter, we utilize a graphic of a text with a reader's eye movements overlaid on it. This particular example comes from the seminal eye-movement researcher Charles Judd (1918, p. 25), but other similar graphics abound (e.g., Paulson & Freeman, 2003, p. 6; Rayner & Pollatsek, 1989, p. 116). The subject is a male university student who read the passage silently. The vertical lines indicate the point of fixation on the word. The numbers above the vertical lines show the order of the fixations (starting over on each line), and the numbers below the vertical lines indicate the duration of the fixation in 50ths of a second.

In the above text concerned in Figure 2.1, the reader fixated approximately 48% of the words, including 39% of the function words and 55% of the content words. A cursory look at these data, then, shows us that half of the words are fixated, with content words more likely to be fixated than function words.[2] There are fixations on the first word in three of the seven lines of the text and fixations on the last word in two of the seven lines. Note that despite the physiological limits of the eye as an information source, the reader still skipped words and looked at words for different lengths of time. The implication of these phenomena for reading theory is discussed. First, however, we address misinterpretations of eye-movement research.

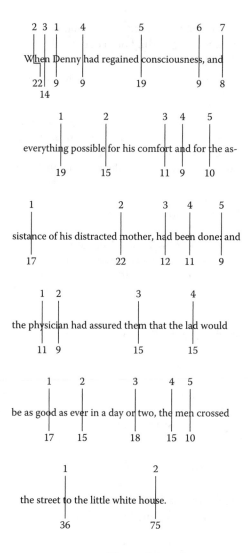

Figure 2.1
Judd's example

Eye-Movement Research Interpretations

Summaries have made interpretive claims of the results of eye-movement research that may fit a given reading model but are many times not supported by the data and the interpretations made by the actual eye-movement researchers. Many times, these statements are made en route to a general refutation of certain models of reading or pedagogical theories growing out of those models, like whole language. For example, Grossen (1997) interpreted eye-movement research to refute a general meaning-construction view of reading:

> Of the three cuing systems frequently mentioned in reading (semantic, syntactic, and graphophonemic cues), the semantic and syntactic cuing systems seem to play a minor role. Recent eye-movement research indicates that good readers do not sample the text and predict to recognize words efficiently, but rather see every single letter on the page. (par. 34)

Similarly, Adams (1990) downplayed the role of context in reading:

> In summary, the eye-movement research lends little support to the notion that skilled readers use contextual constraints to reduce the visual processing involved in reading. To the contrary, when reading for comprehension, skilled readers tend to look at each individual word and to process its component letters quite thoroughly. (p. 102)

This idea is reflected in the theory expressed by Adams and Bruck (1995):

> The letters and words of the text are the basic data of reading. For skillful adult readers, meaningful text, regardless of its ease or difficulty, is read through what is essentially a left to right, line by line, word by word process. In general, skillful readers visually process each individual letter of every word they read, translating print to speech as they go. They do so whether they are reading isolated words or meaningful connected text. They do so regardless of the semantic, syntactic, or orthographic predictability of what they are reading. (pp. 11–12)

Tunmer (1990) explicitly asserted that eye-movement research has provided data that refute "Goodman and Smith" models of reading:

> Research conducted during the past 15 years has not supported the models of skilled reading and reading acquisition advanced by Goodman and Smith. With respect to skilled reading, research on eye movements has shown that rather than sampling words from text, skilled adult readers fixate (i.e., extract information from) the majority of words in text including nearly every content word. (p. 96)

Pressley (1998) argued that eye-movement data are in conflict with whole-language theories of reading:

It is important to process every single letter during reading because letter-level cues are the primary means of recognizing words. This conclusion, based on eye-movement and related analyses, clashes with the whole-language theory of word recognition. ... [T]his perspective [whole language] simply is not supported by outcomes from eye-movement research. (p. 43)

As the quotations illustrate, these conclusions seek to refute transactional or constructivist views of reading. But, are the interpretations supported by the data found in the studies they cite? We examine the conclusions and then look at the studies they claim to represent.

Eye-Movement Research Findings

Number of Fixations

How many words do readers actually look at while reading? In one of the "question-and-answer" sections of her 1990 book, Adams asked, "Do skilled readers skip over any significant number of words in meaningful text? Not really. Normal adult readers fixate most words of a text, regardless of its difficulty" (p. 100). Similarly, Stanovich (1992) stated, "This research is consistent in indicating that the vast majority of content words in text receive a direct visual fixation" (p. 7).

In Judd's (1918) example, only 48% of the words are fixated, which few would argue is a vast majority. Judd's example is on the low end, however; Rayner and Pollatsek's (1989, p. 116) example shows a reader fixating 62.5% of the words in the text, and Paulson and Freeman's (2003, p. 6) text excerpt shows a reader fixating approximately 60% of the words; although these examples show eye-movement percentages that constitute a majority, and it could be argued that therefore literally most of the words in the text are fixated, we should not make the mistake of inferring that this means that every letter of every word must be directly fixated for reading to work. There is a substantial number of the words in a given text that are not fixated by readers; as our examples illustrate, readers can skip half of the words in a text, as in the Judd example, to 37.5% or 40% of the words, as in the Rayner and Pollatsek and Paulson and Freeman examples.

Other eye-movement research has found similar percentages of fixated words. Fisher and Shebilske (1985) reported that "in the 17 records published by Judd and Buswell (1922) we have found that less than two-thirds of the words were fixated in 8 of the records and no more than three-fourths in any of those remaining" (p. 149). In a more recent example, Just and Carpenter (1987) recorded the eye movements of 14 college students reading 15 different short (about 135-word) passages from news magazines. The passages represented examples of writing about scientific discoveries, technical inventions, and biological mechanisms, and most of the readers were unfamiliar with the content of the passages. They found that 68% of the words in the text were fixated. Similarly, Rayner (1997) stated:

> If readers made only one fixation on each word in the text, there would be little problem. Unfortunately, things are not that simple because at least 20% to 30% of the words in text are skipped altogether (i.e., do not receive a fixation) and some words are fixated more than once before the reader moves on to another word. (p. 319)

Eye-movement research has demonstrated that between 50% and 80% of the words in a text are fixated, depending on the difficulty of the text, the reader's proficiency and purpose, and other factors. It should also be pointed out that the directions given in many of these eye-movement studies may actually bias readers toward examining the text more thoroughly than usual, in effect studying the text (Krashen, 1999; Rayner & Carroll, 1984). It is therefore difficult to understand how eye-movement research could be thought to support the notion that readers "tend to look at each individual word and process its component letters quite thoroughly" (Adams, 1990, p. 102).

Skipping Words

Related to the issue of the number of words that are looked at in a given text, there is a misconception about whether readers actually skip words. For example, Adams (1990) stated:

> Readers can discriminate letter-level information as much as seven or eight letter positions to the right of where they are fixated.[3] Do they use this information to pre-process the words to come? Yes, but not in a way that allows them to skip over such words. Readers apparently gain information about the location of the next word in a text and use that information to tell their eyes how far to move. If coupled with contextual clues, the visual information they gain about an upcoming word enables them to recognize the word more quickly when they do fixate it. *Still, they seem not to process its (the word's) identity until it is fixated.* (p. 101; italics added)

Here, Adams seems to acknowledge the role of context in reading only to refute it in the last sentence—erroneously, as is demonstrated in the following discussion. In Judd's (1918) example, the reader "skips" half of the words. Readers do skip words, but do they perceive themselves as skipping words?

To our knowledge, no model of reading seriously implies a "wholesale skipping of words," as Stanovich (1992, p. 7) stated. Indeed, in Goodman's view of reading (1994), the reader constructs a meaning and a personal text parallel to the published text. Having successfully constructed meaning, the reader has the perception that every word has been read. Eye-movement research supports the view that readers do indeed perceive many of the words that are not fixated. Just and Carpenter (1987) explained:

> Some of the words that are not fixated directly are still processed to some extent. The evidence for this claim is that certain words are more likely to be skipped than others. If readers did not process the skipped words, then all words would be equally likely to be skipped. ... Readers were more likely to skip three letter function words (such as *the, and*) than three letter content words (such as *ant, run*). ... This selectivity implies that readers had more information about those words than just their length, even though the words were not fixated. (p. 39)

Readers are thus able to receive some text-level information from the parafoveal region — but how, because the parafovea is not in focus? Predictions play a part in how well these words that are not fixated are processed.

McClelland and O'Regan (1981) explored whether the usefulness of information in the parafovea was dependent on readers' expectations about what the next word in a text would be. One of their experiments that simulated eye movements examined how long it took readers to name target words. The researchers were especially interested in the use of word information available to readers before they looked at the word in question. Subjects read an incomplete sentence (the last word was left out) displayed on a computer screen. When they reached the last word, they pressed a button that initiated a 100-msec preview, followed by a 100-msec blank space, then finally the target word. Subjects were to name the target word as soon as they read it. Preview items were of three types: a series of *x*s (the x condition), an item similar to the target word except that the second and penultimate letters were replaced by other letters of the same shape (the shape-end-letter condition), or the same word as the target word (the word condition). In addition, the sentences the subjects read were of two types: those that enabled a series of judges (who did not take part in the experiment) to accurately predict the last word and those that the judges felt did not allow them to predict the last word. The former condition was termed the constraining context and the latter the neutral context. Their results demonstrate that the speed and ease with which readers could name a target word from a parafoveal preview are dependent on the reader's expectations: "A priori expectations and context greatly increase the benefit subjects gain from a preview of a word in parafoveal vision" (p. 634). They asserted that "our experiments have clarified one point: The ability to derive benefit from the preview we receive of upcoming words in parafoveal vision depends on a prepared mind" (p. 643). That is, readers are able to make use of text information that they have not fixated on but which they have predicted. Fuzzy input is enough to confirm a prediction.

To support the idea that unfixated words are nevertheless perceived and processed, Fisher and Shebilske (1985) performed an experiment that made use of a yoked-control group in which the appearance of the text for one group is changed to reflect the eye-movement patterns on that same text by another group. For example, half of the 60 undergraduate participants had their eye movements monitored while reading sentences (as well as short essays) such as the following:

Pets have funny names such as my favorite dog, Jingles.

If those subjects failed to fixate, for example, the words *funny* and *dog*, the other half of the subjects would see the sentence as

Pets have _____ names such as my favorite _____, Jingles.

The researchers then examined the percentage of words that were skipped that subjects could report versus the percentage of words that were not skipped that subjects could report. The reasoning is that if words that are not fixated are not perceived, then the first group of subjects would recall as many of the skipped words as the second group of subjects. In fact, this was not the case: The ratios of reporting nonfixated words to fixated words in the first group of subjects were 1.0 (sentences) and 0.97 (essays), and the ratios for the group of subjects who received the yoked control materials were 0.40 (sentences) and 0.45 (essays) (that the yoked-control subjects were able to "recall" a word at all is a function of their ability to infer the words from the context). The indication is that even though a word is not directly fixated, it can still be perceived under normal reading conditions. Fisher and Shebilske concluded: "More specifically, the present results support the generality of the hypothesis that expectations based on contextual constraints can interact with parafoveal information to determine the guidance of fixations" (pp. 154–155). In other words, predictions from context are used by the brain to direct the eye where to fixate next.

To further confirm the effects of contextual constraint, or predictability, of text, Rayner and Well (1996) asked readers to read sentences that contained a target word that was classified as high, medium, or low constraint. Their method of determining the predictability of the target words was similar to that of Fisher and Shebilske (1985); judges who did not participate in the study were given a cloze task with the sentence or paragraph presented up to the target word and were asked to fill in the blank. Target words that were produced by the judges over 60% of the time were considered "highly constrained," or predictable, and target words that were produced less than 10% of the time were considered "unconstrained." Eighteen adult participants' eye movements were recorded reading a range of sentences, from highly constrained to relatively unconstrained, with word length and word frequency controlled. The results of the study indicated that the low-constraint words yielded longer fixation times than the medium- and high-constraint words, and readers were more likely not to fixate on the high-constraint target word than the medium- or low-constraint target word. Rayner and Well effectively confirmed findings of other eye-movement studies that show that "highly constrained target words are skipped (i.e., not directly fixated) more frequently than unconstrained words ... [and] when target words are fixated, fixation time is shorter on constrained than on unconstrained words" (p. 504) and concluded that "predictability of a word (or the amount of contextual constraint for that word) ... will affect both fixation time and word skipping" (p. 507). That is, readers' predictions allow them to skip (not to fixate) certain upcoming words. In doing so, they use some parafoveal information about the words. Not all researchers agree with this conclusion; studies by Zola (in McConkie & Zola, 1981) and Hyona (1993) both questioned the usefulness of context in parafoveal processing. However, both of these studies have been criticized as flawed; see Ehrlich and Rayner, 1981; Rayner and Pollatsek, 1989, pp. 223–224; and Rayner and Well, 1996, for a critique of the studies. In addition, more recent studies, such as that of Kennedy (2003), found evidence for parafoveal processing in parallel with foveal processing.

Fixation Duration

Like other eye-movement measures described previously, there are misconceptions about how long readers spend looking at the words in a given text. For example, Adams (1990) asked the following:

> Even if skilled readers look at every word, they might not process every word in equal detail. Do skilled readers sample the visual features of predictable text less thoroughly? No. Regardless of semantic, syntactic, or orthographic predictability, the eye seems to process individual letters. (p. 101)

In the same vein, Stanovich (1992) stated:

> Furthermore, the study of the processing of visual information within a fixation has indicated that the visual array is rather completely processed during each fixation. It appears that visual features are not minimally sampled in order to confirm "hypotheses," but instead are rather exhaustively processed, even when the word is highly predictable. (p. 7)

In Judd's (1918) example (Figure 2.1), there is a difference in fixation duration for words. We saw that prediction explains why some words are not fixated. Does prediction also have something to do with the varying lengths of time different words are fixated?

Differences in fixation duration between words in Judd's (1918) example cannot be explained solely by word length; that is, words with similar durations do not necessarily have the same number of letters, and words with the same number of letters do not necessarily have the same fixation duration. For example, the word *assistance* has more than twice as many letters as the word *good*, but they are both fixated for the same amount of time in Judd's example. By the same token, *men*, *lad*, and *and* all have the same number of letters but are fixated for very different durations. If differences in fixation duration were mostly a function of how many letters are in the word, as Adams (1990, p. 101) suggested, then words with the same number of letters would be fixated for the same amount of time. Obviously, this is not the case. What, then, accounts for the wide variance in fixation durations between words? The answer appears to be the level of predictability of the text and whether the reader's expectations were confirmed by the upcoming information. In their 1996 study described in the preceding section, Rayner and Well demonstrated that "as far as fixation times of words are concerned, words that are unconstrained by context are fixated longer than words that are moderately to highly constrained" (p. 507). Similarly, in 1998 Reichle, Pollatsek, Fisher, and Rayner stated that:

> Reading is a more interactive process, and there may be many situations in which a word will not be predictable in the absence of any information but quite predictable given minimal information such as approximate word length and the first letter. (p. 153)

In short, readers constantly make predictions about upcoming text. The studies show that when readers encounter words that they expect, they need not fixate on those words or only do so for a brief time.

These studies indicate that in the view of reading as meaning construction, when readers confirm their expectations by briefly fixating on a word they expected to be there, they are sampling the text. Smith (1994) pointed out that:

The secret of reading efficiently is not to read indiscriminately but to *sample* the text. The brain must be parsimonious, making maximum use of what is already known and analyzing the minimum of visual information required to verify or modify what can be predicted about the text. (p. 81)

That is, they are using the least amount of text information necessary to create meaning, sampling from the three text-based levels of cueing systems (Goodman, 1994): the graphophonic, lexico-grammatical (structural), and semantic-pragmatic systems. Eye-movement research has demonstrated that readers use the three cueing systems during the parafoveal preview to be able to skip the upcoming word or to facilitate its identification, as the following section demonstrates.

The Cueing Systems

In this section, we provide examples of eye-movement studies that support the use of each of the cueing systems.

The Graphophonic Cue System   The graphophonic cue system consists of phonological and orthographic information available in a text and the information about how the two systems relate to each other. To demonstrate the importance of phonological information, Pollatsek, Lesch, Morris, and Rayner (1992) undertook a project designed to determine whether homophones (words that sound the same) provide a better parafoveal preview than do visually matched controls. Of interest was fixation duration on the target word in a sentence. Each target word had one of four corresponding preview words: a homophone, a visually similar word, a completely different word, or a word identical to the target. The text was displayed on a computer screen. When the subjects began reading the sentence, one of the preview words would be in the target word's position until the reader's eyes crossed the boundary point (the parafoveal preview), at which time the preview word would be replaced with the target word. In other words, the preview word would be in the sentence until the readers began the saccade that would take them to that word, at which time the computer would change the preview word to the target word (remember that the eye picks up no information during a saccade, so the reader was not aware that there was a change). The dependent variable was processing time of the target word once it was reached, with the processing time (i.e., a shorter eye-fixation duration) attributed to the usefulness of the parafoveal preview. The results indicate that the readers fixated for less time after a homophone preview than with a visually similar preview. The authors summarized that, "The central finding of this study is that when a parafoveal preview word was a homophone of a target word, there was a greater preview benefit than when the preview was a non-homophonic control word that was as visually similar to the target word as was the homophone" (p. 158).

The orthographic portion of the graphophonic cueing system was explored by Balota, Pollatsek, and Rayner (1985). Similar to Pollatsek et al. (1992), they utilized a boundary technique to explore the influence of context and parafoveal information that was either visually similar or visually dissimilar to a target word that the reader would subsequently fixate. For example, in the following sentence, *cake* would have as a parafoveal preview *cake, cahc, pies, picz,* or *bomb* that would be changed to *cake* during the reader's saccade immediately preceding the word:

> Since the wedding was today, the baker rushed the wedding cake to the reception.

They found that readers were significantly more likely to skip the visually identical or visually similar parafoveal previews (*cake, cahc*) than when shown the semantically related, visually dissimilar, or anomalous parafoveal previews (*pies, picz, bomb*). They concluded:

> The data imply that when the word is skipped, only the beginning two or three letters of the parafoveal word were actually identified. Thus, on these occasions, a strong context helps readers to fill in information that is not totally available in their parafovea. (p. 374)

Readers are able to sample phonological and orthographic information in the parafoveal field of vision in conjunction with their expectations of the upcoming text either to skip portions of the text or to fixate on it for a shorter-than-average period of time. In the meaning-construction view, this sampling from the text—not thoroughly processing every letter—makes possible efficiently utilizing the least amount of information necessary to make sense of the text and move on. And, if readers are successful in constructing meaning, then they are unaware they have not "seen" all the words. On the other hand, readers are likely to regress and make additional fixations if the meaning is disrupted.

The Lexico-Grammatical (Syntactic) Cue System   In their 1983 study, Carpenter and Just (1983) demonstrated that readers make use of syntactic information in the parafovea. Specifically, readers were more likely to skip three-letter function words such as *and* and *the* than they were three-letter content words like *act* and *two*.[4] Although they cautioned that it is not certain which aspect of a function word a parafoveal preview utilizes, Carpenter and Just described function words as "semantically impoverished," and that, along with word length and shape, "it is possible to recognize a great proportion of the three-letter function words on the basis of the prior syntactic context" (pp. 283–284). Similarly, O'Regan (1979) asked subjects to read pairs of sentences that began the same but ended differently (each subject read one of each pair):

> The dog that growled the most was friendly./ The dog that growled ate many biscuits.
> He claimed the ladies the maid knew lived in New York./ He claimed the ladies met many times to discuss.

Readers skipped *the* substantially more than they skipped three-letter verbs. O'Regan summarized:

> The conclusions to be drawn from this experiment are first, that local eye-movement parameters (saccade size, regression probability, number of fixations, and perhaps fixation duration), are controlled sufficiently rapidly to be influenced from moment to moment by information concerning the lexical category of a word in peripheral vision. ... It is clear that some systematic influence of sentence structure exists. (p. 59)

When readers utilize their implicit knowledge of the structure of language along with their constant predictions about upcoming text, they are sampling from the syntactic cueing system. This enables them to read more efficiently—to skip or spend less time on words that have been confirmed parafoveally.

The Semantic-Pragmatic Cue System One aspect of semantic information that the semantic cueing system conveys is morphological; that is, different parts of words carry different types of semantic information, some of which is more useful than other parts during reading. Underwood, Clews, and Everatt (1990) examined the process by which a fixation location is informed by the information distribution of the word in the parafoveal preview. For example, *underneath* is the only word of its length ending in *neath*, which makes the end of the word a "zone of high information." The end of *engagement*, however, is "redundant," as *ment* can attach to many words. Underwood et al. selected target words that fit several categories of words with zones of high information at the beginning or end of the word and embedded them in short stories. The locations of readers' fixations on the target words were recorded. The researchers proceeded with the expectation that if readers consistently fixated on the zones of high information, then they must be processing morphological information parafoveally. This is indeed what happened. The researchers summarized their results:

> The target words used in our sentences varied in their distribution of information. Being given the first few letters of some words would not be sufficient to identify them, and likewise, the final few letters of some words did not provide a unique suggestion as to the identity of the word. The distribution of the information had its effect upon the location of the first fixation upon the target. ... A redundant beginning induced a first fixation further from the word's beginning. This variation in the initial landing position is evidence of parafoveal processing of the distribution of information in the word, because until that fixation had been made only parafoveal processing could deliver the information necessary to guide the eyes to one location or another. (p. 58)

However, Rayner and Morris (1992) replicated this study and, based on their findings, argued that Underwood et al.'s (1990) claim that the eye initially fixates on the most informative part of a word is too strong a claim:

> Although the results of the present study are consistent with data reported previously ... with regard to the amount of time that readers look at words as a function of where the information for uniquely identifying the word is located, our data are not consistent with the more controversial claim advocated by Underwood and colleagues. ... Our data definitely do not support such a model. Of course, as we acknowledged earlier, semantic processing of parafoveal words does occur. What we are arguing against is a semantic preprocessing model in which the meanings of parafoveal words are unconsciously analyzed, and the information is used to determine where to look next. (pp. 169–170)

Thus, although the research is in agreement that readers are able to sample semantic information from the parafoveal field, how the researchers view the reading process influences how they interpret their data. Yet, in either view, semantic information is shown to enable readers to use as textual cues the most informative part of a word—a good example of one of the numerous ways readers make efficient use of the text.

This section has demonstrated that there is strong experimental evidence for readers using all cueing systems in a text to maintain the most efficient reading process possible. Specifically, readers utilize graphophonic, syntactic, and semantic information in conjunction with their predictions and inferences to more efficiently process upcoming text. This efficiency is demonstrated by readers' ability to skip one of every three or four words yet still perceive them as read. When readers fixate for a short amount of time on a word that they expected to be there, they are confirming their predictions—a process that can be completed by sampling from the most useful cueing systems available.

Conclusions and Implications

Although some reading theorists interpret eye-movement studies as a refutation of current constructivist models of reading, the data and conclusions of the studies by the researchers who undertook the studies do not support that refutation. On the contrary, the research demonstrates that the brain, via the eyes, is less interested in gathering letter-level and word-level information than it is in making sense of the text. Words that the reader did not expect are fixated for longer periods of time than words for which the reader was prepared, and the latter are many times not fixated at all. Function words seem to be fixated less than half of the time that content words are because they are highly constrained: in many positions, only the word *the* can appear, and there is just not enough semantic information in function words for the reader to spend processing time on them. It is also clear that phonological, orthographic, morphological, syntactic, and semantic information all influence eye movements.

It is intuitively seductive to believe that readers see every letter and have read every word on a page of text; after all, the perception is of reading every word in a smooth, continuous motion from left to right. But, the research has not borne this notion out, and in the face of such overwhelming evidence, there is no reason to argue that it must be so. Instead, the focus should be on what the reader *perceives*—as we have alluded to throughout this chapter. Limiting the reader to what is physiologically seen (i.e., whatever is in foveal focus) ignores a vital contribution necessary in a transactional model of reading: the reader. It is the reader's perceptions that result in comprehension. If it were only the sequential visual input that created meaning, then the 10–15% of fixations that are regressions (Rayner & Pollatsek, 1989) would cause serious syntactic problems. Add to that the words in a sentence that are not fixated or in foveal focus, and the visual input quickly becomes incomprehensible gibberish. Paul Kolers (1976), reporting on Buswell's breakthrough eye-movement research, summarized this idea:

> In reading sentences, the visual system samples different parts of sentences at different times, but the perceiver does not necessarily run the sentence parts together in the mind in correspondence to the order in which they are sampled. Rather, he manages to keep track of where in the sentence the different

samples came from. To do so, his brain must tag samples with respect to their location ... mapping temporal order onto structural locations. Hence, neither the perception nor the memory of what is perceived can be the result of a straight-forward listing or recording of samples. ... Disorder is not usually present in the reader's conscious experience; our experience is of coherent and regular messages. The implication is clear, therefore, that the order and clarity of the messages are properties achieved by some powerful cognitive operations, and are not merely reflections of the message the eye picks up from the printed page. ... The mind orders, arranges, supplements, and fills out the information the eye delivers to it. (pp. 390–392)

Throughout this chapter, we have concentrated on refuting misconceptions about eye-movement studies by reviewing and liberally quoting from the actual studies. Perhaps one by-product of this discussion has been to draw attention to the rich data source in a reader's eye movements. However, like other research paradigms, eye-tracking technology, although a powerful research tool, does not provide a complete picture of the reading process. Just and Carpenter (1984) point out the following:

A conceptual limitation, shared with all chronometric approaches, is that eye fixation behavior does not directly indicate the end product of the comprehension process, what the reader has learned from the text. It is usually worthwhile to supplement eye fixation monitoring with another measure like recall, question-answering, or retrospective protocols that indicate more about what has been comprehended. (p. 154)

For this reason, studies in which eye-movement research is combined with miscue analysis have been undertaken (Duckett, 2002, chapter 5, this volume; Ebe, chapter 6, this volume; Paulson, 2002, chapter 11, this volume; Paulson & Freeman, 2003). Although current research considers eye movements in relation to aspects of the text (e.g., content vs. function words), miscue analysis provides a continuous window on the reader's response to the text. It helps make clear why regressive eye movements occur, and it also puts the eye movements in the context of the reader's making sense of the text. That makes it possible to relate what the eye is doing to what the brain is doing in the process of making sense of the text.

Another topic closely related to the information in this chapter is that of the pedagogical implications implicit in the review of this set of studies. If instruction is based on a view of the eye fixating on every word and thoroughly processing the letters, then it will look different from instruction based on a view of eye movements as directed by the brain in the process of constructing of meaning. This seems to be understood by those reading theorists who have misconstrued the data, research, and conclusions of eye-movement studies; consider this final example:

> Goodman means that (presumably skilled) readers merely sample the print, apprehending some words and skipping others .... The point is simply that their ["whole-language people's"] fundamental assumption about skilled reading is contrary to fact. The elegant studies of eye movements during reading by Rayner and his associates have shown conclusively that good readers read every word. (Liberman & Liberman, 1992, p. 352)

If "read every word" can be construed as "perceiving every word," then there is a kernel of truth in that statement. However, tying read every word to "studies of eye movements" and setting this up in opposition to the statement about skipping words in the first part of the quotation implies that the point of this argument is not about understanding every word, but instead about having to look at every word to understand it. If so, then the very researchers Liberman and Liberman cite can refute their basic assertion—remember that previously we pointed out that Rayner himself reports that "at least 20% to 30% of the words in text are skipped altogether" (1997, p. 319). If the intent is to dismiss whole-language teaching philosophy through discrediting its foundational models of the reading process, then the effort is misguided. As the facts reveal, transactive models of reading are supported, not refuted, by eye-movement research.

Notes

A cautionary note: In our eye-movement research, fixations are not always directly on words; often, they occur between words. That would provide partial information about the words to the left and right of the fixation. Some researchers assign such fixations to the word to the right of the fixation; although we accept their data, we do not necessarily accept this convention. Modeling of the reading process that is less word bound would in any case favor a meaning-construction view of the role of perception in reading.

1. Actually, Gough's description of *interactive* models of reading as a "subtle interplay of the conceptual and visual process" (1984, p. 244) is a closer fit to the one Goodman espouses and for good reason: Goodman's model is indeed interactive, not "top down," as it is sometimes characterized.
2. This is a representative example of the eye-movement records of the subjects in Judd's monograph; some readers show more fixations, and some readers show fewer.

3. The foveal, in-focus, field of vision comprises a total of 3-6 letters with the point of fixation in the center of the visual field. Identifying 8 letters to the right of the point of focus puts the print well into the parafovea.

4. We have seen how the reader in the example from Judd (1918) fixated 35% of the function words to 59% of the content words; Just and Carpenter (1987) have recorded a similar ratio (approximately 38% of the function words and 83% of the content words).

References

Adams, M. J. (1990). *Beginning to read: Thinking and learning about print.* Cambridge, MA.: MIT Press.

Adams, M. J., & Bruck, M. (1995). Resolving the great debate. *American Educator, 19*(2), 7, 10–20.

Balota, D. A., Pollatsek, A., & Rayner, K. (1985). The interaction of contextual constraints and parafoveal visual information in reading. *Cognitive Psychology, 17,* 364–390.

Carpenter, P. A., & Just, M. A. (1983). What your eyes do while your mind is reading. In K. Rayner (Ed.), *Eye movements in reading: Perceptual and language processes* (pp. 275–307). New York: Academic Press.

Dodge, R. (1900). Visual perceptions during eye movement. *Psychological Review, VII,* 454–465.

Duckett, P. (2002). New insights: Eye fixations and the reading process. *Talking Points, 13*(2), 16–21.

Ehrlich, S. F., & Rayner, K. (1981). Contextual effects on word perception and eye movements during reading. *Journal of Verbal Learning and Verbal Behavior, 20,* 641–655.

Fisher, D. F., & Shebilske, W.L. (1985). There is more that meets the eye than the eye mind assumption. In R. Groner, G. W. McConkie, & C. Menz (Eds.), *Eye movements and human information processing* (pp. 149–157). Amsterdam: Elsevier Science.

Goodman, K. S. (1994). Reading, writing, and written texts: A transactional sociopsycholinguistic view. In R. B. Ruddell, M. R. Ruddell, & H. Singer (Eds.), *Theoretical models and processes of reading* (4th ed., pp. 1093–1130). Newark, DE: International Reading Association.

Gough, P. B. (1984). Word recognition. In P. D. Pearson, R. Barr, M. L. Kamil, & P. Mosenthal (Eds.), *Handbook of reading research* (Vol. 1, pp. 225–253). New York: Longman.

Grossen, B. (1997). *A synthesis of research on reading from the National Institute of Child Health and Human Development.* Retrieved April 25, 2006, from http://www.nrrf.org/synthesis_research.htm

Huey, E. B. (1968). *The Psychology and Pedagogy of Reading.* Cambridge, MA: MIT Press. (Original work published 1908)

Hyona, J. (1993). Effects of thematic and lexical priming on readers' eye movements. *Scandinavian Journal of Psychology, 34,* 293–304.

Judd, C. H. (1918). *Reading: Its nature and development.* Chicago: University of Chicago Press.

Judd, C. H., & Buswell, G. T. (1922). *Silent reading: A study of the various types.* Chicago: University of Chicago Press.

Just, M. A., & Carpenter, P. A. (1984). Using eye fixations to study reading comprehension. In D. E. Kieras & M. A. Just (Eds.), *New methods in reading comprehension research* (pp. 151–182). Hillsdale, NJ: Erlbaum.

Just, M. A., & Carpenter, P. A. (1987). *The psychology of reading and language comprehension.* Newton, MA: Allyn and Bacon.

Kennedy, A. (1987). Eye movements, reading skill, and the spatial code. In J. Beech & A. Colley (Eds.), *Cognitive approaches to reading* (pp. 169–186). Chichester, U.K.: Wiley.

Kennedy, A. (2003). Parafoveal processing in word recognition. *Quarterly Journal of Experimental Psychology: Human Experimental Psychology, 53A,* 429–455.

Kolers, P. A. (1976). Buswell's discoveries. In R. A. Monty & J. W. Senders (Eds.), *Eye movements and psychological processes* (pp. 373–395). Hillsdale, NJ: Erlbaum.

Krashen, S. D. (1999). *Three arguments against whole language and why they are wrong.* Portsmouth, NH: Heinemann.

Liberman, I. Y., & Liberman, A. M. (1992). Whole language versus code emphasis: Underlying assumptions and their implications for reading instruction. In P. B. Gough, L. C. Ehri, & R. Treiman (Eds.), *Reading acquisition* (pp. 343–366). Hillsdale, NJ: Erlbaum.

McClelland, J. L., & O'Regan, J. K. (1981). Expectations increase the benefit derived from parafoveal visual information in reading words aloud. *Journal of Experimental Psychology: Human Perception and Performance, 7,* 634–644.

McConkie, G. W., & Zola, D. (1981). Language constraints and the functional stimulus in reading. In A. M Lesgold & C. A. Perfetti (Eds.), *Interactive processes in reading* (pp. 155–175). Hillsdale, NJ: Erlbaum.

O'Regan, J. K. (1979). Moment to moment control of eye saccades as a function of textual parameters in reading. In P. A. Kolers, M. E. Wrolstad, & H. Bouma (Eds.), *Processing of visible language* (Vol. 1, pp. 49–60). New York: Plenum Press.

Paulson, E. J. (2002). Are oral reading word omissions and substitutions caused by careless eye movements? *Reading Psychology, 23*, 45–66.

Paulson, E. J., & Freeman, A. E. (2003). *Insight from the eyes: The science of effective reading instruction.* Portsmouth, NH: Heinemann.

Pollatsek, A., Lesch, M., Morris, R. K., & Rayner, K. (1992). Phonological codes are used in integrating information across saccades in word identification and reading. *Journal of Experimental Psychology: Human Perception and Performance, 18*, 148–162.

Pressley, M. (1998). *Reading instruction that works.* New York: Guilford Press.

Rayner, K. (1997). Eye movements in reading. *Scientific Studies of Reading, 1*, 317–339.

Rayner, K., & Carroll, P. J. (1984). Eye movements and reading comprehension. In D. E. Kieras & M. A. Just (Eds.), *New methods in reading comprehension research* (pp. 129–150). Hillsdale, NJ: Erlbaum.

Rayner, K., & Morris, R. K. (1992). Eye movement control in reading: Evidence against semantic preprocessing. *Journal of Experimental Psychology: Human Perception and Performance, 18*, 163–172.

Rayner, K., & Pollatsek, A. (1989). *The psychology of reading.* Hillsdale, NJ: Erlbaum.

Rayner, K., & Well, A. D. (1996). Effects of contextual constraint on eye movements in reading: A further examination. *Psychonomic Bulletin and Review, 3*, 504–509.

Reichle, E. D., Pollatsek, A., Fisher, D. L., & Rayner, K. (1998). Toward a model of eye movement control in reading. *Psychological Review, 105*, 125–157.

Smith, F. (1994). *Understanding reading: A psycholinguistic analysis of reading and learning to read* (5th ed.). Hillsdale, NJ: Erlbaum.

Stanovich, K. E. (1992). The psychology of reading: evolutionary and revolutionary developments. *Annual Review of Applied Linguistics, 12*, 3–30.

Taylor, I., & Taylor, M. M. (1983). *The psychology of reading.* New York: Academic Press.

Tunmer, W. E. (1990). The role of language prediction skills in beginning reading. *New Zealand Journal of Educational Studies, 25*, 95–114.

Underwood, G., Clews, S., & Everatt, J. (1990). How do readers know where to look next? Local information distributions influence eye fixations. *The Quarterly Journal of Experimental Psychology, 42A*, 39–65.

Wolverton, G. S. & Zola, D. (1983). The temporal characteristics of visual information extraction during reading. In K. Rayner (Ed.), *Eye movements in reading: Perceptual language processes* (pp. 41–51). New York: Academic Press.

Section Two

SOCIOLINGUISTIC AND SYSTEMIC FUNCTIONAL LINGUISTIC STUDIES OF READING

INTRODUCTION TO CHAPTER 3

*A*LTHOUGH OUR UNDERSTANDINGS OF reality may change as we study it from different perspectives, and those perspectives may cause us to see different things in it, the underlying structures and processes remain the same.

In this article Peter Fries, a systemic-functional linguist, uses the tools of corpus linguistics to examine the extent to which word-centered and meaning-centered views of reading provide the best fit for the realities of real English texts.

Particularly, he examines the tenets of the two paradigms as they apply to the nature of words in and out of context. A major tool of linguists has been introspection. Using themselves as expert users of the language, they are able to examine how the language works, what its rules are, and what is and is not possible in language. But, modern computer technology has made it possible to use another research methodology to analyze large collections of texts, containing as many as 350 million words. Use of these large corpora has provided linguists with new information on how words and structures combine in language use.

Fries combines these methods in looking at key differences in the theories. He takes on the claim (e.g., Adams, 1990) that readers consider all meanings of each word and only then use context to choose the appropriate meaning. He uses several examples from corpus linguistics to establish that, when considered as isolated items, all words have many meanings, and that as they combine, the combinations themselves add to the possible meanings. However, when one looks at the words and the word combinations in their lexicogrammatical contexts, most of these possible meanings may be eliminated from consideration. In other words, it is both impossible and unnecessary that all meanings be considered in identifying words, or that context could only be used *after* words are identified.

This article demonstrates strongly that much experimental research is based on unexamined theory — in this case, the theory that the word is a self-evident unit of language and meaning. In that view, words are recognized (matched with a kind of mental template) as the basic act in reading. Context is at best an aid in word identification. When that theory is tested against real English texts rather than texts contrived to control words, it is shown to be grossly inadequate.

Fries shows through corpus linguistics that words cannot be recognized except in the multiple contexts of language as readers construct meaning. He demonstrates this by showing the data of corpus linguistics on even the most common words such as *look*. Through his research, he demonstrates that even the issue of what counts as a word is far more complex than the advocates of word recognition theories assume.

Then, Fries goes into another aspect of reading reality. He uses miscue analysis data to examine how readers actually transact with real texts and shows that they treat words differently in different contexts. The actual miscue patterns confirm that the processes readers use in making sense of the texts are those the theory predicts.

Through the lens of these different research methodologies, a much richer theoretical understanding emerges of the structures and processes of reading.

Ken Goodman

3

WORDS, CONTEXT, AND MEANING IN READING

Peter H. Fries

*T*HIS CHAPTER IS WRITTEN in a context in which two contrasting theories concerning the nature of reading are contested: word centered and meaning centered.

A Word-Centered View of Reading

A word-centered view considers reading to entail two steps: First, a reader identifies the words of the text; then, after the words have been identified, the reader relates the words to their context and interprets the text. Several quotations from recent literature represent this view:

> Before you pick this book up, you should understand fully that the topic at issue is that of reading words. Before you put this book down, however, you should understand fully that the ability to read words, quickly, accurately, and effortlessly, is critical to skillful reading comprehension — in the obvious ways and in a number of more subtle ones. (Adams, 1990, p. 3)
>
> The most important skill in early reading is the ability to read single words completely, accurately, and fluently. Context is not the primary factor in word recognition. (Moats, 2000, p. 9)
>
> ... skilled and/or older readers [are] more sensitive to contextual variables when the task that is employed taps comprehension processes but [are] actually less likely to use context to facilitate word recognition. (Stanovich, 2000, p. 8)

Indeed, extreme versions of this word-centered position say that context is not used at all by good readers as they identify the words they are reading:

> Good evidence exists that only beginning and struggling readers rely upon
> context to identify words. (Johnston, 1988, p. 666)

The data that are used as evidence for this word-centered view consist largely of controlled experiments and eye-movement studies that explore the ability of adults to identify words in word lists, sentences, or short passages that have been constructed specifically for the experiments.

Underlying the word-centered position is the theoretical assumption that words (and in the absence of any real discussion of what a word is, we can only assume that what is meant is the orthographic word—a sequence of letters between spaces) constitute the basic unit of language, and that all other units (e.g., sentences, groups, or phrases) can be viewed as structured combinations of words. If context is considered at all, then it is as an aid to word identification.

The view assumes that the theoretical construct 'word' is not a problematic notion, and that the vocabulary of a language is relatively unambiguous and fixed. One can see some of these assumptions at work in this statement of Adams (1990):

> Relevant context generally does speed readers' ability to decide whether
> an item is a word and what it means. For skilled readers, however, it seems
> to do so only **after** they have quite thoroughly identified the word—both
> visually and semantically. Consider the following two clauses.
>> They all *rose*.
>> John saw several spiders, roaches and *bugs*.
>
> Although the meaning of the last (italicized) word of each of these
> clauses is thoroughly ambiguous, the context seems automatically to
> select the correct interpretation. Thus, *rose* means "stood," not "flower";
> and *bugs* means "insects or other arthropods," not "surreptitious listen-
> ing devices." **Intuitions aside, when adults are asked to read sentences
> such as these, they immediately access both meanings of the ambiguous
> words. Only after both (all) meanings have been activated does context
> select the appropriate one.** Very quickly (tenths of a second) thereafter the
> activation of the inappropriate one(s) fade away; in contrast, the appropri-
> ate meaning hangs around at least until it is integrated into the evolving
> interpretation of the clause as a whole. (pp. 102–103; bold added)

In this passage, Adams assumes that words are rarely ambiguous, and when they are ambiguous, they have only a few potential meanings. Further, the typical view of vocabulary within language in this approach is that one can provide a list of the vocabulary, a mental lexicon, of a language. McQueen and Cutler (1997) provide a statement claiming that the vocabulary of a language is finite:

Whatever the exact structure and organization of lexical entries, however, lexical access has to be central to any cognitive model of speech recognition. There is an **infinite** number of possible sentences that a listener might hear, but a **finite** number of words. (p. 566; boldface added)

But, of course, we can only view the vocabulary of a language as finite if we also say that words are relatively unaffected by their contexts. Thus, although it is never stated, a consequence of this position is that words (the lexical entries) are relatively independent units of language. Indeed, vocabulary and grammar are considered different domains of language. One consequence of viewing grammar and vocabulary as different domains of language and viewing vocabulary as a finite construct is that the choice of the grammatical constructions used in a sentence is seen as essentially a different issue from the choice of the words to be used.

A Meaning-Centered View of Reading

A contrasting theory concerning the nature of reading is that reading is a process of creating meaning in some context, based in part on the perception of visual signals and relating these signals to some language system (see Flurkey & Xu, 2003; K. Goodman, 1993, 1994, 1996; Martens, 1995; and Smith, 1994, for examples of this approach). This meaning-centered theory has five essential features:

1. All of perception takes place within some context, and that context is relevant to what is perceived and how it is interpreted.
2. Language is pervasively ambiguous and redundant, and hence the context in which it is encountered is a critical part of the perception and interpretation of language. Of course, there are many types of relevant context. Within language, there are the phonological, orthographic, lexico-grammatical, and semantic contexts. Outside language, there are the context of situation, the context of culture (including the intertextual relations imposed by the readers), and sometimes the physical context, and so on.
3. Words are only one type of linguistic unit. Many other linguistic units (e.g., groups, phrases, clauses, sentences, etc.) also exist. All of these linguistic units are relevant to processing language and hence to the reading process. They are not merely structured combinations of words.

4. There is no major boundary between words and grammar; hence, the term *lexico-grammar* is used here to refer to both vocabulary and grammar.
5. The vocabulary of a language is not finite and fixed. Rather, it is dynamic. As a result, no complete list of the words of a language is possible. Indeed, as conversation analysts often say, participants in a conversation are constantly (re)negotiating the meanings of the terms they use.

The meaning-centered view of reading, particularly in the work of Kenneth and Yetta Goodman, uses systemic functional linguistics as a foundation for its view of language and whole language as its pedagogy. (See Butt et al., 2000; Halliday 1994; and Matthiessen, 1995, for descriptions of systemic functional linguistics.)

The data that underlie this view consist largely of studies of the oral reading of school-age children (kindergarten through Grade 12) as they read complete texts that constitute stories and other genre. Many of these studies were done by teachers who were in the process of teaching some child or children. As a result, the texts that were used were often chosen for pedagogical purposes, not the purposes of the study at hand.

Clearly, these two theories of reading presuppose conflicting views of the nature of language and the role of vocabulary within language. From the point of view of linguistic research on the wording of real texts, the word-centered view of reading cannot work. It places an inordinate demand on mental processing. The Adams quotation on page 54 says that readers access **all** meanings of a word as they identify it, and only later do they use the context to choose one meaning. This process will only work only if words typically have only a few meanings.

The actual situation is quite different. An old study of the *Oxford English Dictionary* (Fries, 1945, pp. 40–41) found that words regularly had from 15 to 20 different meanings, with the most frequent words having the most meanings. The words that have only a few meanings are typically technical words or words that do not get into general use. Table 3.1 illustrates the situation by taking a simple sentence from a children's story and locating the number of meanings of each word in that sentence in the *Collins Cobuild*

Table 3.1   Quantity of Numbered Meanings for Each Entry in the *Collins Cobuild Dictionary* for Each Word in a Sentence From a Children's Story

19	2	5	18	4	10	19	22	2	1	33
The	husband	stayed	home	and	began	to	do	his	wife's	work.

Dictionary, a desk dictionary that contains roughly the number of words that a single educated person might control. The quantity of meanings in this dictionary has been placed above each word. This dictionary lists a total of 102 meanings for the 11 words of this simple sentence. Only a few of these 102 meanings are actually relevant to the text. The position described in the Adams quotation on page 54 would require readers to recover all 102 meanings and then forget all but 11.

This method of counting actually oversimplifies the picture. It does not include the number of meanings for each word as it enters into phrases. For example, *work* enters into 10 phrases (such as *social work, work in, work up,* etc.). Each of these phrases receives separate entries in this dictionary. Adding the meanings for all the phrases in which *work* appears would add 43 additional meanings.

Further, Table 3.1 does not address the fact that a given combination of words may express several potential meanings not discoverable simply by looking at the component words. For example, the genitive and the head noun may be related in any of at least the five ways listed in Table 3.2.

The example sentence in Table 3.1 contains a sequence of two genitives in a row, *his* and *wife's.* Because the word *work* is said to express 33 meanings and *his* is said to express 2 meanings, the phrase *his wife's work* potentially expresses 1,650 (= 5*5*33*2) meanings. The word-centered view of reading implies that readers must access all 1,650 meanings, but most of these 1,650 meanings are totally irrelevant to the actual sentence as it occurred. Of course, longer, more complicated sentences multiply the number of meanings readers would be required to access. Clearly, the human brain cannot process all the potential meanings in the brief time it takes to read a sentence. Information from the context must be used to reduce the task to a manageable size.

Table 3.2 Five Possible Semantic Relations That May Hold Between a Genitive and Its Head Noun

Traditional name	Example	Meaning/Paraphrase
Genitive of possession:	*my pencil*	alienable possession
Inalienable possession:	*my arm*	part-whole relation
Subjective genitive:	*My support* got her through those tough times.	I supported her.
Objective genitive:	*His support* was a real drain on our resources.	We supported him.
Genitive of origin:	*his letter*	He wrote the letter.

The next section presents the results of recent work in corpus linguistics (see Biber, Conrad and Reppen (1998); Biber et al. (1999); Francis (1993); Francis et al. (1996, 1998); Hunston (2002); Hunston and Francis (1999); and Stubbs (1996) for examples) that demonstrates that each word enters into a complex network of redundancy in the text. Focussing on redundancy provided by lexicogrammatical context, we will show that this lexicogrammatical redundancy provides important information about the nature of that word. *Redundancy* is used here to mean multiple text clues to the particular meaning of a word in a particular context.

Words and Their Lexico-Grammatical Contexts

J. R. Firth, a major British linguist said, "You shall know a word by the company it keeps" (1957, p. 11). It turns out that there are two ways in which we can look at the "company a word keeps." We can emphasize the *lexical* of *lexico-grammatical* context and look at the other words in the environment. The technical term for this study is *collocation*. Or, we can emphasize the *grammatical* of *lexicogrammatical* and look at the grammatical patterns in which a word takes part. The technical term for this study is *colligation*. It is important to remember that collocation and colligation are two views of the same phenomena. One cannot have words together without creating some sort of grammatical relation. Similarly, one cannot have grammatical relations unless words give those relations shape.

Looking at the Lexical Contexts: Collocation (Words of a Feather Flock Together)

Let us first look at the company words keep while emphasizing the lexical environment—the other words that tend to occur with a given word, the collocational tendencies of words. Usually, words are compatible because of some commonality in meaning. A search of a corpus of 2 million words of spoken American professional English found 3,803 instances of the lemma LOOK. (A *lemma* is all the various forms of a given word. So, the lemma LOOK includes *look, looked, looking,* and *looks.* Lemmas will be written in small capitals.)

Table 3.3 lists the words that were found within two words (before or after) some form of LOOK. Of these 3,803 instances, 2,220 were followed immediately by the word *at*. Clearly, there is a strong association between LOOK and *at*. Another 317 were followed by the word *like*. Many of the words that are found one word to the right of LOOK are prepositions that indicate some direction. Thus, this corpus contains many instances of sequences, such as

Table 3.3 Major Collocates of the Lemma LOOK (i.e., *look, looks, looking, looked*) in the Corpus of Spoken Professional American English (>2.078 Million Words of Spoken American English and 3,806 instances of the lemma LOOK)

Second Left		First Left		Look	First Right		Second Right	
133	that	637	to		2,220	at	657	The
132	if	297	you		317	like	205	it
117	take	158	a		271	for	195	to
99	when	157	and		158	forward	164	that
99	we	143	we		128	into	127	what
94	and	136	I		71	to	121	a
87	have	88	be		49	back	121	this
75	If	87	it		36	and	70	SP
74	I	82	we're		31	very	64	and
74	you	74	is		25	ahead	62	some
64	to	70	are		19	as	58	—
64	SP	66	of		19	—	56	how
60	as	63	would		19	a	49	in
60	the	60	can		18	through	45	at
59	going	56	will		17	the	43	I
55	And	54	that		17	I	39	all
51	what	49	really		16	more	36	And
48	need	48	they		13	over	36	those
44	want	43	I'm		12	on	33	is
43	it	42	you're		12	across	32	them
41	back	42	SP		12	in	30	these
37	is	38	just		11	good	30	see
32	they	32	were		11	around	29	ways

Note: The data summarized in Table 3.3 and the associated discussion were obtained by searching the Corpus of Spoken Professional American English using Monoconc Pro 2.2 (Barlow, 2002).

look at, look forward, look back, look across, look in, look around, and so on. In addition, it also contains other sequences, such as *look like, look very, look good,* and the like. The frequencies with which these combinations appear indicate an association between the word pairs. I should point out that even frequencies as low as 11 (for *good*) are significant because this corpus contains over 25,000 different word forms that **could** have followed look. Another association that Table 3.3 indicates is the association between LOOK and SEE. SEE is found two words after LOOK some 30 times.

So far, I have merely talked about a statistical association between LOOK and various words that are found in its environment.* Such a statistical association is useful to know about but not interesting if it remains **only** a statistical association. In fact, the associations suggested by Table 3.3 do more than simply suggest the frequencies with which pairs of words are found in text. Specifically, they help us discover the meanings of the word combinations.

For example, the verb LOOK expresses several meanings, which generally fall into one of two large categories. LOOK may express an action, as in *He looked into the room* or *He looked at the picture.* On the other hand, it may express a relation, as in *He looked happy.* When LOOK is followed by a preposition of direction (as *at, into, around, beside,* etc.), it expresses an action. When LOOK is followed by an adjective (*tired, tall, happy,* etc.) or the preposition *like,* as in *He looked like his father,* it is interpreted to express a relation. *Very* from Table 3.3 fits into this second pattern most often because *look very* is most often (21 of 31 instances) followed by an adjective in this corpus.

One of the meanings of LOOK is to turn one's attention in some direction. Prepositions such as *at, around, beside,* and the like all indicate directions. Similarly, the mentioned association between LOOK and SEE can be related to the fact that LOOK describes an action, and SEE can be viewed as the result of that action; so, we get examples such as *If you look, you'll see the ...* and *We'll take a look and see ... .* The situation just described for LOOK, in which other words in the context provide important cues regarding how LOOK is to be interpreted, is typical of words in general.

Looking at the Grammatical Contexts: Colligation

Let us now turn to the discussion of colligation—the grammatical context in which a word occurs. The senses expressed by words are linked to the grammatical patterns in which they are found (their colligations). Although the discussion of the various meanings of LOOK focused on the

---

* I should emphasize that the discussion here only touches on several high points of **one** approach to these redundancies. Other scholars using more statistically based approaches find other sorts of redundancies, variously described as "lexical bundles" (Biber, Johansson, Leech, Conrad, & Finegan, 1998, pp. 990–1024), "lexical phrases" (Nattinger and De Carrico, 1992), or "institutionalized expressions" (Lewis, 1994, p. 94).

collocations of the lemma LOOK, the discussion also illustrated the relevance of grammatical patterns. Francis, Hunston, and Manning (1998) list roughly 30 grammatical patterns for LOOK by itself and for combinations of LOOK plus particle or adverb (e.g., *look forward to, look into, look up,* etc.).* Let us explore a few of these patterns because the case of LOOK illustrates some of the difficulties of using colligation and shows that we need both collocation and colligation.

Table 3.4 illustrates eight of the colligations Francis et al. (1996) find for the verb LOOK. The grammatical environment in which we find a word gives us many cues to its meaning. Thus, only LOOK with an action interpretation is found in grammatical Patterns 1–3; only LOOK with a relational interpretation is found in Patterns 6–8. Pattern 4 is ambiguous.

One of the interesting things about the list of colligations for LOOK in Table 3.4 is the number of sequences that appear to be ambiguous when we consider only the grammatical patterns or the lexical items (the words). Table 3.5 illustrates some ambiguous phrases.

Only by considering both the grammatical patterns into which LOOK enters and the identity of the words that fill those grammatical patterns can we recognize the different meanings of LOOK. For example, there is the sequence LOOK *into* that may be interpreted either as an informal expression of 'investigate' (*I looked into the problem*) or as 'to turn one's atten-

Table 3.4 Eight Sample Colligations for the Verb LOOK

Grammatical Description	Illustrative Example
1. look + preposition of direction *up*	Look at the tall trees. (also *toward, up, around,* etc.)
2. look + particle (up) + NP book	Look up the number in the telephone book.
3. look + particle (after) + NP	Mary looked after the animals.
4. look + preposition (for) + NP	They looked for leaks.
	They looked for an increase in interest rates by the end of the year.
5. look + adverb + to + ing clause	She didn't look forward to visiting Kathy.
6. look + preposition (like) + n	Bill looked like his father.
7. look + adjective	They really looked impressive.
8. look + noun	Tom really looked the part.

Note: NP = noun phrase

---

* The difficulty in providing an exact number lies in deciding exactly what counts as a separate grammatical pattern.

Table 3.5 Pairs of Similar Constructions Involving LOOK That Have Different Grammatical Interpretations

Lexical Sequence	Grammatical Interpretation 1	Example	Grammatical Interpretation 2	Example
LOOK after + NP	LOOK + particle	She looked after the animals.	LOOK + PP	She looked after the dust that the car had raised.
LOOK for + NP	LOOK + PP	They looked for leaks.	LOOK + PP	They looked for an increase in interest rates by the end of the year.
LOOK into + NP	LOOK + PP	We need to look into the question right away.	LOOK + PP	He looked into the room and saw only a bed and a chair.
LOOK over + NP	LOOK + particle + NP	They always looked over new talent.	LOOK + PP	She looked over the wall and saw a well-kept yard.
LOOK up + NP	LOOK + particle + NP	look up the number	LOOK + PP	look up the drain spout

Note: NP = noun phrase; PP = prepositional phrase

Table 3.6 Verbs That Enter Into the Two Grammatical Patterns (a) V -ing and (b) V to-inf

begin	not bother	cease	commence	continue
deserve	dread	fear	forbear	go
hate	intend	like	love	need
omit	prefer	start	try	

Note: V -ing = a verb followed by another verb that takes the -ing suffix; V to-inf = a verb that is followed by a *to* infinitive.

tion in a particular direction within some circumscribed area' (*I looked into the room*). In both cases, the grammatical interpretation involves LOOK followed by a prepositional phrase with the preposition *into*. The fact that both interpretations are found in the same grammatical environment would predict that this phrase would regularly be ambiguous. Yet, in context it is usually easy to discover which interpretation is intended. For example, almost every time that LOOK *into* is followed by an abstract noun particularly by a noun like *issue* or *problem* it is interpreted as 'investigate'. When LOOK *into* is followed by a noun phrase that is interpretable as a location, the phrase is regularly interpreted as 'to turn one's attention in a particular direction'.

In summary, many times phrases that are ambiguous when considered in isolation are actually clearly interpretable when we consider them in their lexical and grammatical contexts.*

In general, only words of a relatively limited range of meanings are found within a given grammatical pattern. Francis et al. (1996, p. 589) mention a group of verbs that enter into the two grammatical patterns V-ing (a verb followed by another verb that takes the -ing suffix, as in *The ladder began falling.*) and V to-inf (a verb that is followed by a *to* infinitive, as in *The ladder began to fall.*). Francis et al.'s list of these verbs is in Table 3.6. They found that the verbs fell into two major groups (plus a residue) based on the sorts of meanings they expressed. One group of verbs expresses the phase of an action, such as beginning, continuing, not doing, and so on. The second group of verbs expresses some sort of mental reaction.

Group 1: Verbs From Table 3.6 That Express Phase of an Action

begin	cease	commence	continue	omit	start
not bother	forbear				

Group 2: Verbs From Table 3.6 That Express Mental Reaction

dread	fear	hate	like	love	prefer

---

* I should note that I have not explored the interactive context in this discussion because of my focus on lexicogrammar in this chapter. Clearly, if we take account of the general social interaction the participants are using the language to encode, that interaction will, through the notions of register, provide strong cues regarding how constructions are to be interpreted. Thus, in a corpus of data that are drawn from faculty meetings, committee meetings, and White House press interviews, it is no surprise to find that LOOK *into* is used almost all the time with the interpretation of "investigate."

Leftovers From Table 3.6 (These Verbs Do Not Form Any Obvious Semantic Group)

deserve	go	intend	need	try

The situation in the list in Table 3.6 is typical* of the sort of situation Hunston and Francis (1999) describe as they summarize their experience analyzing the Bank of English (the corpus of 400 million words that forms the basis of most of their work). They found that "given a list of words occurring with a particular pattern, the majority [of the words] will be divisible by most observers into reasonably coherent meaning groups" (p. 86).

Now, let me move to the next point: The various grammatical patterns may themselves contribute meanings. Hunston and Francis (1999) searched for adjectives that fitted into the pattern Linking verb + Adjective + about + noun phrase (v-link ADJ about NP). (An example of such a structure might be *He was quite reasonable about it, you know.*) They found the list provided in Table 3.7.

Hunston and Francis (1999, p. 87) comment that the list of words is quite varied and does not seem to have a common semantic thread. They say the following:

> With this pattern, they [the words in Table 3.7] all indicate that someone reacts to a situation in a particular way. It is not the **words** in the list that have this precise meaning, but the whole **phrase** of which they are a part. (p. 87; bold added)

In other words, the pattern itself adds or contributes meaning. Actually, we can see the active contribution of pattern when we look at individual words in collocation and colligation with others.

Table 3.7 Words That Fit Into the Adjective Slot in the Pattern v-link ADJ About NP

adult	foolish	marvelous
beastly	funny	mature
brave	good	nice
brilliant	gracious	odd
cool (= reasonable)	great	ok/okay
excellent	heavy (= unreasonable)	reasonable
fine	lovely	sweet

---

* I should say here that, because of limitations of space, I have chosen one of their examples that contains only two semantic groups plus a leftover category. This is an unusually small list of categories. However, the general point remains valid: The meanings of the words that fit into a given pattern generally express a limited range of meanings.

Table 3.8 Pattern of Constructions Related
to 'I have known him for ___'

I have known him for ___
five months
two days
ten years
yonks

I encountered an example several years ago. An Australian friend of mine once said of someone else, "I have known him for yonks." I had never heard *yonks* before, and so it was essentially a nonsense word for me, yet I was able to interpret the entire sentence with no difficulty because I placed it into a set of related constructions such as those in Table 3.8. Specifically, I interpreted *yonks* to refer to an extended period of time. (Note that I would have been surprised if my friend had said something like *I have only/merely known him for yonks*.)

Of course, old words that we already know may be given new meanings by their contexts just as well as new words. People entering fields that are new to them regularly encounter "familiar" words used in new ways. For example, people beginning the study of medicine may find the use of *present* unusual when they find it in a sentence such as the following medical headline: *A 63-year-old man presents to the emergency room with episodes of shaking and difficulty concentrating.* Many of us know how to present a paper at a meeting or to present a gift; few of us know how to present at an emergency room.

*Words Are Not Independent Units but Are Chosen in Groups
Based on Their Collocational and Colligational Properties*

Suppose you are asked where someone is, and you want to reply that you have no information.* There are several ways available for you to make that point, including the sentences in Table 3.9. Example 1 is a simple expression of lack of knowledge. Examples 2–6 all emphasize the lack of knowledge. These utterances fit into a preexisting pattern; the choice is of the pattern as a whole, and the words used are chosen because they fit into that pattern.

It turns out that if we look at the range of similar phrases, we find that there are relatively strong limitations on what occurs. However, *I haven't the faintest idea* is not an idiom, a form that is chosen as a single item at one time. It is not created in a way that is similar to a phrase such as *He got his*

---

* The discussion of this example is based on the work of Tucker (1996).

Table 3.9   Sentences That Express Extreme Lack of Information on Some Subject

1. I don't know where she is.
2. I don't have any idea of where she is.
3. I don't have any idea.
4. I haven't the faintest idea of where she might be.
5. I haven't the slightest idea.
6. I haven't the faintest.

dander up. That phrase has few possibilities for altering it other than creating appropriate substitutes for *he* and *his.* Idioms are merely at the extreme end of a range of possibilities. Rather, in the case of *I haven't the faintest idea*, the construction is formed by using the grammatical resources of the language. But, as each choice is made, it is made as part of an interlocking web of associations in which a choice in one place affects and restricts the choices available at other points. It is quite normal for a choice in one part of a sentence or of a text to have implications for the choices made at other parts of the sentence or text. Producers of text (speakers and listeners) as well as receivers of text (listeners and readers) make use of these redundancies in choices as they produce, receive, and interpret the texts involved.

Do Readers Actually Make Use of the Lexico-Grammatical Redundancy Available to Them as They Read? Evidence From Precorrection Miscues

General Issues

As discussed, the lexico-grammatical context in which a word is found provides a great deal of information concerning the identity and interpretation of the word. But, do readers actually **use** that information as they read?

It is important to notice that the advocates of the word-centered view do **not** claim that context is **never** used in reading. Stanovich (2000) divides the reading process into (at least) two steps: (a) word identification and (b) text comprehension.

> Skilled and/or older readers [are] more sensitive to contextual variables when the task that is employed taps comprehension processes but [are] actually less likely to use context to facilitate word recognition. (p. 8)

The theory is that good readers automate their response to letter patterns and are able to identify words accurately with little effort and little reference to the context in which the words are found. Because that initial identification is achieved with little mental effort, good readers are able to devote most of their mental energy to **interpreting** the words in context. Thus, a major difference between the two theories concerns the extent to which context is used in the **initial perception** of the words of the text.

Miscue Analysis of 14 Readings of "The Man Who Kept House"

Miscue analysis provides a means of exploring the issue of whether readers use information about the lexico-grammatical context as they initially perceive the words of the text. In miscue analysis readers, are asked to read a complete text aloud into a tape recorder, and then they are asked to retell the text from memory. The miscues, which are places where the **observed** response of the reader differs from the **expected** response based on the printed text, are then analyzed.

The study of miscues that are made **before** readers attempt to correct them (what I will call "precorrection miscues") provides insight into the information that the readers used for their initial identification of words. As a means of examining the relevance of context to the initial perceptions of readers, I examined the oral reading of a group of 14 readings of the story "The Man Who Kept House" (1962). The 13 readers (1 child read the story twice) ranged from first grade to seventh grade and illustrated a variety of reading abilities. These children were asked to read the story aloud while they were tape recorded and then to retell the story in their own words. All children understood the text reasonably well. The tape recordings of the oral readings were then studied to locate miscues. Finally, the miscues were analyzed to discover how they fitted in with the grammatical context.

Table 3.10 summarizes the miscues produced by all the readers. Columns in Table 3.10 are numbered for ease of reference. With one exception, each reader read the story only once. Zach, the only exception, read the story twice. Zach 93 summarizes the analysis of his first reading, and Zach 94 summarizes the analysis of his second reading. Column 2 of Table 3.10 shows the total miscues produced by each reader on the entire story. Columns 3 through 6 summarize the effect of the miscues on the grammar of the sentences as read. The numbers in Column 3 indicate how many miscues preserved the grammar of the original sentence. The numbers in Column 4 indicate how many miscues resulted in grammar that differed from the original but was perfectly acceptable in the context as read. The numbers in Column 5 provide the number of miscues that changed the grammar and resulted in a grammatical construction that was only partially acceptable in

Table 3.10 Summary of the Readers and Their Miscues

1	2	3	4	5	6	7	8
		Effect of Miscue on Grammar					
Reader	Total Miscues	Same Grammar	Different and Acceptable	Different and Partially Okay	Different and Unacceptable	Corrections	Abandon Correct
1. Able	15	4	5	6	0 (0%)	6	0
2. Alex	142	54	14	26	48 (34%)	43	5
3. Barbara	35	12	8	11	4 (11%)	13	0
4. Betsy	86	23	17	41	5 (6%)	38	0
5. Brooke	62	25	12	21	4 (6%)	16	1
6. Catherine	41	9	20	10	2 (5%)	6	0
7. Elizabeth	125	30	8	35	52 (41%)	31	4
8. Edward	52	16	4	18	14 (27%)	13	2
9. Jeremy	52	33	2	10	7 (13%)	12	0
10. Karen	18	12	1	3	2 (11%)	7	0
11. Robert	102	33	27	23	19 (18%)	16	7
12. Terrence	40	14	7	11	8 (20%)	6	0
13. Zach 93	54	28	9	14	3 (6%)	18	1
14. Zach 94	29	16	5	4	4 (14%)	12	0
Total	**853**	**309**	**139**	**233**	**172**	**237**	**20**
		36%	16%	26%	20%	28%	2%

Note: See text for discussion.

context.* Column 6 shows how many of the miscues changed the grammar into a sequence that was totally unacceptable. Columns 7 and 8 indicate how many times the reader corrected a miscue and how many times the reader abandoned a correct form.

---

* A miscue that results in a grammatical construction that is partially acceptable is acceptable with only part of the sentential context. For example, when Alex saw <We'll do it tomorrow>, he read "we'll do the," then he stopped and corrected *the* to *it* and went on. If we look at *the* and its relation to the remainder of the sentence, we see that it fits well with the preceding words. (For example, the sentence could continue as *we'll do the dishes.*) However, *the* does not fit with the following word (*tomorrow*). That miscue creates a grammatical construction that is partially acceptable. See Y. Goodman, Watson, and Burke (1987, pp. 82–84) for a more careful description.

To explicate the table, I use Alex (Row 2) as an example. He produced 142 miscues. Of these miscues, 54 preserved the grammar of the original sentence, 14 changed the grammar into something that was acceptable in context the way that he read it, 26 produced a grammatical construction that was partially acceptable, and 48 miscues produced unacceptable grammar. Of the 142 miscues, only 43 were corrected. In 5 cases, Alex abandoned a correct form.

Types of Evidence That an Analysis of Miscues May Provide

In what ways can precorrection miscues shed light on the dispute concerning the reading process? I see four types of evidence that are relevant to this argument:*

1. Insertions
2. Complex miscues
3. Miscues on repeated words
4. Comparison of the precorrection miscues of readers who differ in proficiency

Insertions   An *insertion* is a miscue in which a reader has added a word to the expected response. Thus, when Catherine read the title of the story <The man who kept house> she said "the man who kept the house" inserting *the* before *house*. Similarly, when Able encountered <Out the door went the pig>, he read "Out of the door went the pig," inserting *of* after *out*. We even have an unintentional experiment in the data. Because of a typographical error, sentence 58 was written as <It was not very long before woodman's wife came home.>, omitting *the* before *woodman's* in 13 of the 14 scripts for the readings. Of the 13 readers, 7 inserted *the* in front of *woodman's*.† Overall, roughly 6% of the miscues produced in the 14 readings involved insertions. Further, 11 of the 14 readings in the data contained at least one insertion.

---

* A fifth factor seems possibly relevant to the argument, although the relation to the issue at hand is complex. Specifically, Kenneth Goodman reports in conversation that miscues tend to cluster. That is, if a reader produces one miscue on a sentence, particularly a miscue that interferes with syntactic or semantic acceptability, that same reader is likely to produce other miscues elsewhere in that same sentence with a greater-than-chance probability. This phenomenon is interpretable as implying that if the first miscue leads the reader to lose track of the lexico-grammatical and semantic context, then the reader has to rely solely on the orthographic shape of the word. In that case, the reader is more likely to produce further miscues. Unfortunately for the discussion here, other interpretations of this phenomenon are possible.

† One reader corrected herself when she noticed that *the* was absent and reread the sentence omitting that word.

Insertions are relevant to the argument because they **cannot** be considered to be improperly automated responses to word shapes. No word is present in the original to improperly identify.

Complex Miscues   *Complex miscues* are miscues that involve a reader producing a reading in which several words differ from the expected response. However, the changes produced by the reader are related in that producing the first miscue virtually required the reader also to produce the other miscues. For example, when Terrence encountered the sentence <It was not very long before … .> he read "It *had not been* very long before … ." If we treat reading as the identification of **words**, then we are required to treat the two miscues in the verb phrase as unrelated. We are forced to say that in this sentence Terrence has replaced *was* with *had* and then, as a **separate** process, has inserted the word *been* into the sentence. But, that analysis seems to misrepresent what has happened. Rather, Terrence has substituted a past perfect form of the verb for a simple past tense. It is an accident that in English the past perfect involves one more orthographic word than does the simple past tense. A similar example occurs when Betsy reads <We'll do it tomorrow> as "well, you do it tomorrow." By changing *we'll* into *well* she deletes the original subject and changes the word into a sentential adverb. By deleting the subject, she allows herself to supply a different subject, and by making *we'll* into the adverb *well*, she allows herself to separate *well* rhythmically and grammatically from the rest of the sentence.

Finally, a third example occurred when Jeremy read the sentence <… he ran outside to look for her.>. He read this sentence as "… he ran outside *and looked* for her". Here, Jeremy changed two words. He changed *to* to *and* and *look* to the past tense *looked*. However, if we consider the phenomenon on a larger scale, it is merely **one** change in which a subordinate clause of purpose has been changed to a finite clause that is coordinated with the preceding finite clause.

Thirty-two miscues (slightly less than 4% of the miscues in the data) involved complex miscues. A theory that constrains us to consider reading as a process of identifying **words**, and words alone, has no way to account for the fact that quite a few miscues produced by readers involve more than one word.

Miscues on Repeated Words   The third type of evidence concerns what happens when a word recurs in the text several times in different lexico-grammatical contexts.

As we have seen, the word-centered view of reading claims that reading involves the automatic identification of word shapes independent of context. The implication of this view is that the patterns of miscues on repeated instances of the same word shape should be uninfluenced by context. That is, if a word shape (e.g., <l o o k>) occurs repeatedly throughout a story, then because readers are reacting to the same shape uninfluenced by the context in which it is encountered, each instance of that shape should occasion about the same number of miscues and the same types of miscues.

By contrast, the meaning-centered view of reading regards reading as creating meaning **in context**. The implication of this view of reading is that different instances of the same word shape are likely to engender different numbers of miscues and different types of miscues because readers are influenced by the context in which they perceive words as they read.

K. Goodman (1996) reports on his data in which children's ability to read different instances of the same word is indeed affected by the context in which the word is found. He describes his data informally:

> In a story about a circus coming to town young readers produced far fewer miscues on *circus* used as a noun, as in *The circus is coming*, than when it appeared as a noun modifier, as in *He liked the circus clowns*. They found it easier to read *vines* in *He hid in the rose vines* than in *Mr. Vines' candy store*. Miscues were more likely on *river* in *He lived in River Town* than *He fell into the river*. (p. 77)

In this section, I compare the miscues produced on multiple examples of several major lexical items (nouns, main verbs, or adjectives) and three function words. It turns out that only eight major lexical items are repeated seven or more times in this story. Further, in few cases do these repetitions involve different lexico-grammatical constructions. As a result, the data provide trends at best. As a means of discovering why few distinct patterns of miscues are found, it is useful to provide some statistics on the story and the miscues in the current database. As can be seen in Table 3.10, the 14 readings produced 853 miscues. Against that number, we need to consider all the opportunities to create a miscue that are available in this story. The story contains 796 words. Of course each word is a potential site of a miscue. However, many miscues were insertions, so they were coded as a miscue on a space. Because every word division constitutes a potential site of an insertion, we need to add the 795 spaces to our number of words. Finally, many miscues were coded as involving punctuation. For example, Able saw the words <She cut the rope from the cow's neck. As she did so, ...> on the page and read them as "She cut the rope from the cow's neck, as she did so. ...">. There were 159 punctuation marks; each constituted a potential site for a miscue. In sum, there were a total of 1,750 opportunities to miscue for each reading. There were 14 readings, so even by

Table 3.11 Distribution of Miscues on Items

No. of Miscues on Item	No. of Items	Total Miscues
0	1,243	0
1	318	318
2	108	216
3	45	135
4	17	68
5	9	45
6	5	30
7	1	7
8	2	16
9	2	18
Totals	1,750	853

conservative estimates there was a total of 24,360 opportunities to miscue. The 14 readings produced 853 miscues; thus, there was an average of 0.035 (= 853/24,360) miscues per opportunity to miscue.

Table 3.11 presents the distribution of the miscues on the various items (words, spaces, or punctuation). There are 1,243 items (by far the majority of items in the story) that occasion no miscues at all; 318 items occasion only 1 miscue on each item; 108 items occasion 2 miscues each and thus account for a total of 216 miscues of the 853 miscues; and so on. Only 36 items occasion four or more miscues.

Miscues on Two Major Lexical Items　All major lexical items that occurred seven or more times were examined. Few lemmas produced sufficient numbers of occurrences in different lexico-grammatical contexts to be of interest. One exception is the lemma HOUSE. This lemma is of interest because it occurred 14 times: 7 times in the phrase KEEP *house*, once in *clean house*, and 6 times in prepositional phrases such as *in the house* or *to the house*. Table 3.12 summarizes the miscues on HOUSE in these three environments. The first column presents the sentence number of each instance of the word *house* in the story. The second column gives the immediate phrase in that sentence that includes the word *house*. The third column gives the number of miscues that occurred on that instance, and the final column gives the miscues that the readers produced on the word *house* in each instance.

On the whole, Groups 1 and 2 produced more miscues than Group 3. Further, the one miscue produced on an instance of *house* in Group 3 is a rather different sort of miscue than the miscues in Groups 1 and 2. Finally,

Table 3.12   Miscues on the Word *house* in Three Environments

Sentence No.	Phrase	Miscue No.	Miscue Items
	Group 1		
0	who kept house	1	houses
3a	I keep house	2	houses, horses
3b	keeping house	2	houses, horses
9	keep house	2	houses, horses
33	keeping house	1	(___)
65	keep house	1	houses
67	keep house	2	houses, houses
	Group 2		
10	clean the house	2	houses, horses
	Group 3		
21	in the house	0	
23	to the house	0	
25	to the house	0	
47	on top of the house	1	roof
51	into the house	0	
59	near the house	0	

Note: (___) indicates the omission of a word.

it is worth noting that the issue is not simply one of readers getting practice in identifying the word *house* as they read the story. Group 1 contains two instances of *house* that are found in the last two sentences of the story, and these instances occasion the same sorts of miscues as the other instances in this group. Apparently, for these children, the word *house* in the phrases KEEP house and *clean the house* seem to provide a difficulty in this story that the other occurrences of *house* do not. In other words, at least some of the children are having difficulty with a phrase in spite of the fact that they know and are able to process the component words in other contexts.

A different example occurs in the miscues on the lemma SAY. In this case, *said* occurs nine times, and *say* occurs once. Table 3.13 presents the miscues on these items. The items are grouped according to the order of the subject and the predicate.

It is interesting to see that the items that begin with the predicate or the finite are the ones that create problems for the readers. Further, *say* in Sentence 66

Table 3.13   Miscues on the Lemma SAY

Sentence No.	Phrase	Miscue No.	Miscue Item
	Subject + Predicate		
2	He said to his wife	0	
16	He said	0	
44	He said to the cow	0	
	Predicate + Subject		
4	Said the husband	2	Is, the husband said (i.e., transposition)
7	Said the wife	2	$sayed, (___)
10	Said the wife	0	
31	Said the man	1	He
36	Said the woodman	0	
53	Said the woodman	1	this
	Finite + Subject + Predicator		
66	Never again did the woodman say to his wife	3	Stay ((3)

Note: (___) indicates the omission of a word

occasions an unusual number of miscues and miscues that are quite different from the other miscues produced for *said*. One factor that contributes to the presence of and the nature of these miscues is the fact that Sentence 66 is the first of two sentences that summarize the outcome of the story.

66.   Never again did the woodman say to his wife, "What did you do all day?"

67.   Never again did he tell his wife that he would stay home and keep house.

As can be seen from Sentence 67, it would have been quite appropriate for the book to say something such as "Never again did the woodman stay home and keep house." Apparently, three of the readers predicted that the story would end with that sort of information.

Miscues on the Function Words in, into, and to   As a comparison, it may be instructive to examine miscues on words that occur more frequently in this story and

Table 3.14 Summary of Miscues on *in*, *into*, and *to*

into	7	in	6	to				27			
								Infinitival *to*		19	
Prep.		**Prep.**		**Prep.**	8	**Complex vp**	7	**Adverbial of Purpose**	6	**Qualifier**	6
Miscue	**#**	**Miscue**	**#**	**Miscue**	**#**	**Miscue**	**#**	**Miscue**	**#**	**Miscue**	**#**
to	3	(__)	2	(__)	5	(__)	1	(__)	4		
in	1	and	1	in	3			and	3		
inside	1			into	3			into	2		
(__)	1			home	1			the	1		
				on	1						
				onto	1						
Total Miscues	6		3		14		1		10		0

Note: See text for discussion. (__) indicates the omission of a word..

that provide some more interesting variation in the lexico-grammatical context. One group of similar but interestingly different words are the function words *into*, *in*, and *to*. The miscues on these words are summarized in Table 3.14. These words are interesting partly because they involve similar graphic shapes. *Into* combines the form of *in* and *to*. However, this similarity of form is complicated by the special grammatical functions of *to*. All three words are (in the case of *in* and *into*) or may be (in the case of *to*) prepositions. *To,* however, also functions as a marker of the infinitive. Further, its function as an infinitival marker may be complicated by the role of the infinitive in the larger construction. In the story analyzed in this chapter, the infinitive construction fills three different functions: (a) The infinitive may be part of a complex verb phrase as in (10b) … *you'll have to make butter … .* (b) The infinitive may function as part of a qualifier following the head of a noun phrase or adjective phrase as in (31) *Now I've got more work to do.* (c) The infinitive may function as part of an adverbial clause of purpose as in (10a) *If you stay home to do my work … .*

We may use the presence of different grammatical functions for *to* as a sort of test of the degree to which readers use contextual information in their reading. If readers identify each word individually and then later relate those identified words to their contexts, then we should see essentially the same pattern of miscues on the word *to* regardless of the grammatical context. If, on the other hand, readers use context (and more specifically lexico-grammatical context) as they make sense of the graphic signals on the page, then we should find that the various uses of *to* should receive different patterns of miscues. Indeed, we could expect the pattern of miscues for the prepositional use of *to* to resemble the miscues for *in* and *into*. However, we would expect to find a different pattern of miscues for infinitival *to*.

Table 3.14 summarizes the miscues on all the occurrences of these words. The numbers in the top row indicate the number of instances of each of the words. In the case of *to*, the miscues produced in each grammatical function are separated, and the total number of instances is given for each function in the second row of the table. The fourth through ninth rows give the various miscues produced for each type of word, and the total number of miscues produced on that type of word is provided in the bottom row.

Numbers are small, but we can see some patterning in the miscues produced. When we compare the miscues produced on the three prepositions (*in, into,* and *to*), we find there is no statistical difference in the number of miscues produced on the different prepositions. In addition, the actual miscues produced on each of the words often involve substituting one of the three prepositions for another. Thus, 4 of the miscues produced on *into* are either *in* or *to*. Similarly, 6 of the miscues produced for *to* are either *in* or *into*. In fact, 11 of the 23 miscues produced on these three prepositions involve some similarity of graphic shape, so we could say that the graphic form is relevant to the production of these miscues. However, the similarity of graphic shape cannot be seen as the single determining factor because most of these miscues preserve a larger lexico-grammatical pattern. Thus, *on* and *onto* are read for *to* in a context in which those words make perfect colligational and collocational sense (... *the cow fell down to the ground,* ...). Similarly, *home* is read in a context in which the reader said "Never again did the woodsman stay home his wife." Once the reader said "stay," it was quite appropriate (colligationally and collocationally) for him also to say "home." Only when he reached the phrase *his wife* did he encounter something that did not fit the pattern he had begun. In summary, most of the miscues produced on the three prepositions not only preserve graphic shape to some degree but also preserve the larger lexico-grammatical patterns either entirely as in *on* and *onto* for *to* or partially as in the case of *home* for *to*.

When we consider the miscues produced on the three infinitival uses of *to*, we find different sorts of miscues. On all seven occurrences of infinitival *to* when it is part of a complex verb phrase (e.g., *have to make butter, began to do,* and *is not going to be*), only one miscue was produced. This lack of miscues relates to the high predictability of *to* in this context. Of the three constructions (HAVE *to*, BEGIN *to*, and GOING *to*), only BEGIN allows two different sorts of verb forms to follow it. Not only is it quite common for BEGIN to occur before *to* infinitives (as in *began to do it*), but also it is quite common for BEGIN to precede *-ing* participles, as in (*began doing it*). Further, the two constructions express similar meanings. It is of interest that the only miscue in this set involved a complex miscue in which *to* was omitted and *doing* was substituted for *do*. That is, the reader simply substituted one grammatical construction for another with a similar meaning.

A similar pattern exists for the six examples in which the *to* clause functions as a qualifier of a noun phrase or adjective phrase. None of these six examples of *to* engenders a miscue. It is worthy of note that infinitival modifiers follow these particular head words (*glad, grass, something, time, water, work*) relatively frequently in the language as a whole. For example, in the corpus of Spoken Professional American English, *glad* occurs 80 times, of which 36 (almost half) are followed by a *to infinitive* clause. This is an extreme case. Other examples (e.g., *time to*) are relatively less frequent but still occur more frequently than chance would predict.

When *to,* introduces an adverbial clause of purpose, an entirely different pattern of miscues occurs. First, we find more frequent miscues. There are six instances of this use of infinitival *to*, and these six instances occasion a total of 10 miscues (an average of almost 2 miscues per instance). More striking is the pattern of miscues produced. Of the miscues, 3 involve replacing *to* with *and*, 4 involve omissions of *to*; 2 miscues each replace *to* with *into*, and 1 replaces *to* with *the*. Only 2 of these miscues involve graphic similarity. All of the miscues respond to a larger lexico-grammatical pattern. All the instances in which *to* is replaced with *and* involve cases in which the readers have changed the infinitive clause into a finite clause. Even the reader who substituted *the* for *to* (saying "... wife stayed home to keep houses and the look after the child") produced a structure that could have been completed grammatically as in (*... wife stayed home to keep houses and the husband went to the forest*).

Comparison of the Precorrection Miscues of Readers Who Differ in Proficiency

As was seen in the Stanovich and Johnson quotations on pages 53 and 54, the word-centered theory claims that only poor readers use context as they identify the words they are reading. By contrast to the poor readers, proficient readers (and proficient adult readers) are said **not** to use context to identify words. We can use miscue analysis to examine this claim. Of course, we expect adult proficient readers to make far fewer miscues than children. However, they **will** make miscues, and an analysis of the patterns of miscues that they make will tell us something about those adult readers' attention. Specifically, if a great proportion of their miscues displays graphic or

Table 3.15 Initial Miscues and Story Content, Sentence Syntax, and Sentence Semantics

	Story Content		Sentence Syntax		Sentence Semantics	
	Accept.	Unaccept.	Accept.	Unaccept.	Accept.	Unaccept.
Average number of miscues	45.541	6.875	49.042	3.375	45.958	6.458
Average percentage of miscues	86.9	13.1	93.6	6.4	87.7	12.3

phonological similarity to the expected response, then they are probably paying great attention to the letter shapes and identifying the words with little reference to context. By contrast, if a great proportion of the miscues preserves the sentence grammar and the local semantics of the sentence, then the readers are probably using the sentential context as they initially make sense of the words in the text.

Kucer and Tuten (2003) investigated the precorrection oral reading miscues of 24 advanced graduate students enrolled in a doctoral program in language, literacy, and learning or a professional diploma program (post-master's) in school psychology as they read the 21-page short story "Poison" (Roald Dahl, 1958). Table 3.15 (their Table 1) reports the frequency with which the miscues produced by these adult readers preserved story content, sentence syntax, and sentence semantics. Table 3.16 (their Table 2) reports the frequency with which the adult readers preserved the graphic or phonological shape of the expected response.

Clearly, the adult readers in this study paid a great deal of attention to the syntactic and semantic environment of the words they were reading. Over 93% of the precorrection miscues created acceptable grammar within the sentence. Similarly, over 87% of the miscues were acceptable with the previous meaning

Table 3.16 Initial Miscues and Graphics and Sound

	Graphics			Sound		
	High	Partial	None	High	Partial	None
Average number of miscues	18.417	5.917	28.083	17.292	6.042	29.083
Average percentage of miscues	35.1	11.3	53.6	33	11.5	55.5

of the sentence in which they were located. Finally, over 86% of the miscues expressed meanings that were acceptable within the terms of the story. By contrast, these readers paid less attention to the graphic and phonological shapes of the words. Over 53% of the miscues showed no graphic similarity with the expected responses, and over 55% of the miscues showed no sound similarity with the expected response.

It is instructive to compare the results for Kucer and Tuten's (2003) readers with the results for the young readers in my data. In my data, the 14 readings preserved acceptable grammar in 84.2% of the cases (compare this with Kucer & Tuten's 93% for the adult readings). The averages for individual readers ranged from 58% of miscues that preserved acceptable grammar for one reader, to 100% of the miscues that preserved acceptable grammar for a second reader. Clearly, the readers who were graduate students maintained acceptable syntax **more** regularly than the readers who were elementary school students. In other words, the older and more proficient readers were **more** sensitive to the lexico-grammatical context than the younger, less-proficient readers. These results clearly call into question whether proficient readers use context-free techniques as they identify the words they read.

Conclusion

In the second section of this chapter I described some of the basic conclusions concerning language reached by corpus linguists based on their explorations of very large corpora (corpora that contain hundreds of millions of words). Their evidence documents the strong and pervasive lexico-grammatical redundancy that exists within naturally occurring language. This work can be summarized by saying that the lexico-grammatical context in which words are found regularly provides important information about the identity of the words and the meanings of those words.* Simply put, language is pervasively redundant.

The third section of this chapter addressed the question of whether readers actually use the linguistic redundancies available to them as they read natural texts. This study investigated the precorrection miscues produced by a group of 14 readers as they read a children's story. The assumption

---

* I should emphasize here that **only** the lexico-grammatical redundancies have been explored here. I have ignored information provided by generic structure, by patterns of opposition created by the text, or by semantic prosodies (see Louw, 1993; Sinclair, 1991, p. 112) within a text, and I have not included information gained from the interaction that the text is used to encode. All of these other aspects of language in use, as well as still other aspects not mentioned here, regularly provide important evidence about the nature of the words and phrases used in a particular text.

behind this study was that the children used the same sort of processes to produce miscues as they did when they were reading and produced expected responses. The simple presence of a significant number of insertions and of complex miscues provides evidence that these readers were not simply identifying the words of the text purely on the basis of the identification of the letters seen on the page. Neither insertions nor complex miscues can be explained as a process of word identification gone wrong. Rather, these miscues require an explanation that addresses the perceived relation between the miscue and its lexico-grammatical context.

Similarly, when we examined the miscues produced on different instances of the same word in different contexts in the story, we found evidence that suggested that the number and nature of the miscues changed depending on the lexico-grammatical environment. Again, this could not happen unless the readers were paying considerable attention to the lexico-grammatical environment as they read.

Finally, when we compared the results of our study with a study of adult readers in a graduate program at a university, it was found that the older, more proficient readers were even more influenced by the lexico-grammatical context than the younger readers. In short, not only is language pervasively redundant, but also readers **use** these redundancies as they make sense of the texts they are reading.

References

Adams, M. J. (1990). *Beginning to read: Thinking and learning about print*. Cambridge, MA: MIT Press.

Anonymous (1964). The man who kept house. (1962). In J. McInnes, M. Gerrard, & J. Ryckman (Eds.), *Magic and make believe* (pp. 282-287). Don Mills, Ontario: Thomas Nelson.

Barlow, M. (2002). Monoconc pro 2.2. <www.Aethelstan.com>

Biber, D., Conrad, S., & Reppen, R. (1998). *Corpus linguistics: Investigating language structure and use*. Cambridge, U.K.: Cambridge University Press.

Biber, D., Johansson, S., Leech, G., Conrad, S., & Finegan, E. (1999). *Longman grammar of spoken and written English*. Harlow, U.K.: Longman.

Butt, D. Fahey, R., Feez, S., Spinks, S., & Yallop, C. (2000). *Using functional grammar: An explorer's guide*. Macquarie University, Sydney, Australia: NCELTR.

Dahl, R. (1958). Poison. In R. W. Inglis & J. Spear (Eds.). *Adventures in English literature* (pp. 604-611). New York: Harcourt, Brace & Jovanovich.

Firth, J. R. (1957). A synopsis of linguistic theory, 1930–1955. *Studies in Linguistic Analysis, special volume,* 1–32.

Flurkey, A., & Xu, J. (Eds.). (2003). *On the revolution of reading: The selected writings of Kenneth S. Goodman.* Portsmouth, NH: Heinemann.

Francis, G. (1993). A corpus-driven approach to grammar — principles, methods and examples. In M. Baker, G. Francis, & E. Tognini-Bonelli (Eds.), *Text and technology: In honour of John Sinclair* (pp. 137–156). Amsterdam: Benjamins.

Francis, G., Hunston, S., & Manning, E. (Eds.). (1996). *Collins COBUILD grammar patterns 1: Verbs.* London: HarperCollins.

Francis, G., Hunston, S., & Manning, E. (Eds.). (1998). *Collins COBUILD grammar patterns 2: Nouns and adjectives.* London: HarperCollins.

Fries, C. C. (1945). *Teaching and learning English as a foreign language.* Ann Arbor: University of Michigan Press.

Goodman, K. (1993). *Phonics phacts.* Portsmouth, NH: Heinemann.

Goodman, K. (1994). Reading, writing and written texts: A transactional sociopsy-cholinguistic view. In R. Ruddell, M. Ruddell, & H. Singer (Eds.), *Theoretical models and processes of reading* (4th ed., pp. 1093–1130). Newark, DE: International Reading Association.

Goodman, K. (1996). *On reading: A common-sense look at the nature of language and the science of reading.* Portsmouth, NH: Heinemann.

Goodman, Y., Watson, D., & Burke, C. (1987). *Reading miscue inventory: Alternative procedures.* New York: Owen.

Hunston, S. (2002). *Corpora in applied linguistics.* Cambridge, U.K.: Cambridge University Press.

Hunston, S., & Francis, G. (1999). *Pattern grammar: A corpus-driven approach to the lexical grammar of English.* Amsterdam: Benjamins.

Johnston, F. R. (1998). The reader, the text, and the task: Learning words in first grade. *The Reading Teacher, 51,* 666–675.

Kucer, S., & Tuten, J. (2003). Revisiting and rethinking the reading process. *Language Arts, 80,* 284–290.

Lewis, M. (1994). *The lexical approach: The state of ELT and a way forward.* Hove, U.K.: Language Teaching.

Louw, B. (1993). Irony in the text or insincerity in the writer? The diagnostic potential of semantic prosodies. In M. Baker, G. Francis, & E. Tognini-Bonelli (Eds.), *Text and technology* (pp. 157–176). Amsterdam: Benjamins.

Martens, P. (1995). Empowering teachers and empowering students. *Primary Voices K-6, 3,* 39–44.

Matthiessen, C. M. I. M. (1995). *Lexicogrammatical cartography*. Tokyo: International Language Sciences.

McQueen, J. M., & Cutler, A. (1997). Cognitive processes in speech perception. In W. J. Hardcastle and J. Laver (Eds.) *The handbook of phonetic sciences* (pp. 566-585). Oxford: Blackwell.

Moats, L. K. (2000). Whole language lives on: The illusion of "balanced reading instruction." Retrieved May 12, 2006, from http://www.usu.edu/teachall/text/reading/Wholelang.htm

Nattinger, J. R., & DeCarrico, J. S. (1992). *Lexical phrases and language teaching*. Oxford, U.K.: Oxford University Press.

Sinclair, J. (Ed.). (1987). *Looking up: An account of the COBUILD project in lexical computing*. London: Collins ELT.

Sinclair, J. (1991). *Corpus, concordance, collocation*. Oxford, U.K.: Oxford University Press.

Smith, F. (1994). *Understanding reading* (5th ed.). Hillsdale, NJ: Erlbaum.

Stanovich, K. (2000). *Progress in understanding reading: Scientific foundations and new frontiers*. New York: Guilford Press.

Tucker, G. (1996). So grammarians haven't the faintest idea: Reconciling lexis-oriented and grammar-oriented approaches to language. In R. Hasan, C. Cloran, & D. Butt (Eds.), *Functional descriptions: Theory and practice* (pp. 145–178). Amsterdam: Benjamins.

INTRODUCTION TO CHAPTER 4

S TEVEN STRAUSS, WHO IS BOTH LINGUIST and neurologist as well as a good friend, came to me some years ago with a video of one of his aphasic patients exhibiting an odd behavior. The patient had a stroke, and his language abilities were severely impaired. When he was asked to read a list of short words, he responded by counting the letters in each word. "One, two, three, four, five," for example, for a five-letter word. He never named the word but occasionally threw in a letter name. I suggested that he thought he was spelling, and that perhaps letters and numerals are somehow connected in his mind. We discussed the possibility of giving him some real texts, such as newspaper ads, and sure enough, although he did not read them accurately, his responses sounded more like real language, and he did not count out letters. We began an informal collaboration looking at the reading of his patients with various forms of language impairment, both productive and receptive. Our concern was to look at what they did in meaningful contextualized language rather than the bits and pieces typical of speech therapy for such patients.

When I shared this in one of my classes, a teacher told me about a colleague whose young husband had a stroke a few months earlier. I made contact with the man, Stuart Carter, and we began a long-term collaborative study of his reading and how it had been affected by his stroke. Andrea García-Obregón analyzed the videotapes of these sessions for her doctoral dissertation. She was uniquely qualified to do so having worked as a speech therapist in Mexico.

In this chapter, García-Obregón refers to the two participants in the collaborative study by our first names. That is fitting because it makes clear that we were not subject and researcher but collaborators in this study. I brought to it my expertise as a reading researcher and theoretician, and Stuart brought his as an educated, literate, thoughtful, and introspective man with aphasia. We have used his real name at his suggestion.

From the beginning, I made clear that I made no promises that anything we did would result in any improvement in his condition other than helping him to understand it. And, Stuart made clear that he was pleased to be part of a study that could help others who had been similarly impaired and enlighten those who worked with them.

Stuart is a remarkable man. He is determined to live as normal a life as possible. He maintained a strong sense of humor, often laughing at his own clumsiness, and showed no signs of depression. His supportive wife always came with him and sat in our sessions. The study very much depended on his insights into his own performance as a reader.

In research based in scientific realism, the questions come first, and then the methodology and research design evolve to answer them. That contrasts with what has been called the hammer approach: First you have a hammer, and then you look for things to bang on.

In our study, the key question was how a massive stroke on the brain hemisphere that controls language had affected Stuart's reading competence and his performance. The literature often refers to the condition Stuart had as *acquired dyslexia*, but Stuart was not dyslexic. He was a competent reader whose ability to perform as a reader had been impaired. Our joint goal was to find out what he could and could not do as a reader and writer over time as he worked at regaining his strength. We tried to understand why he performed as he did.

It was an opportunity for me to test my reading theory in the context of Stuart's aphasia. So, the methodology emerged. García-Obregón has used miscue analysis to look at the relationship of his reading performance and competence. I involved Stuart in a number of reasonably authentic reading and writing tasks drawn if possible from the literacy acts important to him. Each event suggested others, and my analysis during the ongoing study was always informal. Often, we would check out one insight by trying a slightly different type of text or zeroing in on certain phrases or word types in and out of context. The conversations we had before and after each such authentic probe were an important part of the study, as were the comments he made during each activity and the experiences he shared, such as taking 45 minutes to write a two-line note to the day person on his job at the cotton gin where he worked nights or how he figured out how to change a tire with his one good arm.

What made this collaborative study so fruitful is that we explored together real literacy activities in one real person's attempts to perform them.

Ken Goodman

4

REIMAGINING LITERACY COMPETENCE
A Sociopsycholinguistic View of Reading in Aphasia

Andrea García Obregón

In the hospital in Willcox, so it is from the ... the second day, or [...] week until the five, fifth week, after the stroke. There again the ... the lady had asked if I wanted to have a book and I said, "Yea, I guess so." And I would just open it and pick ... pick up the day, the words, and that was the only way I could do it 'cause everything else was gibberish, more or less.

Stuart Carter, November 29, 1995

*I*N THE SPRING OF 1994, Stuart Carter was working at his house when he suffered a stroke. He was 36 years old at the time and owned a pecan farm in the Southwest. He remembers working on the books for the farm on a Friday night, when he suddenly felt that something was wrong. Medical records indicate that on April 8, 1994, Stuart suffered a unilateral intracerebral hemorrhage on the left side of his brain, which resulted in expressive aphasia and hemiplegia, with weakness in the right side of his body. Not long after the stroke, Stuart learned that one of the most upsetting consequences of aphasia is that both oral and written language processes suffer as a result of the neurological shifts experienced by the brain (Nadeau, Gonzalez Rothi, & Crosson, 2000).

What happens when there is a sudden event that inevitably affects the structure of the human brain? What happens when someone experiences a stroke, for example, and is left unable to use language to communicate? How does a competent language user face the loss of the ability either to produce or to understand oral or written language as a result of a cerebral vascular injury? Ewing and Pfalzgraf (1990) describe a stroke as a "swift, unexpected, and devastating" (p. 11) event that most commonly causes loss of communication. When this traumatic event takes place, how is literacy affected? How is the reading process transformed?

Based on a longitudinal and qualitative case study of literacy in aphasia (García Obregón 2002), this chapter presents an investigation of Stuart's literacy competence after the onset of aphasia, concentrating on his reading process across time. Using miscue analysis as a research tool to investigate Stuart's oral reading, it supports and extends Ken Goodman's (1994) transactional and sociopsycholinguistic model of reading, offering a new perspective to reimagine the meaning of literacy competence in the case of readers with aphasia.

This chapter begins with a review of related literature and a discussion of the main theoretical influences that frame this inquiry. I then present Stuart's reading profile and supportive miscue analysis data to describe his miscue patterns and his use of reading strategies after the stroke. Finally, the chapter concludes with a discussion of implications for future inquiry in the area of reading and aphasia.

Theoretical Framework: Literacy Processes and Aphasia

Aphasia: An Introduction

For the present research, *aphasia* is defined as an acquired disorder of previously intact language ability resulting from brain injury (Kirshner, 1995). The most common cause of aphasia is a stroke, which results from disruptions in the blood supply of the brain tissue from blood clots, aneurysms, or trauma. The extent of the brain injury varies depending on where the flow of blood was interrupted. Receptive or productive language processes can be affected. These include any or all of listening, speaking, reading, writing, and signing.

Physical movement may also be impaired depending on the location of the brain injury. As a result of the cerebral hemorrhage in the left hemisphere of his brain, Stuart experienced hemiplegia on the right side of his body. This condition had important consequences for his use of written language. As a right-hand-dominant, but somewhat ambidextrous, individual, Stuart had to learn to write with his left hand after the stroke. A number of other related psychological and emotional disorders, like depression, are commonly experienced by individuals affected by a stroke. These psychological disorders are usually faced by their family members and close friends, as the loss of language has significant implications for the overall structure of social and relational networks. At the time this research was conducted, Stuart seemed surprisingly free of depression and had strong support from his family and friends.

There is a variety of language disorders associated with aphasia, many of which are still a matter of great debate within the field of aphasiology (Goodglass, 1993; Nadeau et al., 2000). Overall, oral and written languages are usually very much affected by the onset of aphasia. In some cases, people lose the ability to comprehend oral language while maintaining the ability to produce oral language or to understand what is written. Other times, it is the inability to produce oral or written texts that is most evident, while the ability to understand oral language is maintained. In some cases, unfortunately, both receptive and productive processes are affected by the cerebrovascular event.

In Stuart's case, the type of trial and error evidenced in his oral and written language is most commonly associated with motor, or expressive, aphasia. In this type of aphasia, the ability to understand both oral and written language remains mostly untouched; it is the expression of meaning through oral or written language that is problematic as both productive forms of communication are altered. Stuart's speech is commonly characterized by numerous paraphasias, "the unintended use of another word in lieu of the target" (Goodglass, 1993, p. 78). These semantic, syntactic, and phonological oral miscues are sometimes associated with either *agrammatism*, "a distinctive form of linguistic breakdown" within the grammatical dimension of language (Goodglass, 1993, p. 102), or *apraxia*, a term used to identify disorders in the sphere of purposeful movement, which may or may not be related to oral language. Apraxia in Stuart's case caused him minor difficulty in articulating some sounds to form his desired oral messages. At the same time, a minor degree of agrammatism influenced his speech production and his construction of grammatically conventional English structures.

It is important at this point to mention that throughout this narrative I use quotations to indicate Stuart's speech as transcribed from videotaped interviews. All grammatical structures are represented as Stuart spoke at the time of the interview. The quotations have not been modified to reflect conventional grammar because it was important to leave his words as evidence of his recovery and development across time given that this research presents data collected at different moments in time since the onset of aphasia. In addition, as a coparticipant in this research, Stuart made it clear he wanted readers to know that the presence of unconventional grammatical structures is not representative of his underlying language competence. Even in the early weeks after the stroke, Stuart was able to identify when he had made a mistake in his choice of words or syntactic constructions. However, often his aphasia prevented him from fully correcting his unconventional grammar, especially in the months following the stroke. Within quotations, other transcription marks include hyphens to indicate partial attempts at a word, and ... to indicate a pause in Stuart's speech.

In aphasia, the severity of any resulting communication problem changes with time. The most severe communication difficulties become evident in the days and weeks immediately following the stroke. Cases vary considerably from each other, and there are some who believe that variability in aphasia is as broad as the diversity among individuals living in this world (Lesser & Milroy, 1993).

Transactional and Sociopsycholinguistic Perspective of Literacy Processes

My investigation of the reading process in aphasia is informed by the "Copernican revolution" Ken Goodman started almost 40 years ago when he first explained his conceptualization of reading as a "psycholinguistic guessing game" (Goodman, 1967/1982). Goodman's research helps us understand reading as an active process of making sense during which a reader uses information gathered from the language cueing systems in the text in conjunction with psycholinguistic reading strategies (sampling, predicting, confirming, and disconfirming) to make sense of print. While transacting with printed texts, the reader creates a parallel text, a "personally constructed reader text" (Goodman, 1996, p. 91) that is informed by the reader's previous experiences, background knowledge, and cognitive schema.

Goodman's (1994) transactional and sociopsycholinguistic model of reading provides a way of understanding how readers use all the cueing systems when reading, and that reading miscues, unexpected oral reading responses to expected printed text, are a natural part of the reading process for all readers. His research throughout the past decades has demonstrated how miscues are not random responses, but psycholinguistic responses that demonstrate the complex transaction between the text's linguistic system and the reader's linguistic knowledge and psycholinguistic reading strategies.

By investigating the oral reading process of readers transacting with real texts, Goodman (1994) defines reading in terms of proficiency, which has at its center a concern with the effective construction of meaning through the efficient use of linguistic cueing systems and cognitive reading strategies. "Effective reading is making sense of print, not accurate word identification," Goodman writes. He then elaborates, "Meaning is in the reader and the writer, not in the text" (p. 1094), and it is through the transaction between the two that a meaning potential is constructed and open for interpretation.

Reading and Aphasia

Throughout the decades, and even as far back as the 16th century, researchers have used aphasia as a source of clinical experimentation (Roth & Heilman,

2000). Classic case studies go back to 1864, when medical doctors described for the first time patients who had oral language difficulties following a cerebral lesion. Results from these studies led to the construction of models of language and learning that generally deal with the brain as a language-processing center. This highly descriptive medical arena documents exceptional language stories. Most concentrate on the unique expressive and receptive oral language difficulties presented by particular individuals (Jacyna, 2000). Since the early 1970s, research related to written language and aphasia has slowly emerged in the literature.

Much of the resistance to investigating written language comes from the commonly held belief that written language is not as important as oral language. As Carlomagno and Iavarone (1995) point out:

> Writing disturbances in aphasic patients have usually been considered a secondary aspect of their communication disorder. This point of view was supported by the (quite general) assumption that writing is a mere graphemic translation of spoken language. (p. 201)

The majority of the research reported on written language and aphasia deals with closely controlled experimental tasks in which researchers attempt to map or to document the performance of those who suffer from aphasia while they participate in reduced clinical reading and writing activities with decontextualized language (Andreewsky & Cochu, 1995; Greenwald, 2000; Webb & Love, 1983). The literature presents descriptive symptoms and extensive comparisons with previously published accounts to inform reading models based on cognitive information-processing analysis (Carlomagno & Iavarone, 1995; Rapcsak & Beeson, 2000; Rieff Cherney, 2004).

Competence as Socially Constructed

The present research is a psycholinguistic exploration of the reading process in aphasia, moving away from the use of standardized tests in favor of using texts of everyday life to document and investigate Stuart's reading competence. A guiding argument in this work is the belief that literacy competence is socially constructed through our daily participation in multiple literacy events and practices. My use of the term *competence* in this research does not follow the classic distinction between competence and performance described by Chomsky (1957). Rather, it is based on the work of Hymes (1972) and Kovarsky, Duchan, and Maxwell (1999).

Hymes (1974) describes the ethnography of communication as "a science that would approach language neither as abstracted form nor as an abstract correlate of a community, but as *situated* in the flux and pattern of communicative events" (p. 5). Within this context, it is possible to locate literacy as situated in the flux of literacy events and shaping literacy practices. Hymes believes that knowledge about language does not include only knowledge about the underlying grammatical structures. He criticized Chomsky's definition of competence by stating that "it is restricted to … knowledge of grammar. Thus, it leaves other aspects of speakers' tacit knowledge and ability in confusion" (p. 93). According to Hymes, communicative competence includes knowledge about the appropriateness and the rules of language use within a given sociocultural context. Hymes's recognition that any discussion of competence should take into consideration "not only knowledge, but also ability to implement it" (p. 96) is a powerful indicator of the situated nature of competence.

The conceptualization of competence delineated by Hymes is further developed by Kovarsky, Duchan, and Maxwell (1999), who argue for an interactive and contextualized understanding of competence, "a view that allows us to see and understand how competence gets constructed, evaluated, and revised in the course of everyone's everyday life experience" (p. 20). Writing about communicative competence within clinical discourse settings, these authors believe that "displays of competence rely heavily on the conditions that prevail in particular occasions" (p. 18). Their view is one that highlights the situated nature of competence and the influence of social interaction in the construction of a competent or incompetent identity.

I locate my understanding of competence following this situated framework, in which competence is not something static and quantifiable but a dynamic and complex display of abilities that emerge depending on the contextual features that frame social communicative interactions. In particular reference to reading, a similar argument was set forth by Goodman (1975/1982) in the initial stages of conceptualizing his reading model:

> Competence, what readers are capable of doing, must be separated from performance, what we observe them to do. It is competence that results in the reader's control and flexibility in using the reading process. Their performance is simply the observable result of the competence. … Researchers may use performance or behavioral indicators of underlying competence but they err seriously in equating what readers do with what they are capable of doing. (p. 7)

This line of thinking is supported by Strauss (1999) in his research specifically with aphasic adults. Strauss's research indicated that, "Data from adult aphasic language provide striking support for Goodman's notion that language performance is optimized in social contexts that involve authentic texts and prompt language users to have particular communicative purposes" (p. 405). Kovarsky, Kimbarow, and Kastner (1999) extend this further when they write, "Speakers with severely impaired language abilities are able to communicate quite effectively, given the right interactional circumstances" (p. 291).

Research Context

This research presents results from a collaborative inquiry conducted by Ken Goodman and Stuart Carter in 1994 through 1995. During that time, they engaged in a longitudinal case study of reading and writing processes in aphasia from a transactional and sociopsycholinguistic perspective. Data were collected for a period of approximately 15 months during weekly 2-hour meetings between October 1994 and December 1995.

Stuart was 37 years old when he began collaborating with Ken. Born June 22, 1957, in Portales, New Mexico, he grew up in Lovington, New Mexico, located about 90 miles from Portales. He married Kathy, his high school sweetheart, and is the father of two children, Caitlin and Cameron. His parents were born in the United States from immigrant families. His father earned degrees in the areas of economic and political sciences and was an active local and state politician when Stuart was young.

Stuart's personal history reflects his expertise in multiple work domains, including farming, construction, and politics, in addition to his work as treasurer of a regional electric cooperative, among others. He completed 88 hours toward a bachelor of science degree in geology at Abilene University and Texas Tech University. He was an active member of Western Pecan Growers Association, attending yearly seminars and annual gatherings. When this research story began, Stuart was the president and general manager of High County Pecans Incorporated, as well as a board member and treasurer of the cooperative.

Data and Analysis Strategies

Over 40 hours of tapes were produced during the course of the study between 1994 and 1995, plus additional data were collected between 1998 and 2001, when I joined the research study. The resulting database includes written documents and videotapes, which contain a multitude of oral and written language events (i.e., oral and silent readings, writing, dictation, informal interviews, dialogue) as Stuart and Ken engaged in an ongoing dialogue and investigation of language and literacy. An in-depth analysis of this database can be found in García Obregón (2002).

The data reported in this research comes from the archived data set of videotaped interactions between Ken and Stuart. The analysis of the data took place through a combination of strategies looking at the macro- and microcontexts of the research. At the macrolevel, the first step was to identify units of analysis within the videotaped data. I selected to code the interactions looking at what I define as *exploratory literacy events*, instances in which Ken presented specific activities to understand, or explore, Stuart's strengths and weaknesses in his construction of meaning through reading and writing.

During the course of each exploratory event, Stuart displayed metalinguistic awareness of his strengths and difficulties with reading and writing. The sophistication of his metalinguistic understandings were an invaluable resource as he continuously provided insightful responses on what was difficult, what was easy, and what had been transformed as he read and wrote after the stroke. Through participating in a "dialogic inquiry" (Wells, 1999) with Ken exploring literacy processes and transactions with texts, Stuart consciously manipulated linguistic information, which in turn served as a mediating tool, in the Vygotskian tradition (Moll, 1990), for making sense of the experiences of reading and writing with aphasia. Thus, an exploratory literacy event includes the actual transactions with texts in which Stuart participated as a reader or a writer as well as the conversations and dialog about reading and writing surrounding the event.

There were three different kinds of exploratory events involving reading: (a) oral reading, (b) silent reading, and (c) shared reading events. Each of these reading events took place using a wide variety of texts. Table 4.1 presents the type of texts utilized within each of the observed types of reading events across the study.

Miscue Analysis and Aphasia

The second level of analysis consisted of a more micro- and in-depth analysis of a series of reading events representing Stuart's performance over the course of the study.

From the video database, I analyzed a total of seven different exploratory oral reading events using modified miscue analysis procedures (Goodman, Watson, & Burke, 1987) to understand Stuart's use of the linguistic cueing systems and his reading strategies while transacting with different types of texts. The selected events purposely present a wide range of texts. This variety makes it possible to document the delicate and

Table 4.1 Texts Used During Exploratory Reading Events

Type of Reading	Type of Text Used
Silent Reading	Magazine articles and indexes
	Newspaper articles
	Maps
	Charts
	Stock reports
	Agenda/Journal
Oral Reading	Newspaper articles
	Baby book excerpts
	Children's books
	Recipes
	Words
	Letters
	Catalogue prices
	Numbers
	Agenda/Journal
Shared Reading	Children's books
	Newspaper articles
	Agenda/Journal

complex relationships that exist between the linguistic nature of the text and Stuart's literacy performance while reading aloud. In addition, these events were taken from different points in time during Stuart's process of recovery. The events are summarized in Table 4.2, and results of this analysis are presented in Table 4.3.

Table 4.2 Exploratory Reading Events Analyzed Using Miscue Analysis Procedures

ID	Date	Title	Type of Text
1	10/8/94	"A Passage to Antiquity"	Newspaper article
2	10/8/94	Isolated words	Words and letter
3	10/23/94	*Soccer Game*	Children's book
4	10/23/94	*Time for Bed*	Children's book
5	11/19/95	"Drake Didn't Lie"	Newspaper article
6	11/19/95	His job at the cotton gin	Self-produced journal entry
7	11/29/95	"Critter Contest"	Newspaper article

Table 4.3 Analyzed Exploratory Reading Events and Miscue Analysis Statistics

| | | | | | | | Procedure II Language Sense | | Procedure III | | | | | | | | | | | | |
| | | | | | | | | | Syntactic Accept. | | Semantic Accept. | | Meaning Change | | | Graphic Similarity | | |
Id	Date of Reading	Title of Selection	No. of Words	No. of Miscues	Miscues per Hundred Words	No. of Sentences	Strength	Weakness	Y	N	Y	N	N	P	Y	H	S	N
1	10/8/94	Passage to Antiquity	34	23	67	3	0	100	33	67	0	100	n/a	n/a	n/a	62	23	15
2	10/8/94	Isolated Words	19	5	26	-	-	-	-	-	-	-	-	-	-	33	67	-
3	10/23/94	Soccer Game	61	12	19.6	22	91	9	100	0	91	9	100	0	0	33	50	17
4	10/23/94	Time For Bed	62	17	27	8	75	25	88	12	75	25	100	0	0	64	21	14
5	11/19/95	Drake Didn't Lie	121	28	23	7	71	29	100	0	71	29	20	80	0	68	32	0
6	11/19/95	His Job–Cotton Gin	42	6	14	6	100	0	100	0	100	0	100	0	0	50	17	33
7	11/29/95	Critter Contest	135	18	13	12	67	33	83	17	67	33	100	0	0	67	17	17

The use of miscue analysis procedures served as a heuristic tool for understanding Stuart's reading process (Goodman et al., 1987). Miscue analysis is used as a research tool to inform and interpret the available recorded data from Stuart's oral readings throughout the archived data set. Given that miscue analysis is a performance-oriented analysis of oral reading, it became important to use it as a tool in combination with other qualitative and descriptive tools for investigating reading in aphasia, particularly given Stuart's difficulties as a result of his expressive aphasia. I use miscue analysis data in conjunction with other ethnographic research strategies to contextualize the data and get at the relationship between his competence and performance.

Take, for example, miscue analysis data from Stuart's reading of a newspaper article, "A Passage to Antiquity," the first oral reading Ken invited Stuart to do. Looking at his statistics for language sense in Procedure II (Table 4.3), he obtained a score of 100% for language sense weakness, which would reflect a reader who was unable to make sense from the printed text. That made Stuart look ineffective and inefficient. But, Stuart reported he had already read the article silently in the comfort of his home that same morning prior to his meeting with Ken; reading the Sunday morning paper is part of his posttrauma literacy practices. Stuart knew that the article was about a newly found tunnel under the Sphinx in Egypt, evidenced from his conversation with Ken and his written response to the content of the article.

After reading the first couple of sentences aloud, Ken invited Stuart to write something about what the story was about. Stuart paused for a moment, began writing TUNNELS (Figure 4.1), and then stopped. Ken provided a prompt, "Why don't you write something like 'They found the tunnel under the Sphinx?'" Ken suggested. Stuart agreed and began writing. His final sentence read 'WE FOUND THE TUNNEL UNDER THE SPHINX.'

Stuart's productive language difficulties made it almost impossible for his oral reading performance to demonstrate his underlying literacy competence and his ability to make meaning through his transactions with text. Thus, miscue analysis data were necessary in light of descriptive observation of literacy processes in use. Ken provided multiple opportuni-

Figure 4.1
Prompted writing in response to reading of the article
"Passage to Antiquity," October 8, 1994.

ties for Stuart to share his interpretations of the texts through either oral or written language. Because both of Stuart's productive language processes were affected by the stroke, either of the proposed retelling forms proved to be a challenging situation for Stuart. Yet, comprehension was demonstrated throughout their ongoing exploratory conversations. In this research, comprehension of the stories, articles, and diverse passages was interpreted from the resulting oral conversations as well as from any written responses Stuart produced. In addition, miscue analysis statistics of analyzed events informed interpretations of Stuart's comprehension of written texts.

Finally, in the case of aphasic literacy processes, the use of miscue analysis as a research tool proved to be an invaluable resource for understanding the underlying linguistic principles of Stuart's miscues. This in-depth analysis of his reading provides an opportunity not only to understand Stuart's literacy development with aphasia but also to gain new knowledge about the nature of literacy processes.

Discoveries

Stuart's Reading Process

Ken: When did you begin to feel that you were understanding what you were reading? It seems like you were reading all along. Were there any periods where you gave up?
Stuart: Every day.
Ken: Every day you would be frustrated?
Stuart: No, I didn't do that. ... I'd say ok, I can't, not today. I can't. I'll try it again. (Transcript, October 16, 1994)

During the immediate days and weeks following the onset of aphasia, Stuart remembered his inability to understand written language. "I couldn't," Stuart said, "I tried, but there is nothing in that." Stuart regained his ability to understand written language as the edema from the bleeding subsided, which in some cases may take as long as year (Ewing & Pfalzgraf, 1990). But, the process of regaining control of his reading began in the early stages of his hospitalization. Stuart recalled his daily struggle to keep trying to read while he stayed at a halfway house in Tucson. Seven years after the stroke, Stuart highlighted his determination to read again, even though the initial attempts seemed to be somewhat discouraging.

Stuart: But I didn't give up. ... And boy, it was hard to read the page, without reading it. You know what I mean? I went though the whole page though ... and put it away and pull it out again the next day.

Andrea: When you say that you went through it, did you identify the words that you knew? Were the other words blank and you just kept going?

Stuart: Yes ... had no ... it mean, meant nothing [...]. But then I understood with time that it will be better. (Transcript, August 1, 2001)

By the time Stuart and Ken started collaborating, approximately 6 months after the stroke, Stuart demonstrated a relatively strong ability to understand printed texts when he read both silently and orally. In the case of oral reading, one crucial discovery was that his ability to understand printed texts was not affected by his laborious oral reading, given the resulting verbal apraxia associated with his expressive aphasia. Starting with the assumption that Stuart was a reader, Ken introduced a number of exploratory reading events to understand better his underlying literacy competence as well as to explore some of the contextual features that supported or hindered his process of transacting with texts.

On October 23, 1994, Stuart shared some of the texts read by Cameron, his youngest son. Prior to this meeting, Ken and Stuart had been discussing Stuart's participation in shared reading events with Cameron, given that 6-year-old Cameron was in the process of learning to read at the time. Stuart selected one of these books to read aloud to Ken, called *Soccer Game*. This text has a predictable structure, with one sentence per page and complementing colored illustrations. Although the text is much too simple compared to Stuart's usual reading materials, like the newspaper or historical novels, I use this reading to introduce Stuart's reading profile because this particular reading event provides evidence of Stuart's negotiation of meaning through his use of psycholinguistic reading strategies as well as his use of syntactic, semantic, and graphophonic language cueing systems.

A note on the markings of miscue examples, as seen in Figures 4.2 to 4.7, is necessary before I elaborate on Stuart's reading profile: C indicates self correction; - indicates a partial attempt; UC indicates unsuccessful attempt to correct; PC indicates prompted correction if Ken provided support; and $ indicates the production of a nonword.

When reading the first sentence of the text the interaction in Figure 4.2 took place. Stuart's first attempt at reading the word *game* resulted in the word *time*, a miscue that maintains the same grammatical function with the expected response (i.e., a noun for a noun), with only some degree of graphic and sound similarity between the miscue and the expected response. When Ken probed further and asked about the meaning of the word, Stuart was

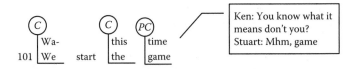

Figure 4.2
Miscues on game.

able to produce the expected response. I describe this type of self-correction as *prompted correction* to denote the supportive nature of Ken's intervention during the reading event. Prompted corrections did not occur frequently in the analyzed data, but whenever present, Ken's support was not intended to penalize Stuart's observed responses or miscues. Rather, this type of probing was instrumental for investigating Stuart's ability to comprehend the text when the oral rendering of the text was difficult. Stuart's production of the expected response 'game' notes not only the interactional nature of the reading event but also the dynamic displays of performance that provide hints to Stuart's underlying competence.

Analysis of Stuart's miscues from his reading of *Soccer Game* (Table 4.3) indicate that of a total of 61 words in the story, Stuart produced a total of 12 miscues, which represent 19.7 miscues per hundred words (MPHW). Statistics from Procedure III (Goodman et al., 1987) indicate that 100% of his sentences were syntactically and semantically acceptable, which provides evidence of his control of the English language syntactic system as well as his concern for meaning while reading the text. Although he persevered sometimes with specific words, he was able to correct 75% of his substitutions when these changed or affected the meaning of the text. An example is provided in the sentence in Figure 4.3.

The substitution of *many* for *fun* in this particular context does not produce a syntactically acceptable structure, and it does not make sense within the context of the sentence or the whole text. Stuart's correction of this miscue demonstrates his ability to monitor and confirm or disconfirm his predictions. In this substitution, his prediction of the word *many* does not work syntactically or semantically, thus forcing Stuart to disconfirm his prediction and correct the miscue.

In this reading event, only 17% of his substitutions remained uncorrected, and the remaining 8% of his corrections were prompted by Ken. In most instances, whenever

Figure 4.3
Miscue on fun.

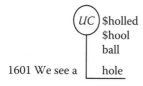

1601 We see a

Figure 4.4
Miscues on hole.

his miscues remained uncorrected, Stuart made several attempts at producing the expected response before moving along in the text. Other times, Stuart's use of correction as one of his reading strategies sometimes caused him to abandon high-quality miscues in pursuit of an accurate oral reading. *High-quality miscues* can be defined as those miscues that result in syntactically and semantically acceptable structures without changing the meaning of the story (Goodman et al., 1987).

Stuart's first substitution of *ball* for *hole* (Figure 4.4) provides an example of his ability to predict an alternative linguistic structure that fits nicely with the overall pattern of the text. It shows that he is constructing his own parallel text and its meaning. It would have been acceptable at both the sentence and the story level if Stuart had chosen to leave the word *ball* and continue reading. However, Stuart decided to stay close to the printed text and attempted to correct his miscue. Unfortunately, the word *hole* proved to be difficult to articulate, and the resulting nonwords $hool and $holled illustrate Stuart's approximations at producing the expected response. In this case, Stuart made inefficient use of correction as his reading strategy.

Stuart's oral reading throughout the analyzed data provides multiple instances to problematize the relationship between oral production and comprehension in reading with aphasia. It became important to distinguish between those miscues that were caused by difficulties at the moment of executing, or articulating his response, with those miscues that were caused by a breakdown in accessing the desired response. In some instances, as in the first two examples provided in Figures 4.2 and 4.3, Stuart's substitutions of the words *time* or *many* did not seem to be related to any evident difficulty in articulating the expected responses *game* or *fun*, respectively. These miscues seemed to originate from his difficulty in accessing the expected response in his first attempt at reading the text.

C $dibble
de-
1601 We dribble

Figure 4.5
Miscue on dribble.

On the other hand, there were instances in which the miscue seemed to be solely related to Stuart's inability to articulate the desired word, such as in the case of his multiple unsuccessful attempts at producing the word *hole*. The example in Figure 4.5 also illustrates this same pattern because his nonword substitution of $*dibble* for *dribble* may have been influenced by his apraxia.

As far as Stuart's use of the graphophonic cueing system, 33% of his word-for-word substitutions in his reading of *Soccer Game* were coded as high for graphic similarity between the observed response and the printed text. Of his substitutions, 50% were coded as having some graphic similarity and the remaining 17% as having no graphic similarity with the expected response. In this last category, Stuart's substitutions included only two miscues, both involving function words: The word *we* was substituted for *it,* and *we* was substituted again for *this.* When looking at the rest of his substitutions within the seven analyzed reading events, I found it interesting that whenever his substitutions were coded as having no graphic similarity with the expected response, these substitutions involved for the most part function words, such as pronouns, conjunctions, prepositions, and the like. Stuart's reading of function words throughout the study is an area that requires more detailed analysis because of the particular ways in which certain patterns emerged. I make reference to some of these patterns when discussing Stuart's reading development throughout his recovery from aphasia in the section entitled Change Across Time.

Patterns of Miscues

Through miscue analysis of the seven reading events reported in Table 4.3, certain patterns of miscues emerged, patterns that shed light on Stuart's experiences as a reader with aphasia. Similar to miscue research with nonaphasic individuals, Stuart's miscues throughout the different reading events maintain the same grammatical function as the expected response most of the times. For example, in his reading of a brief article, "Drake Didn't Lie," in November 1995, 88% of his substitutions maintain the same grammatical function as the expected response, substituting nouns for nouns, verbs for verbs, and so on. In some cases, he maintains grammaticality of the sentences with the production of nonwords that also reflect his awareness of syntactic structures. His use of nonwords in these instances serves as a strategy to produce an approximation of the expected response when the target words are challenging. Consider the example in Figure 4.6 from his reading of "Drake Didn't Lie."

In this example, Stuart's substitution of *regarding* for *regarded* maintains the same grammatical function, but the tense does not work in the syntactic structure, causing Stuart to correct the miscue and continue reading. I found this and other miscues in which Stuart only changed the morphemic part of the expected word, turning –ed into –ing, or singular

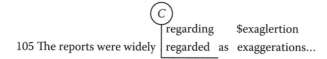

Figure 4.6

Miscue on regarded.

nouns into plural nouns by adding the plural marker –s. These miscues have been documented in the literature relating to aphasia as reading difficulties associated with the linguistic sphere of aphasic difficulties (Ewing & Pfalzgraf, 1990). In this same sentence, Stuart produced the nonword substitution $exaglertion as his approximation of the target word *exaggerations*. In this case, Stuart's miscue serves as a grammatical place holder that supports him in moving along the text (Goodman et al., 1987).

Ewing and Pfalzgraf (1990) describe that, "It is important to remember that an aphasic person's ability to say the word out loud is not an indication of understanding" (p. 102). I think the opposite is also applicable in the case of reading with aphasia; for example, Stuart's inability to say a word aloud was not an indication of lack of understanding of the meaning of a particular word. This phenomenon was repeatedly observed in Stuart's reading and represents an interesting feature of Stuart's literacy competence. He consistently confirmed that he knew what he wanted to say even when he had trouble saying it.

Miscue analysis research presents evidence that readers deal with concepts, not with words, as they read texts, and that it is easier to read words in context than in isolation (Goodman & Goodman, 1994). Stuart's miscues are in most cases not words that are unknown to him, but words that he is unable to produce or to access. In terms of accessing information, Stuart had the sense that sometimes his miscues involve words that have not been used that frequently or that he has not seen since the stroke. He believed that once he had seen a word and read it, it became easier to access the word later on. This pattern did not hold true, however, in those cases when he was able to read aloud a word one day and then was unable to say it the day after, hinting at the situated nature of language use versus the isolated recognition of words while reading. Stuart described that his successful production of the expected printed text often seemed to follow uncertain and capricious conditions. Some days, he would have complications with a word, and other days he would not. In the reading of the article "Drake Didn't Lie," the interaction in Figure 4.7 took place.

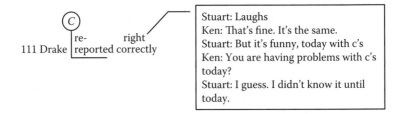

Figure 4.7
Miscue on correctly.

Further analysis of his substitution miscues during this reading event revealed that Stuart's intuition was on the right track. In his reading of "Drake Didn't Lie," he had produced a number of substitution and partial miscues involving 'c,' or rather the two different phonemes associated with this grapheme: \k\ and \s\. These included *Frank* for *Francis*, *$conductions* for *conditions*, *$forthmaking* for *forthcoming*, and corrected partials in his reading of *account* and *curator*. This pattern was not observed in any of the other events analyzed.

One pattern that was consistent throughout the analyzed data was his difficulties with function words. According to Stuart, even in the years following the stroke, he still has to concentrate to produce the function word appropriate for the syntactic structure when reading either orally or silently.

It could be said, then, that there were different types of miscues associated with Stuart's reading process in the presence of aphasia:

1. Miscues associated with the Stuart's apraxia: These miscues often lead to semantic paraphasias and nonwords. Although his use of nonwords often served as placeholders to maintain grammaticality at the sentence level, Stuart was not pleased with this aspect of his reading performance and would engage in multiple unsuccessful attempts at producing the target word.

2. Miscues associated with the *linguistic* breakdowns: This type of miscue emerged since the onset of his aphasia and was manifested at the level of accessing the deep structure of language, which resulted in Stuart's challenge by function words and bound morphemes.

3. Miscues associated with the natural reading process: Although it took time for Stuart to feel comfortable when producing high-quality miscues, miscue analysis data indicate that, even in the presence of aphasia, Stuart engaged in the psycholinguistic making of meaning through his transactions with texts.

Change Across Time

Since the beginning of Ken and Stuart's collaboration, most of the conversations about the reading process involved engaging in a discussion about how Stuart read, what he found difficult, and how his reading had evolved through time. As mentioned, in their first meeting in October 1994 Stuart read aloud a section of a newspaper article, "A Passage to Antiquity." The headline of the article read, "Newly Found Tunnel Adds to Mystery of the Sphinx." Stuart made a number of miscues in this first sentence, including the substitution of *we* for *Newly,* and *add* for *adds.* When he got to the word *to,* Stuart paused and said, "This is my worst," pointing to the word with his left index finger. Stuart explained how he had a difficult time reading and writing "little words." Nevertheless, Stuart also indicated that it was much worse at the beginning of the aphasia, and that he recognized that there had been growth in his ability to deal with written language since the stroke. In this section, I retrace some of the most evident changes in his reading process across time.

Quantitative data from the reading events analyzed indicate that Stuart's miscues per hundred words decreased from 67 MPHW in the reading of "A Passage to Antiquity" in October 1994, to 12 MPHW in the reading of an article, "Critter Contest," in November 1995 (see Table 4.3). Keeping in mind that miscue analysis is the exploration of that small percentage of unexpected responses while the rest of the text is read accurately, these data provide striking evidence of his development as a reader and his control over the linguistic and grammatical structures and productive aspects of reading aloud. The same is true when one compares his statistics for language sense in Procedure II from these two readings: 100% of the resulting structures in his oral reading of "A Passage to Antiquity" were coded as weaknesses, and 67% of the resulting structures in his reading of "Critter Contest" resulted in strengths. In classic studies of aphasia, this lack of initial observable performance is sometimes, more often than not, equated with lack of competence.

In general, Stuart encountered different types of challenges when reading texts orally. His articulation difficulties made it challenging to pronounce certain words; thus, his oral reading was characterized by the production of a number of nonwords with high graphic and sound similarity with the expected response. Stuart's patterns of miscues evolved through time. In later readings, he stopped persevering so much with producing the accurate pronunciation of the expected response. He had an increased tolerance for using nonwords to serve as placeholders whenever he was unable to produce the desired word. This made him become more effective in getting to the meaning and more efficient in his use of his reading strategies (Goodman, 1996).

In addition, his early oral reading included numerous omissions, mostly of function words. In this case, it was not an articulation difficulty that caused the miscue. Rather, Stuart seemed to have difficulties dealing with the underlying syntactic structure of the text. In the case of handling function words during his oral readings, his omissions became substitutions, which demonstrate his prediction of syntactic structures influenced by the printed text. When reading the article "Passage to Antiquity" in October 1994, omissions accounted for 43% of his miscues, and the remaining 57% were word-for-word substitutions. By November 1995, while reading "Critter Contest," 100% of his miscues were substitutions.

There were other issues to consider when looking across time at his performance as a reader with aphasia. Since the beginning of the research, Stuart described that he found it difficult to concentrate when there was noise around him. This condition got better with time, but fatigue was always an issue in terms of his performance in reading, or writing and speaking for that matter. In the literature related to aphasia, it has been reported that noise overload and fatigue negatively affect reading performance (Ewing & Pfalzgraf, 1990). If Stuart was tired, then he found it challenging to concentrate on reading, and his reduced tolerance to noise went hand with hand with fatigue. However, in the 2-hour sessions with Ken, he never complained of fatigue.

Discussion

In "Drake Didn't Lie," read in November 1995, Stuart encountered the word *paleoclimatological* in the text. As he worked his way through the text, Stuart saw the word *paleoclimatological* and stopped. Then, he said the following:

Stuart: Ahh, I know what it means (laughing) the paleo- is old (underlining **paleo-** in the text), and the, cal- cal- , this one (pointing to clima-) I can't get ... cl- weather, weather type, and then ...
Ken: You know that word (pointing to climatological) has to do with weather forecasting.
Stuart: And how they can do it three, no four ... centuries after. (Transcription, November 6, 1995)

Stuart's sophisticated metalinguistic explanation of his understanding of the meaning of the word *paleoclimatological* represents one of the many instances throughout this research when Stuart found ways to make evident his underlying literacy competence after the onset of aphasia.

Research done with aphasic individuals, as reported by Strauss (1999), supports the notion that performance varies depending on the contextual situation. Strauss believes that recovery from aphasia seems to be a process of learning language for a second time. Engaging in exploratory conversations, like the one just described, seems to provide an ideal situational context to make use of oral and written language as mediational tools to support individuals with aphasia in the process of relearning language. They also allow talk about language to mediate abstract understandings about the nature of the reading process.

This chapter has examined Stuart's meaning–making process as a reader after suffering a stroke. Throughout this process, Stuart's inventions as he learned to read with aphasia emerged from the analysis of his miscues and the conversations surrounding each reading event analyzed. In many ways, by documenting closely how Stuart read, Ken created opportunities for his reading process to be captured on tape for later analysis, in as much a "natural context" as possible within an exploratory event.

Roth and Heilman (2000) provide an interesting review of the history of aphasia. They write that "the history of aphasia is revealing of how methodologies *influence the course of science*, and how political and social milieus can change the reception of finding and shape the efforts within a scientific field" (p. 3; italics added). Kovarsky, Kimbarow, et al. (1999) write about "particular models of language and cognition that influence the discipline of speech-language pathology" (p. 308). They argue that implicit models for interpreting language and cognition guide evaluation judgments of competence. Although writing about oral language, they do speak of the fragmentation of language and the problems of recontextualization of language into something different from the way it would normally be used outside clinical settings.

Analysis of miscue data collected over time reveals that Stuart became more proficient at handling the linguistic and articulation breakdowns associated with his expressive aphasia. At the performance level, he became more proficient in his use of reading strategies, allowing nonwords to serve as placeholders, which raised the efficiency of his reading. Miscue data also revealed that the more support he had from both the text and the context, the better the portrait of his ability that was documented. With fragmented texts, or when only allowed to provide oral rendition of his understanding of a text, Stuart's performance did not provide accurate representation of his literacy competence. Reading texts of everyday life, participating in mediated talk during readings events, and the ability to write to aid his retelling of the content of his reading were all contextual features of this research through which a more competent literacy performance was documented.

Was reading the same for Stuart after the stroke? Research revealed that he continued to use reading in his life to fulfill different functions and as part of his daily literacy practices. There were changes and adaptations that he had to make. But, in general, Stuart's reading process continued to be driven by meaning making, by an attempt to comprehend text.

The present research contributes to the field by investigating reading in aphasia using a particular research methodology informed by a sociopsycholinguistic understanding of the reading process. Looking at Stuart's reading through the use of miscue analysis helps explain how miscues that disrupted the flow of the reading event, for the most part, did not disrupt Stuart's underlying competence to understand texts. The findings of this work help to "influence the course of science" by helping us *reimagine* landscapes of literacy competence in the life of one man living with aphasia and to consider the universality of the reading process (Goodman, 1994) when reading has been transformed by a neurological shift, such as in the case of a stroke.

References

Andreewsky, E., & Cochu, F. (1995). Reading theories and their implications for rehabilitation. In C. Code & D. Muller (Eds.), *The treatment of aphasia: From theory to practice* (pp. 187–200). San Diego, CA: Singular.

Carlomagno, S., & Iavarone, A. (1995). Writing rehabilitation in aphasic patients. In C. Code & D. J. Muller (Eds.), *The treatment of aphasia: From theory to practice* (pp. 201–222). San Diego, CA: Singular.

Chomsky, N. (1957). *Syntactic structures.* The Hague, The Netherlands: Mouton.

Ewing, S. A., & Pfalzgraf, B. (1990). *Pathways: Moving beyond stroke and aphasia.* Detroit, MI: Wayne State University Press.

García Obregón, A. (2002). *Landscapes of competence: A case study of literacy practices and processes in the life of one man with aphasia.* Unpublished doctoral dissertation, University of Arizona, Tucson.

Goodglass, H. (1993). *Understanding aphasia.* San Diego, CA: Academic Press.

Goodman, K. S. (1982). Reading: A psycholinguistic guessing game. In F. V. Gollasch (Ed.), *Language and literacy: The selected writings of Kenneth S. Goodman* (Vol. 1, pp. 33–43). London: Routledge & Kegan Paul. (Original work published 1967)

Goodman, K. S. (1982). The reading process. In F. V. Gollasch (Ed.), *Language and literacy: The selected writings of Kenneth S. Goodman.* (Vol. 1, pp. 5–16). London: Routledge & Kegan Paul. (Original work published 1975)

Goodman, K. S. (1994). Reading, writing and texts: A transactional socio-psycholinguistic view. In R. B. Rudell, M. R. Rudell, & H. Singer (Eds.), *Theoretical models and processes of reading* (pp. 1093–1130). Newark, DE: International Reading Association.

Goodman, K. S. (1996). Principles of revaluing. In Y. Goodman & A. Marek (Eds.), *Retrospective miscue analysis* (pp. 13–20). New York: Richard C. Owen.

Goodman, Y. M., & Goodman, K. S. (1994). To err is human: Learning about language processes by analyzing miscues. In R. B. Rudell, M. R. Rudell, & H. Singer (Eds.), *Theoretical models and processes of reading* (pp. 104–123). Newark, DE: International Reading Association.

Goodman, Y., Watson, D., & Burke, C. (1987). *Reading miscue inventory: Alternative procedures*. Katonah, NY: Richard C. Owen.

Greenwald, M. L. (2000). The acquired dyslexias. In S. E. Nadeau, L. J. Gonzalez, & B. Crosson (Eds.), *Aphasia and language: Theory to practice* (pp. 159–183). New York: Guilford Press.

Hymes, D. (1972). On communicative competence. In J. B. Pride and J. Holmes (Eds.), *Sociolinguistics: Selected readings* (pp. 269–293). Baltimore: Penguin.

Hymes, D. (1974). *Foundations in sociolinguistics: An ethnographic approach*. Philadelphia: University of Pennsylvania Press.

Jacyna, L. S. (2000). *Lost words: Narratives of language and the brain 1825–1926*. Princeton, NJ: Princeton University Press.

Kirshner, H. (1995). *Handbook of neurological speech and language disorders*. New York: Dekker.

Kovarsky, D., Duchan, J., & Maxwell, M. (1999.). *Constructing (in)competence: Disabling evaluations in clinical and social interaction*. Mahwah, NJ: Erlbaum.

Kovarsky, D., Kimbarow, M., & Kastner, D. (1999). The construction of incompetence during group therapy with traumatically brain injured adults. In D. Kovarsky, J. Duchan, & M. Maxwell (Eds.), *Constructing (in)competence: Disabling evaluations in clinical and social interaction* (pp. 291–311). Mahwah, NJ: Erlbaum.

Lesser, R., & Milroy, (1993). *Linguistics and aphasia: Psycholinguistics and pragmatic aspects of Intervention*. London: Whurr.

Moll, L. C. (Ed.). (1990). *Vygotsky and education: Instructional implications and applications of sociohistorical psychology*. New York: Cambridge University Press.

Nadeau, S. E., Gonzalez, L. J., & Crosson, B. (Eds.). (2000). *Aphasia and language: Theory to practice*. New York: Guilford Press.

Rapcsak, S., & Beeson, P. M. (2000). Agraphia. In S. E. Nadeau, L. J. Gonzalez Rothi, & B. Crosson (Eds.), *Aphasia and language: Theory to practice* (pp. 185–220). New York: Guilford Press.

Reiff Cherney, L. (2004). Aphasia, alexia and oral reading. *Topics in Stroke Rehabilitation, 11*, 22–36.

Roth, H., & Heilman, K. (2000). Aphasia: A historical perspective. In S. E. Nadeau, L. J. Gonzalez Rothi, & B. Crosson (Eds.), *Aphasia and language: Theory to practice* (pp. 3–28). New York: Guilford Press.

Strauss, S. (1999). Learning a first language for the second time: "Goodman contexts" and "Vygotskyan zones" in recovery from aphasia. In A. Marek & C. Edelsky (Eds.), *Reflections and connections: Essays in honor of Kenneth S. Goodman's influence on language education* (pp. 403-419). Cresskill, NJ: Hampton Press.

Webb, W. G., & Love, R. J. (1983). Reading problems in aphasia. *Journal of Speech and Hearing Disorders, 48*, 164–171.

Wells, G. (1999). *Dialogic inquiry: Towards a sociocultural practice and theory of education.* Cambridge, U.K.: Cambridge University Press.

Section Three

STUDIES OF BEGINNING READING

INTRODUCTION TO CHAPTER 5

A MAJOR OBJECT OF SCIENTIFIC realism is to produce a theory that can explain the structures and processes found in the real world. As such a theory develops, it must be tested against reality in further research. At the same time, the theory suggests to the researcher what to look for and how to design further research.

Peter Duckett used eye movement/miscue analysis (EMMA) methodology to study how relative beginners read picture books. His research tests my transactional theory of reading at the same time that it provides insight into how beginning readers make sense of picture books.

Some theorists have suggested that although a transactional model of reading may fit proficient reading, it may not fit developing readers, and others argue that words must be identified automatically before comprehension can occur. Such a stage theory of reading development proposes that readers must first learn to decode words letter by letter until they can identify words. In the research that Duckett summarizes, others have argued that pictures distract young learners from the task of making sense of print.

Duckett had first graders read a short picture book of the type used in beginning reading programs. They read out loud for the purposes of the miscue analysis, but he also used eye tracking equipment to record and analyze their eye movements. Using EMMA methodology, he was able to study what the eyes were doing in relationship to what the readers were saying as they read orally. He was able to see the relative amount of time and energy the readers devoted to the print and the pictures and how the readers were constructing meaning using both sources of input. He saw his young readers acting much like more proficient readers, not distracted by the pictures but actually using them to clarify points in the text where they seemed to need more information.

This theory-based study stands in sharp contrast to the small number of studies that see pictures in books as an aid to word identification. In those studies, the texts are often constructed artificially to provide for controlling known and unknown words. However, Duckett's young readers show the same concern as older readers for making sense of what they are reading.

This study also shows another strength of scientific realism. It provides a baseline of data for many further questions to be answered in subsequent studies. These will further test the theory and further explain the processes of reading development.

Ken Goodman

5

SEEING THE STORY FOR THE WORDS
The Eye Movements of Beginning Readers

Peter Duckett

Introduction

*I*T IS THE FIRST day of the school year, and Luke, a first-grader, is reading a Sunshine Series book published by the Wright Group. The book is *Are You a Ladybug?* by Cutting and Cutting (1988). Before he starts, he tells me that he really does not know how to read because he does not "know all the words." With encouragement, he agrees to try. On numerous occasions while reading, he encounters challenges. At times, he pauses, looks at the pictures, goes back to the print, and sounds out the first letter of the next word. Other times, he goes back to the picture and scans it. Eventually, Luke says something that fits multiple parameters: the graphophonic information that he has accessed, his current syntactic understandings, his semantic knowledge, his understandings of the picture, and his background knowledge and life experience about story and picture books. He offers me a view through the window onto his reading process and demonstrates "how texts teach what readers learn" (Meek, 1988).

The Research Question

My observational experience with Luke, in conjunction with many similar experiences with beginning readers, sparked a point of curiosity: How do first-grade beginning readers use print and pictures as they read? It also encouraged me to go beyond just surface observation by using tools that would allow me to find out where young readers' eyes were focused, so that, in conjunction with the oral text they produced, I would be able to gain a deeper understanding of reading as a systemic process.

Rationale

There are a multitude of instructional practices for beginning readers; these range from masking out pictures because they are viewed as distracters from print to encouraging students to use pictures and print in strategic ways when reading. There is also an extensive array of diagnostic tools used to examine reading performance and to suggest instructional responses. Each instrument collects observational data that are viewed as informative of readers' competence when reading aloud. Readers' oral responses are one form of data collected and assessed. Readers' eye movements in conjunction with the oral texts that they produce can help create a more complex picture of what readers are doing as they read so that we, as instructors, better understand readers and provide them with effective and appropriate support. Therefore, in this chapter I intentionally focus on the eye movement and eye movement/miscue analyses findings and interpretations of my study.

Background Literature

In a footnote (Footnote 92, p. 367) in her book *Beginning to Read,* Adams (1990) remarks that there is virtually no information on the constructive use of pictures with print by beginning readers. However, there is a wisdom that guides the children's literature industry. Authors and illustrators of children's literature create pictures and texts that are purposefully considerate of the wedding of two sign systems. Kiefer (1995) references a well-known Caldecott Award winner:

> Illustrator Barbara Cooney (1988) likened the picture book to a string of pearls. She suggested that the pearls represent the illustrations, and the string represents the printed text. The string is not an object of beauty on its own, but the necklace cannot exist without the string. Although in picture books a verbal text should certainly be beautiful and bring pleasure in and of itself, Cooney's analogy supports the idea of the *interdependence* of pictures and text in the unique art object that is a picture book. (p. 6)

Together, the subtle weave of words and pictures allows both to tell one seamless tale (Scieszka, 1998). Children are aware of this weaving of pictures and print into one story and offer demonstrations of this awareness in their own writing and conversations about pictures and print (Hubbard, 1989; Yaden, Smolkin, & Conlon, 1989).

Empirical Research Studies

Empirical research regarding the relationship between print and pictures in early reading falls into two large categories, with one or two additional studies falling outside these major categories: word identification/picture studies and comprehension/picture studies.

The first set of studies involving word identification and pictures generally focuses on finding out whether pictures are beneficial in the teaching of sight words (Samuels, 1977; Singer, 1980; Willows, 1978a, 1978b). The second set of studies involves older proficient readers reading complete illustrated texts to determine the effects of pictures on comprehension. Vernon's (1953, 1958) studies typify such research in that the focus is one of determining the effects of the treatment of including pictures in a text on reading comprehension (Holmes, 1987; Koenke, 1968, 1980; Koenke & Otto, 1969; Weintraub, 1960, 1966).

Falling outside these two broad categories is a single study conducted by Denburg (1976); this study examines end of first-grade readers' use of pictures in reading complete texts. The study suggests that pictures have a positive influence on reading (when defined as word identification), and that beginning readers do use pictures and print together when reading. However, the study does not provide detailed information about how beginning readers use both pictures and print as they read.

Eye-Movement Research

Eye-movement research has been an informative research tool in studies of reading for over a century; see Paulson and Goodman's chapter 2 in this volume for a review of eye-movement research findings. During the early 1920s, Buswell (1922) conducted eye-movement studies involving first-grade beginning readers. His study explored readers' eye movements relative to the texts, two methods of instruction (word analysis focused and meaning focused), and differing pathways toward experienced reading. He found that although readers exhibited different eye movements related to the method of instruction experienced, these eye movements were not significant (better or worse) if considered in relation to the ultimate goal of mature reading habits.

Similarly, Hegarty's (1992) study examined how readers used pictures and print together as they read.

Paulson (2000, 2002) used eye-movement research in conjunction with miscue analysis to create a hybrid form of analysis that he has called eye movement/miscue analysis (EMMA) (see Ebe, chapter 6, this volume; Paulson, chapter 11, this volume). EMMA uses both miscue analysis and eye-movement data to examine the relationship between eye movements and miscues that readers produce as they read to reveal the complex relationships between where the eye has been directed by the brain and what the voice is producing as an oral text.

Methodology

Informants

Participants reported in this study are six first-grade, beginning readers I call Cory, Esmeralda, Javier, Kimberly, Mac, and Rashaun. Esmeralda and Mac are Spanish/English bilingual and biliterate. The six readers represent three ethnic ancestries — Hispanic American, African American, and Anglo American — as well as a range of socioeconomic groups.

Materials

The text *I Saw a Dinosaur* is used here; this is a Literacy 2000 Stage 2 Set D book published by Rigby, written by Joy Cowley (1988), and illustrated by Phillip Webb. This text is commonly used for instruction in the first grade. The text is short (55 running words), which can be problematic because miscue analysis is applied to texts that are longer than 250 words; some research (e.g., Menosky, 1971) has shown that the quality of miscues changes substantially after the first 250 words. However, I have intentionally chosen the short text used in this study because I wanted to work with the type of text commonly used in classrooms for instructional purposes in first grade.

Data Collection

The data were collected using an ASL model 5000 eye-tracking machine, a computer to record oral data, and an audiocassette recorder to collect backup and additional oral data. I collected three sets of data for each reader: one primary data set in the form of the oral reading with the eye-movement data and two secondary sets of data—a modified Burke Reading Interview (Y. Goodman, Watson, & Burke, 1987) and retellings that were used to uncover readers' conceptualizations of reading and to confirm their comprehension of the stories that they read. Retellings are a standard component in any miscue analysis (Y. Goodman et al., 1987).

Analyses

I performed three levels of analysis: miscue analysis of the reading, eye-movement analysis of the reading, and EMMA of the reading (in which the oral response of the reader is compared with the expected response as indicated by the text; see Ebe, chapter 6, this volume; Paulson, chapter 11, this volume). As the present study was focused on understanding what beginning readers focused on while reading, eye-movement analysis and EMMA are the focus of this chapter.

Findings

Eye-Movement Findings

Across all readers, a total of 53 miscues and 2,347 eye fixations were examined and analyzed. First-grade beginning readers in this study fixated print, pictures, and other areas as they read the complete text. They fixated print more frequently than pictures. On average, 55% of the fixations were in print, and 36% of the fixations were in pictures. The remaining 9% of fixations were in other areas outside the print and picture fields.

In terms of time spent fixating (fixation duration) these three areas, the readers devoted 73% of their time viewing print, 21% of their time on pictures, and 6% on other areas outside the print and picture fields. K. Rayner (personal communication, 2001) has replicated this finding in a print/picture study with adult readers viewing magazine advertisements; he reports that the four subjects he studied spent 67%, 73%, 72%, and 77% of their time reading the text. A number of patterns were common to all the beginning readers in the current study:

- All readers had average fixation durations in print that were greater than their overall average fixation durations of the three categories combined (print, pictures, and other).

Figure 5.1
Readers do not look at (fixate) every word as they read.

- All readers had average fixation durations in pictures that were less than their average fixation durations of the three categories combined (print, pictures, and other).
- All readers had average fixation durations in print that were almost double their average fixation durations in pictures.

None of the readers fixated every word in the text as previous eye-movement research has found (Hogaboam, 1983; Just & Carpenter, 1987; Paulson, chapter 11, this volume; Rayner, 1997); their nonfixation rate varied from 9% to 34% of the words in the text. The dots in Figure 5.1 illustrate where Rashaun fixated as he read page 6. The lines between dots represent saccades—eye movements between fixations—during which no useful graphic information is transmitted to the brain (see Paulson & Goodman, chapter 2, this volume).

The first-grade beginning readers in this study orally produced words that they did not fixate 100% of the time. This finding would seem to indicate that the readers in this study could predict with a great deal of certainty particular words and therefore did not need to fixate them.

Like Paulson's (chapter 11, this volume) readers, the first-grade readers in this study did not always fixate words serially from word to word, left to right.

As they read, readers engaged in regressive eye movements within print or transitioned from print to pictures and then back to print. They also engaged in fixations that shifted vertically from line to line and diagonally across the print field. Readers did not always fixate words for the same amount of time. They did not always fixate at the center of words, horizontally and vertically. There was a low incidence of fixations that fell between lines of print, between words, and in the blank margins of the page.

All readers spent less than 1.5 s in fixating pictures prior to entering print. For monolingual speakers, this amount of picture-viewing time prior to entering print was even further reduced to less than 0.5 s.

Bilingual readers in this study fixated pictures and print more frequently and for longer periods of time than their monolingual counterparts. Bilingual readers' average fixation times were longer than those of monolingual readers. These findings related to bilingual readers do not constitute new eye-movement research: Cattell (1886) found that second-language readers take more time to read texts. Almost a century later, Oller and Tullius (1973) further substantiated this finding. Although bilingual readers fixated pictures and print more frequently and for longer periods of time, their fixation durations were proportionally similar (in terms of percentages) to monolingual readers.

All readers transitioned from pictures back to print by moving to a word prior (20%), to the same word (45%), to a word beyond (26%), and to other areas outside word boundaries (9%).

On average, regressive eye movements (i.e., eye movements that move backward in the text) accounted for 14% of all eye movements. Regressions within sentences (moving backward across word boundaries within a sentence) accounted for 52% of all regressive eye movements. Regressions within words (moving backward within word boundaries) accounted for 46% of all regressive eye movements.

As Table 5.1 illustrates, in instances of words with multiple occurrences, readers fixated the same word (in this example, the word *a*) in different contexts for different amounts of time. In some contexts, they did not fixate the word at all.

When sampling pictures, readers devoted a majority of their time (90% of fixation duration time) and fixations (89% of fixations) sampling major components such as characters and objects within the pictures.

The first-grade beginning readers in this study were more likely not to fixate function words compared to content words (see Paulson & Goodman, chapter 2, this volume, for a more detailed description of this tendency). On average for all readers, 82% of nonfixated words were function words. This is a common finding within eye-movement research (Just & Carpenter, 1984;

Table 5.1 Total Fixation Durations (in Seconds) on the Word *a* in Multiple Contexts

Word	Page	Cory	Esmeralda*	Javier	Kimberly	Mac	Rashaun	Average for All Readers
a	2	0.85	1.16	0	0	1.07	0	0.51
a	3	0	0.53	8.99	0.71	0.94	0	1.86
a	5	1.33	0.31	0	0	1.36	0	0.50
a1	6	0	2.59	0	0.52	0.58	0	0.61
a2	6	0.46	0	0	0.95	0.9	0	0.38
a	7	0.56	1.56	0	0.73	0	0	0.55
a	8	0.48	4.31	2.33	1.57	1.93	0.18	1.52
Total fixation duration		3.68	10.46	11.32	4.48	6.78	0.18	6.02
Average for reader		0.52	1.49	1.61	0.64	0.95	0.02	.86

* Bilingual reader.

Paulson & Goodman, chapter 2, this volume). For example, Just and Carpenter found that 74% of content words were fixated, and 40% of function words were fixated. Readers were also more likely to transition from print to pictures at content words: On average, 91% of all transitions from print to pictures were from content words.

Eye Movement/Miscue Analysis Findings

EMMA analyses involved examining readers' oral miscues relative to eye fixations within the eye-voice span—the phenomenon that readers' eye fixations are generally ahead of their voice as they read—across the reading of the complete text. The eyes sample graphic information from the page, the brain makes sense of it, and the voice produces an oral rendering of the sense that is made by the reader. EMMA analyses revealed that first-grade beginning readers in this study engaged in picture sampling prior to producing a miscue 86% of the time; for omission miscues, readers sampled from pictures prior to producing the miscue 91% of the time. This does not mean the readers were not paying attention to the print when the miscue was produced, however, as all readers fixated miscued words well beyond their personal average fixation duration prior to miscue production 94% of the time. When miscues were corrected, postmiscue fixations on the same word occurred 100% of the time. Readers also engaged in regressive eye movements or transitioned to pictures 100% of the time when miscues were corrected. When readers produced oral repetitions, regressive eye movements or picture sampling preceded the oral repetition.

During oral pauses, readers engaged in fixations of extended durations or multiple fixations. In most cases, these extended fixations or multiple fixations included picture sampling. During oral pauses, all readers were active in terms of eye movement, indicating related brain activity. The data analyses related to oral pauses and eye movements show clearly that although readers' voices may be inactive, their eyes are not. Because eye movement is brain directed, this can only mean that not only readers' eyes are active during oral pauses, but also their brains are as well.

Discussion

The eye movements of the readers indicate evidence that they are engaged in the complex process of making meaning. When they are reading, their brains are directing their eyes to go to places in the text that they can use to construct meaning. They fixate for differing periods of time during which they devote the majority of their time to print.

In going back and forth between pictures and print, the readers in this study sampled both media in ways that were strategic and systematic to orally construct a text that made sense. The readers demonstrated awareness of the systematic nature of their actions. They used pictures and print in ways to construct meaning that transmediated (Leland & Harste, 1994) both media. The readers employed a variety of reading strategies for making sense of the text as they read. They used their knowledge of oral language, their knowledge of written language, information from the printed text, and information from the text that they were constructing in their heads as they read.

As they read, the readers made decisions about where useful information would be located. Their brains directed their eyes to fixate in these places. These decisions were based on information that the text offered and the evolving text that the reader was constructing.

In relation to picture and print use, readers spent more time sampling print than pictures. They knew that print would provide strongly constraining information in making sense of the story. However, to imply that the pictures were without value would be simplistic. Readers sampled from pictures in ways that were purposeful and systematic. Their sampling of pictures relative to print indicates that they are well aware of the relationships between pictures and print and how to access those relationships effectively. In sampling pictures and print, they devoted the majority of their time to the major meaning carriers in both media. In pictures, they sampled from the major components (characters and objects). Within pictures, the major components are key sources for information regarding who and what are central to the story as well as the actions between characters and objects. Thus, the sampling of major components in pictures provides the reader with information regarding nouns, adjectives, and verbs. Within print, readers implicitly knew enough to sample more frequently from content words (nouns, adjective, adverbs, and verbs) because these words are the major meaning carriers in print. Readers' systematic transitioning from content words to major components in pictures indicates that they are well aware of the fact that content words in print and major components in pictures are related in terms of informational value.

The sampling of pictures and print played key roles in correction strategies. Readers regressed and refixated the miscued word and generally resampled the picture. Readers' knowledge of the relationship between content words and major components in pictures proved informative in the correction process. They knew where they would find useful information to confirm or disconfirm the text that they were producing and where to get cues to textual constraints in building meaning.

By contrast, readers were less likely to fixate function words. As readers progressed throughout the text, they learned more about how the text was constructed. As a result, they were able to make more informed predictions about what was coming next and where valuable information would be located in the print. They arrived at places in the text where constraints of the text and their implicit knowledge of English were so strong that they were able to predict function words, making it unnecessary to fixate those words to produce them orally.

The first-grade beginning readers in this study used the same reading process as that of experienced readers; that is, regardless of the level of the reader, reading as a process is constructive in nature. The behaviors of the readers in this study demonstrate this constructive process. They use the same strategies as older readers. However, they are not as experienced and therefore sample the pictures and print more frequently than older more experienced readers typically do.

Implications

Beginning readers have always faced high scrutiny regarding their reading performance within educational institutions. Based on their performance, educational decisions are made regarding the types of instruction they will receive and which learning opportunities will be made available to them. This study, other eye-movement studies (Jacobson & Dodwell, 1979; Rayner & Pollatsek, 1989), and reading studies (Flurkey, chapter 12, this volume) suggest that readers' performance is variable within texts, and that text construction influences reading performance. Therefore, readers' proficiency is variable within texts and is highly influenced by elements within the construction of the text.

Although recent instructional researchers (Pinnell & Fountas, 1999) have addressed the issue of matching readers' knowledge bases with the content of books or readers' diagnosed proficiency with text difficulty, the issue of internal variability of text construction has not been highly featured in discussions about reading assessment and instruction.

Because the data revealed that first-grade beginning readers in this study used pictures in methodical and purposeful ways, educators need to be aware that pictures do not constitute a distraction in the reading of picture books. Therefore, such practices as covering the pictures to force readers to focus on print only create further fracturing of the reading experience for readers and makes reading even more problematic. Pictures were shown to be a valuable resource used in the correction process. Some educators have used pictures to activate schema prior to reading by engaging readers in "picture walks." However, because the data showed that pictures also play a vital role in the correction process, educators will do well to support readers' use of pictures to develop Goodman, Watson, and Burke's (1996) strategies of "rereading a portion of the text to sample additional semantic/pragmatic cues (also syntactic and graphophonic), confirm inferences, make new or additional predictions, and integrate their new understandings with established meanings" (p. 76).

This study, reading research (Flurkey, chapter 12, this volume), and eye-movement research (Jacobson & Dodwell, 1979; Rayner & Pollatsek, 1989) show that texts offer varying degrees of support for readers within the text. Educators need to realize that the variability of readers' performance within each reading is influenced by the structural contours of the text. If the text is marked by structural elements that contradict each other or the reader's linguistic or pragmatic knowledge, then the text will present difficulties and weaken the reader's performance. Educators may interpret poor performance as a sign that the reader has reading problems. However, this is a misinterpretation if the problem resides within the construction of the text or a mismatch between the text and the reader's linguistic and pragmatic knowledge.

The fact that readers in this study (and proficient adult readers) do not fixate every word as they read implies that reading is not a word-by-word identification process. If instruction focuses on having readers fixate every word in print, then the reading process will be influenced in ways that run contrary to what proficient readers do when reading. Instructional practices that demand that readers look at every word (or every letter) will slow the reading process, making comprehension more difficult.

Educators need to realize that when readers miscue it is not because of a less-than-thorough examination of the word on which the miscue occurs. The data from this study and Paulson (chapter 11, this volume) shows that miscues often occur after readers have thoroughly examined the text and rejected what it offers because it does not fit with the syntactic, semantic, or pragmatic knowledge that the reader brings to the text.

Some educators believe that a word is a word is a word; that is, good readers are characterized by their ability to identify words in any context in an equal amount of time. By this definition, good readers are accurate automatic word identifiers. However, the data from this study strongly refute this idea. Instead, the data show that readers make contextually influenced adjustments to the time devoted to viewing words based on the printed text and the oral text that they are producing as they read. There are instances when the reader's oral text and the printed text conjoin, and the reader predicts words without ever fixating them. Likewise, there are instances when the reader's oral text and the printed text strongly diverge. The data in this study show that at such points, readers have exhaustively examined the print and picture resources offered and rejected what does not make sense or fit with the oral text that they are producing. In both cases, the contextual and textual constraints conjoin to support the dynamic emergence of text (the oral text of the reader).

EMMA analyses found the readers in this study exhibited the phenomenon of eye-voice span that has been historically reported in eye-movement research. The concept of eye-voice span calls into question instructional practices that ask readers to match oral text to print. If flexible eye-voice span is the mark of proficient readers, then is it effective to ask readers to match voice to print? If so, under what conditions is this practice effective, for what purposes, and for how long? In addition, teachers need to realize that the concept of eye-voice span challenges the idea that when readers' voices are producing an oral text, the point of oral production and the location of the eye in collecting information are synonymous. They are not.

The data from this study indicate that when readers pause in oral reading, they are sampling picture and print resources to make sense of the text. Traditionally, educators have been encouraged to see oral pauses as a sign of readers' inactivity and a plea for help. However, the data from this study reveal this as a myth. Instead of interrupting readers' reading and thought processes during oral pauses, educators might wait to see what readers decide to do or to acknowledge that readers are working and then ask them what *they* want to do. An oral pause is a strategic learning opportunity in which readers integrate information from the three cueing systems (Goodman et al., 1987) to make sense of pictures and print. These are the moments during which readers make decisions regarding strategies that they can employ to make meaning. If educators interrupt to "tell them the word," then they may be robbing the reader of an important strategic learning opportunity. What the educator has identified as the cause of the oral pause may also be inaccurate. The reader may actually be thinking about something else entirely different.

The data from this study stand as further evidence that a word recognition model of reading does not adequately explain the eye movement and oral reading performances of beginning or proficient readers. Numerous facets of the data analyses reveal reading behaviors that do not fit with the word recognition model.

The data in this study support a transactional sociopsycholinguistic model of reading (Goodman, 1996) because the model accounts for and explains reasons for readers' performances in this study, including nonfixated words, words with multiple occurrences with varied fixation times ranging from 0 to 8.99 s, textual influences on readers' production of miscues in one context and not another on words with multiple occurrences, regressions across large linguistic units, and readers' extended fixation times on words prior to miscue production.

Limitations

The study is limited in terms of the number of informants involved. It serves as a baseline study to which subsequent reading research may add.

The study is limited by the small number of miscues produced by its readers. Miscue analysis researchers generally agree that at least 25 miscues are needed to be able to gain insight into the reader's miscue patterns and reading strategies. A contrastive study involving trade books and instructional texts might prove informative and beneficial.

Finally, analyses within this study involved the use of traditional eye-movement research in which eye fixations were ascribed to words and within word boundaries. Technically speaking, eye fixations do not always fall neatly within word boundaries. At times, the graphic information that falls within the foveal field (the area of greatest visual acuity) falls across word boundaries or even across boundaries of lines of print. Therefore, the traditional use of word boundaries in ascribing the location of fixations is an additional limitation of this study. The practice of ascribing fixations to words and ignoring beyond-word boundary or multiple-word boundary fixations has not been challenged within eye-movement research. The idea of arbitrarily forcing eye movements to fit within word boundaries distorts the data. To what degree, eye-movement researchers will not know until we begin to examine and compare fixations based on foveal boundaries and fixations arbitrarily ascribed at word boundaries.

References

Adams, M. (1990). *Beginning to read: Thinking and learning about print.* Cambridge, MA: MIT Press.

Buswell, G. (1922). *Fundamental reading habits: A study of their development.* Chicago: University of Chicago.

Cattell, J. (1886). The time it takes to see and name objects. *Mind, 11,* 62–65.

Cooney, B. (1988). *Remarks made at a symposium, "Ways of Saying, Ways of Knowing."* Paper presented at the New England Reading Association annual conference, Portland, ME.

Cowley, J. (1988). *I saw a dinosaur.* Crystal Lake, IL: Rigby.

Cutting, B., & Cutting, J. (1988). *Are you a ladybug?* Bothell, WA: Wright Group.

Denburg, S. (1976). The interaction of picture and print in reading instruction. *Reading Research Quarterly, 12,* 176–189.

Goodman, K. (1996). *On reading.* Portsmouth, NH: Heinemann.

Goodman, Y., Watson, D., & Burke, C. (1987). *Reading Miscue Inventory: Alternative procedures.* New York: Owen.

Goodman, Y., Watson, D., & Burke, C. (1996). *Reading strategies: Focus on comprehension.* New York: Owen.

Hegarty, M. (1992). The mechanics of comprehension and the comprehension of mechanics. In K. Rayner (Ed.), *Eye movements and visual cognition* (pp. 428–443). New York: Springer-Verlag.

Hogaboam, T. (1983). Reading patterns in eye movement data. In K. Rayner (Ed.), *Eye movements in reading* (pp. 309-332). New York: Academic Press.

Holmes, B. (1987). Children's inferences with print and pictures. *Journal of Educational Psychology, 79,* 14–18.

Hubbard, R. (1989). *Authors of pictures, draughtsmen of words.* Portsmouth, NH: Heinemann.

Jacobson, J., & Dodwell, P. (1979). Saccadic eye movements during reading. *Brain and Language, 8,* 303–314.

Just, M., & Carpenter, P. (1984). Using eye fixation to study reading comprehension. In D. Kieras & M. Just (Eds.), *New methods in reading comprehension research* (pp. 151-182). Hillsdale, NJ: Erlbaum.

Just, M., & Carpenter, P. (1987). *The psychology of reading and language comprehension.* Newton, MA: Allyn and Bacon.

Kiefer, B. (1995). *The potential of picturebooks.* Englewood Cliffs, NJ: Prentice-Hall.

Koenke, K. (1968). *The effects of a content relevant picture on the comprehension of the main idea of a paragraph.* Paper presented at the Wisconsin Research and Development Center for Cognitive Learning, University of Wisconsin.

Koenke, K. (1980). Pictures and reading. *Journal of Reading, 7,* 650–653.

Koenke, K., & Otto, W. (1969). Contributions of pictures to children's comprehension of the main idea in reading. *Psychology in the Schools, 6,* 298–302.

Leland, C., & Harste, J. (1994). Multiple ways of knowing: Curriculum in a new key. *Language Arts, 71,* 340.

Meek, M. (1988). *How texts teach what readers learn.* Woodchester Stroud, U.K.: Thimble Press.

Menosky, D. M. (1971). *The psycholinguistic description of oral reading miscues generated during the reading of varying positions of text by selected readers from Grades 2, 4, 6 and 8.* Unpublished doctoral dissertation, Wayne State University, Detroit, MI.

Oller, J., & Tullius, J. (1973). Reading skills of non-native speakers of English. *International Review of Applied Linguistics in Language and Teaching, 11,* 69–79.

Paulson, E. J. (2000). *Adult readers' eye movements during the production of oral miscues.* Unpublished doctoral dissertation, University of Arizona, Tucson.

Paulson, E. J. (2002). Are oral reading word omissions and substitutions caused by careless eye movements? *Reading Psychology, 23,* 45–66.

Pinnell, G., & Fountas, I. (1999). *Matching books to readers: Using leveled books in guided reading, K–3.* Portsmouth, NH: Heinemann.

Rayner, K. (1997). Understanding eye movements in reading. *Scientific Studies of Reading, 1,* 317–339.

Rayner, K., & Pollatsek, A. (1989). *The psychology of reading.* Hillsdale, NJ: Erlbaum.

Samuels, S. (1977). Can pictures distract students from the printed word? A rebuttal. *Journal of Reading Behavior, 9,* 361–364.

Scieszka, J. (1998, March/April). Design matters. *The Horn Book Magazine,* pp. 196–208.

Singer, H. (1980). Sight word learning with and without pictures: A critique of Arlin, Scott, and Webster's research. *Reading Research Quarterly, 15,* 290–298.

Vernon, M. (1953). The value of pictorial illustration. *The British Journal of Educational Psychology, 23*(Part 3), 180–187.

Vernon, M. (1958). The instruction of children by pictorial illustration. *The British Journal of Educational Psychology, 24*(Part 3), 171–179.

Weintraub, S. (1960). *The effect of pictures on the comprehension of a second grade basal reader.* Unpublished doctoral dissertation, University of Illinois.

Weintraub, S. (1966). Illustrations for beginning reading. *Reading Teacher, 20,* 61–67.

Willows, D. (1978a). Individual differences in distraction by pictures in a reading situation. *Journal of Educational Psychology, 70,* 837–847.

Willows, D. (1978b). A picture is not always worth a thousand words: pictures as distractors in reading. *Journal of Educational Psychology, 70,* 255–262.

Yaden, D., Smolkin, L., & Conlon, A. (1989). Preschoolers' questions about pictures, print conventions, and story text during reading aloud at home. *Reading Research Quarterly, 24,* 188–214.

INTRODUCTION TO CHAPTER 6

*A*LONG-STANDING CONTROVERSY IN LITERACY instruction is whether reading is the same or different in different languages and whether reading instruction should be different if the reading processes are different.

Ann Ebe designed an eye movement/miscue analysis (EMMA) study to look at whether the processes of reading English and Spanish were actually different or essentially the same. In this, she was testing my theoretical view that there is a single universal process for making sense of print for both Spanish and English.

Using EMMA, the integration of miscue analysis and eye-movement research, on oral reading by biliterate readers, Ebe demonstrates that her readers are making sense of both Spanish and English in the same way. She conducted an experiment in which biliterate readers read from the same text with one chapter in English and the other in Spanish. But, unlike empirical studies, which use some manipulation of texts to control variables and are hypothesis testing, her study used in-depth miscue analysis and eye tracking of the actual reading of real texts The texts are real in the sense that they were not expressly created to fit the experimental design but rather written as a book for children to read by the same author in either Spanish or English.

Ebe's readers are in fact making sense of the text in both languages but are somewhat more efficient in their first language. So, her answer to the question of whether the process of making sense in English and Spanish is the same or different is that the languages do in fact show the same processes and structures. They are really the same.

Ebe's strong inference from the study is that if the reading process is the same in Spanish and English, then optimal instructional methodology should also be the same. That is a justifiable inference and eliminates an important claim of those who argue for Spanish instruction as different from English, but it should be noted that she did not study reading instruction in this study. She also did not study how readers become literate in two languages, that is, how they learn to read in each language. Reading instruction should be based on the reality of how people make sense of print and how they learn to do so, but there is another kind of reality in reading instruction that can be studied through scientific realism that would go beyond experimental studies that compare test performance by students instructed in two or more different ways. Such studies may show one method statistically superior to another, but they cannot show why or under which circumstances one would be superior over the other. This requires building a theory, which is the object of scientific realism.

Ken Goodman

6

WHAT EYE MOVEMENT AND MISCUE ANALYSIS REVEALS ABOUT THE READING PROCESS OF YOUNG BILINGUALS

Ann Ebe

Introduction

*W*ITH THE INCREASING NUMBERS of English language learners (ELLs) in U.S. schools, there is a serious need for current research that seeks to understand the process these students engage in while reading in both their native languages and in English. The study presented in this chapter examines the reading processes of fourth graders as they read in English and in their native language, Spanish. Through miscue analysis, eye-movement analysis, and a combination of the two, eye movement/miscue analysis (EMMA), this study contributes to the field of biliteracy by expanding and refining the research base on the reading processes of young bilinguals who are developing literacy in two languages.

The Research Question

The study was guided by the following question: What do miscue analysis, eye-movement analysis, and EMMA reveal about differences and similarities of the reading in Spanish and English of fourth-grade biliterate readers? By analyzing students' oral reading and studying their eye movements as they read in two languages, it is possible to gain a more complete picture of what readers do as they process text in each language.

I have taught reading in both Spanish and English and have worked with bilingual students from kindergarten through high school. In my classes, the methods that I used were underpinned by the assumption that the reading process is the same for students regardless of the language in which they are reading. My teaching was guided by the understanding that reading is a meaning-making process, and my methods are based on Goodman's universal theory of reading. As Goodman (1984) explains, "Though written language processes appear to vary greatly as they are used in the wide range of functions and contexts they serve, reading and writing are actually unitary psycholinguistic processes" (p. 81).

However, both coteachers and teacher educators I worked with challenged my approach, especially my teaching in Spanish. They believed that I should use traditional methods of teaching reading in Spanish. Synthetic methods such as the alphabetic, onomatopoeic, phonetic, and most commonly, the syllabic method were among the most common approaches used by my coworkers in teaching reading in Spanish.

These synthetic approaches to teaching reading begin with small parts, such as sounds, letters, or syllables, and move to wholes, which usually consist of words. A common rationale for using such methods is explained by Freeman and Freeman (1996): "Since phonics patterns are more consistent and less complex in Spanish than in English, most methods for teaching reading in Spanish emphasize using sound clues to identify words" (p. 61). Although publications about literacy in Spanish such as *Lectura y Vida* reflect a growing understanding of reading as a meaning-making process (i.e., Freeman & Serra, 1997), many of the synthetic approaches to teaching reading in Spanish continue to be used both in Latin America and in the United States.

Bilingual students taught to read in two languages, then, may experience two different approaches to teaching reading, even from the same teacher. Diaz, Moll, and Mehan (1986) found this to be true in their case study involving third- and fourth-grade Spanish-speaking children. They observed these students in two different contexts, a Spanish reading lesson and an English reading lesson. In this case, the Spanish teacher focused on comprehension, and the English teacher focused on having the students decode sounds.

In light of the different approaches used in teaching reading to bilinguals, the following question emerges: Do bilinguals read differently in their two languages, or as Goodman (1984) suggests, is reading a unitary process that operates similarly in any language? As a bilingual reading teacher and as a researcher, I saw the need to learn more about the reading process of bilingual students to connect reading theory to bilingual reading instruction.

Background Literature

Although few research studies examine the combination of eye movements with the oral reading of bilinguals, many studies exist in the literature that use these two methodologies separately. As early as 1886, James Cattell found through his eye-movement studies that readers took more time processing text when reading in a second language. In 1908, Huey (1908/1968) wrote about the work of Landolt, who discovered that while reading texts in a foreign language, readers made more fixations, and their eye movements were slower. This finding is logical as the readers needed more time and visual data to make sense of text in a new language. These readers relied more on the visual information provided by the text because the foreign language limited their ability to use the syntactic and semantic cue systems. Readers often bring less background knowledge to foreign language texts. In 1973, Oller and Tullius conducted an eye-movement study with nonnative English speakers reading in English that revealed similar findings.

In their eye-movement study, Oller and Tullius (1973) compared the reading skills of nonnative and native English-speaking university students from a variety of linguistic backgrounds. The results revealed that the native English readers read more rapidly in their native language. The eye-movement data showed that these readers made fewer fixations and shorter fixations than the nonnative readers. The native English readers also made fewer regressions, or backward fixations, overall as they read. As with many modern eye-movement studies, however, only a single sentence was used as the text unit of analysis in this study, limiting its applicability to authentic reading, that is, reading complete texts that have not been altered for experimental purposes.

The first group of studies presented above describes eye-movement research conducted with bilingual readers. A second group of studies involves listening to and examining the oral reading of text. In miscue analysis studies, complete, meaningful sections of texts are used to explore the reading process. A growing number of these miscue analysis studies have been conducted with bilingual readers from a variety of language backgrounds. One group of studies (Hatch, 1974; MacNamara, 1970; Malik, 1990; Oller, 1972; Rigg, 1977a, 1977b, 1986; Tucker, 1975; Zhang, 1988) involves subjects reading in English as a second language. A second group of studies (Clarke, 1980; Crowell, 1995; Eaton, 1983; Favreau & Segalowitz, 1982; Hodes, 1981; Miramontes, 1987; Rodriguez-Brown & Yirchott, 1983; Romatowski, 1981) compares the readings of bilingual readers as they read in both their first and second languages. In these two groups of studies, researchers analyzed the miscues and retellings of the readers to learn the degree to which readers used each cue system and what meaning they made from the text. In general,

miscue analysis studies have shown that readers are more effective and efficient as they read in their first language. Effective readers make balanced use
of the cue systems as they read, and efficient readers make minimal use of the
cues as they maneuver through text. Often, second-language readers are less
effective in their reading because they overrely on one of the cueing systems.
Similar results are found for second-language readers and general readers
who struggle through a particular text. Second-language readers tend to rely
more on the graphophonic cue system, the visual data from text, and less on
the semantic and syntactic systems as they read in a second language.

The combination of eye movement and miscue analysis (EMMA) was first
developed by Paulson (2000) when he combined the oral data from miscue
analysis with the visual data from eye-movement analysis to create a more
complete picture of the reading process. By analyzing the patterns of eye
movements and miscues of adult readers, Paulson was able to gain insights
into the processes used to construct meaning. To date, EMMA research has
been conducted with readers who range from as young as first grade (Duckett, chapter 5, this volume) to adult readers (Paulson, 2002, chapter 11, this
volume). EMMA studies involving readers of various linguistic backgrounds
are relatively new, and several are in progress. The present EMMA study,
which analyzes bilingual students reading in two languages, has no prec-
edent in the research literature.

Participants

The participants are fourth-grade Spanish and English readers who attend a
local Spanish/English bilingual school. This school is located in a low socioeconomic neighborhood on the south side of an urban city. The dominant
language of the neighborhood is Spanish, which is reflected by the signs on
restaurants and shops and the language spoken on the streets.

The four participants included in this study (Andrea, Juan Antonio, Angel,
and Jazmin) are Mexican American, and their primary language is Spanish.
Andrea, Juan Antonio, and Jazmin were born in the United States. Angel
was born in Mexico and attended school there prior to coming to the United
States. Although all four readers show higher levels of reading proficiency in
Spanish, they read and communicate in English as well.

Materials

The participants read two consecutive book chapters, providing readers a more
authentic reading experience than the many eye-movement studies in which

participants read only single sentences. The two book chapters are from a fictional story written by Alma Flor Ada (1993a, 1993b). The first chapter of the story was read from the English version of the text, *My Name Is María Isabel*. The second chapter of the story was read from the Spanish version of the story, *Me llamo María Isabel*. Both chapters are approximately the same length.

These two texts were selected because they are authentic, are of the same genre (as the chapters come from the same story), and are close in length. Also, *My Name Is María Isabel* is a story to which fourth-grade bilingual readers may relate because it involves a young girl who is becoming bilingual and biliterate.

In the first chapter of the story, the protagonist, María Isabel, who is from Puerto Rico, is nervously thinking about her first day of school in the United States. Her parents reassure her and send her off to school with her older brother. Unfortunately, on her way to the bus stop, María Isabel trips and falls, scraping her knee and ruining her special dress.

In the second chapter, read from the Spanish version of the story, María Isabel arrives at school and is shown to her new classroom. Because there were already two girls named María in her class, María Isabel's teacher decides to name her Mary. María Isabel then sits at her desk and begins to think about the importance of her name and daydreams about the relatives for whom she was named. The chapter ends with María Isabel's teacher impatiently trying to get María's attention and not understanding why María was not responding to her numerous calls: "Mary!"

I selected English and Spanish texts that were as similar as possible to eliminate the number of variables in the comparison of the two readings. I also had to choose texts short enough so that the participants could read and retell both in one session. The English chapter contains 793 words, and the Spanish chapter contains 808 words. Each text is 10 pages long.

Each text was typed onto PowerPoint slides. Each of the two chapters contained one illustration, which was scanned and included along with the text. The chapters were typed to maintain a 2-page open-spread format just as a reader holding the open book would see them. This was done to make the electronic texts look as close to the original as possible. The text was enlarged to an 18-point font so that it could be read comfortably on the computer monitor. The readers sat directly in front of the computer monitor in a comfortable chair.

Data Collection

Eye movements were recorded using an Applied Science Laboratories 504 eye tracker. This eye tracker measures the reader's pupil diameter and point of gaze on the stationary text, which is displayed on a computer monitor.

The eye-tracking device measures pupil and corneal reflections from the reader's eye with a harmless infrared beam and uses those measurements to tell exactly where a reader looks on a page of text. The recording device is accurate to within 0.5° of visual angle. Because the autofocus eye camera and eye illuminator are contained in a pan/tilt module, the camera moves automatically with the readers' slight head movements as they read. This camera, which rests on a table next to the monitor from which the participant reads, eliminates the use of more intrusive means of capturing eye movements, such as having the participants wear a head-mounted tracker, use of a chin rest, or use of a bite bar to ensure accurate recordings.

The eye-movement data are captured by the eye tracker control unit, which is accessed by a second computer. That computer produces raw-eye movement data in the form of a series of X,Y coordinates. During the reading, the computer from which the participant reads makes a video recording of a picture of the text that is read; the picture has a cursor superimposed on it to show where the reader's eye movements are. This video recording also records the reader's voice, which is used for the miscue analysis. The reading is also audiotape recorded as a backup for the miscue analysis.

Once the system is calibrated to the reader to ensure an accurate eye-movement record, the participant reads the first chapter of the story in English. After the first chapter, the reader provides a retelling in either English or Spanish to ensure comprehension. The system is then recalibrated, and the participant reads the second chapter of the story in Spanish. Again, a retelling is provided in the participant's language of choice.

Analyses

To compare the readings in English and Spanish, the data were analyzed on three levels. The first was the miscue analysis using Procedure I (Goodman, Watson, & Burke, 1987) along with analysis of the retellings. The second was eye-movement analysis. The third level of analysis was EMMA, for which the eye movements and miscues were analyzed together for the readings in both Spanish and English.

Findings and Interpretations

Miscue Analysis

In miscue analysis Procedure I, the miscues are coded, and the retelling is scored. Next, a reader profile is created by adding the results from the

Table 6.1   Miscue Analysis Procedure I Reader Profile Summaries for English and Spanish

	Meaning Construction		Grammatical Relationships		Relations Graphic/Sound		
	No Loss/Partial Loss	Loss	Strength/Partial Strength	Weakness	High/Some	High/Some	Holistic Retelling Score (1–5)
Andrea (English)	76%	25%	87%	13%	100%	100%	4
Andrea (Spanish)	100%	0%	67%	0%	100%	86%	4
Juan Antonio (English)	36%	64%	53%	45%	95%	87%	3
Juan Antonio (Spanish)	63%	37%	72%	28%	89%	87%	4
Angel (English)	24%	76%	33%	64%	100%	81%	4
Angel (Spanish)	75%	25%	65%	15%	93%	87%	4
Jazmin (English)	27%	73%	55%	44%	95%	83%	3
Jazmin (Spanish)	38%	62%	52%	46%	98%	95%	4

coding of each miscue for meaning construction, grammatical relationships, graphic similarity, and sound similarity and determining, for the entire reading, percentages for each score. Retelling scores are also included on reader profiles. Table 6.1 summarizes the data from the English and Spanish reader profiles for each of the four readers in this study.

The first section shown in Table 6.1 summarizes the data on meaning construction. The patterns for meaning construction are determined by combining information that deals with semantic acceptability of miscues, meaning change caused by miscues, and correction of miscues. These patterns indicate how closely the meaning the reader makes of the text matches the expected meaning. The second column in this section represents the percentage of miscues that reflect a loss of meaning. In the grammatical relationships of miscues section of Table 6.1, we see the degree to which readers produce sentences that are syntactically acceptable or corrected. In the leftmost column of this section, the percentages of grammatical relationships that show strength or partial strength are displayed. The percentages of weakness of grammatical relationships are shown in the right column of that section. The graphic and sound relations of miscues are shown in that section of Table 6.1. The percentage of miscues that show high or some graphic similarity to the expected response is shown in the leftmost column of the section, and the rightmost column shows the percentage of miscues with high or some sound similarity to the expected response. The farthest right column of Table 6.1 shows the holistic retelling scores for the retellings provided after each reading. Although the miscues provide information about how the readers are comprehending during the reading, the retelling provides information about what readers have comprehended at the end of each reading. Each retelling was scored holistically on a scale of 1 to 5.

The miscue analysis revealed that Andrea, Juan Antonio, Angel, and Jazmin are proficient in their comprehension of text in both English and Spanish, as shown by their retellings of each text. Their reader profiles, however, show that they are more proficient in their comprehending strategies for these texts in their primary language, Spanish, than in English. For example, the four readers generally make more use of graphophonic cues when reading English than when reading Spanish. The readers' overreliance on the graphophonic system in English is revealed partly through their production of more nonwords in English. The readers' higher proficiency in Spanish is revealed by their higher percentages of no loss of meaning construction and strength of grammatical relations in Spanish than in English. Although the four readers' proficiency in Spanish is stronger than in English, all four fourth graders included in this study are biliterate. They can read, comprehend, and discuss texts written in both English and Spanish.

The miscue-analysis data also reveal that the four readers included in this study vary greatly in how proficiently they read the Spanish and English texts. Andrea, for example, makes fewer than 10 miscues when reading each text; Jazmin makes over 100 miscues in reading each chapter. The qualitative analysis of the miscues produced by these four readers also reveals that there are differences in the effectiveness and efficiency of each reader. However, the four readers appear to be using the same strategies as they read. All four readers integrate their knowledge of syntax, semantics, and graphophonics, as well as their background knowledge, as they read. Some of the readers in this study do so more effectively than others for these texts.

The data also demonstrate that even though overall the four readers were more proficient in their reading of the Spanish text, there appeared to be more differences between the readers than across the two languages. In other words, readers who were proficient in their Spanish reading were also proficient in their English reading. Likewise, readers who were less proficient in reading the Spanish text were also less proficient in reading the English text. This supports the idea that although there is diversity among the proficiency of the readers in this study, there is a universal reading process for Spanish and English.

Eye-Movement Analysis

Eye movements in reading consist of pauses and movements between the pauses called *saccades*. The pauses, or fixations, are places where the reader samples from the visual text. During saccades, when the eye moves to the next section of text from which the reader will sample, no visual data are picked up (Dodge, 1900; Wolverton & Zola, 1983). Because the brain only receives useful visual data from the eyes when the eyes are fixating, eye-movement research concerns itself with the study of fixations and what the reader samples during these pauses.

An analysis of the fixations made during the readings reveals that the fourth-grade bilingual readers in this study did not fixate every word in either the English or the Spanish texts. In addition, words were not all fixated sequentially from left to right. All four readers made regressive, or backward, eye movements during their readings in both Spanish and English. Figure 6.1 clearly illustrates these two findings.

Figure 6.1 shows the first part of the English text read by Juan Antonio; indications of his eye movements are superimposed on the text. The round dots represent the places where Juan Antonio fixated the text. The lines between the dots are the saccades, and the numbers under each fixation represent the order in which the fixations on this text were made. In his oral reading of this portion of text, Juan Antonio made no miscues. The eye-movement data show that Juan Antonio clearly did not look at every word, and he did not look at every word sequentially in order. For example, while reading the title, he fixated the word *Way* before regressing to the word *the*.

Table 6.2 summarizes the combined eye-movement data collected for all four readers. Of the words in the English text, 56% were fixated, and of the words in the Spanish text, 59% were fixated.

The higher percentage of fixations in Spanish was surprising as typically readers make fewer fixations while reading in their native language. Overall,

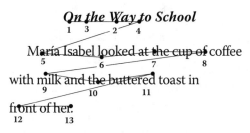

Figure 6.1
Juan Antonio's fixations and regression.

Table 6.2 Percentages of Words Fixated for All Four Readers

	% Total Words Fixated	% Content Words Fixated	% Function Words Fixated
English	56	67	45
Spanish	59	75	43

however, the percentages of words fixated by the participants were lower than the percentages typically found in the literature for adults. Studies show that adult readers typically fixate between 60% and 75% of words in a text (Hogaboam, 1983; Just & Carpenter, 1987). It appears that as these young readers are gaining control of the three cueing systems in reading, they are sampling less from text than adult readers. As more eye-movement studies are conducted with developing readers, we may begin to find that there is an optimal rate of fixation for efficient reading. This optimal rate would be closer to the percentage of words fixated for adults, between 60% and 75%. As the readers in this study increase in oral reading proficiency, their rate of fixations may increase as they move toward this optimal rate.

This helps explain why the readers in this study made more fixations in Spanish, their native language, than in English. As the readers are more proficient in their Spanish reading, as reflected in the miscue analysis of their readings, they were closer to the optimal rate of fixation while reading in their native language. These bilingual readers may be moving toward the optimal rate more quickly in Spanish than in English.

It is important to note, however, that the optimal rate of fixations includes both a lower and an upper limit. Instruction for readers who lack proficiency tends to lead readers to focus on the graphophonic cueing system. It is important to understand that once the optimal fixation rate is reached, readers should continue to make balanced use of the three cueing systems in their integration of the three to avoid overreliance on the graphophonic system as seen with many nonproficient readers.

In reviewing the types of words that participants fixated, the data revealed that readers fixated more content words than function words in both English and Spanish. When combining the percentages for all readers, 67% of the content words were fixated; 45% of the function words were fixated in the English text. A t test showed that this difference is statistically significant ($p = .003$). In the Spanish text, 75% of the content words were fixated, and 43% of the function words were fixated. This difference was also statistically significant ($p < .001$).

The data also revealed that readers fixated a higher percentage of content words in Spanish, their primary language, than in English. Of the content words in the Spanish text, 75% were fixated; 67% of the content words in the

English text were fixated. This difference is statistically significant ($p < .05$). These data suggest that the bilingual participants sample more effectively in Spanish than in English because they fixate on the words that carry the most meaning more often in Spanish than in their reading of the English text.

Eye Movement/Miscue Analysis

In combining the miscue analysis data collected from the four readers with the eye-movement analysis of the readings, further findings have been reached. In both Spanish and English, readers fixated miscued words more often and for longer periods of time than the other words in the texts.

As discussed, 56% of the words in the English text and 59% of the words in the Spanish text were fixated for all of the readers combined. As shown in Table 6.3, when miscued words are eliminated from the total and only fixations on nonmiscued words are examined, the percentage fixated is slightly less. Of the nonmiscued words, 54% were fixated in English, and 58% of the nonmiscued words were fixated in Spanish.

For miscued words, however, the percentage of words fixated is higher than the percentage of nonmiscued words fixated in both languages. A t test showed that these differences are statistically significant for both English ($p < .05$) and Spanish ($p < .05$). In English, readers fixated 77% of miscued words, and in Spanish they fixated 70% of miscued words.

Because these readers fixate English words that are miscued at a higher rate than Spanish words that are miscued, we can see that they are seeking more visual information in English when they miscue. It looks as though the readers are relying too much on the visual information. Because spending more time sampling from the graphic, or visual, information does not help these readers make fewer miscues, these data suggest that they are less confident in their nonvisual information (i.e., reader knowledge) than when reading in Spanish.

Figure 6.2 shows how Jazmin samples the visual data from the text, making many fixations and two miscues as she works to make sense of this portion of text. The numbers in the figure represent the order of the fixations. While reading this portion of text, Jazmin fixates the word *kept* two times

Table 6.3 Percentages of All Words and Miscued Words Fixated

	Mean % of All Words Fixated	% of Nonmiscued Words Fixated	Mean % of Miscued Words Fixated
English	56	54	77
Spanish	59	58	70

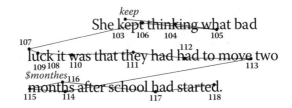

Figure 6.2
Jazmin's fixations and miscues.

and orally produces the word *keep*. Further along in the sentence, she fixates the word *months* three times and produces a nonword substitution, perhaps thinking that this was an object she was not familiar with, when she says "monthes." The oral reading analyzed through miscue analysis alone might suggest that Jazmin was not looking carefully at the words *kept* and *months*. Through an EMMA analysis, however, we see that Jazmin is relying heavily on the graphic information in these portions of text as she works to make sense of it as she reads. In fact, she may be relying too much on the visual information and not enough on the other cueing systems.

Although miscued words in general are fixated more often and for longer periods of time than words in the text that are not miscued, analysis of different types of miscues reveals further information.

When examining different types of miscues, the data, shown in Table 6.4, reveal that the expected responses for omission and substitution miscues in the English text were fixated more often than the expected responses for the omission and substitution miscues made in the Spanish text. However, the expected responses for nonword substitution miscues were fixated at an equal rate in both languages. This suggests that nonword substitutions like the monthes miscue produced by Jazmin represent places where readers are using graphophonic and syntactic information to consider possible text meanings. Jazmin does put in a word that shows use of graphics and syntax (because it has an inflexional suffix s, typical of nouns). However, because it is a nonword, she is not using semantic information as monthes does not have referential meaning.

Table 6.4 Percentage of Fixated Words in Each Language by Miscue Type

	Omissions		Substitutions		$ Nonword substitutions	
English	50%	N = 8	80%	N = 95	84%	N = 38
Spanish	13%	N = 8	70%	N = 91	85%	N = 26

In miscue analysis, miscues are coded for their amount of graphic similarity to the expected response. This measure helps identify when readers are using the graphophonic cueing system. Although in miscue analysis researchers can infer that readers are visually sampling from the text when they produce miscues with high graphic similarity to the expected response, eye-movement analysis provides researchers with evidence regarding whether readers fixated the expected response. The findings from this study show that miscues with high or some similarity to the expected response have a higher percentage of fixations than the miscues with no graphic similarity in both English and Spanish.

The EMMA data also show that readers fixate a slightly lower percentage of the *high* and *some* graphically similar miscued words in the Spanish text than in the English text. This provides evidence that these biliterate readers integrate the three cueing systems—syntax, semantics, and graphophonics—in Spanish to a greater degree than in English.

When the readers in this study produced semantically acceptable miscues, the expected responses for those miscues tended to be fixated less often than the expected responses for miscues that were semantically unacceptable. This means that when the text the readers produced made sense, they were relying less on the graphophonic cueing system and were integrating the cueing systems.

In addition, the more proficient readers of the texts used in this study made fewer regressions, or backward eye movements, around miscued words than the less-proficient readers. All four readers made more regressive fixations around miscued words in English than in Spanish.

Finally, not all corrected miscued words had regressive eye movements around them. In fact, few did, and those miscued words that did have regressive eye movements around them came primarily from the English readings. The readers relied more on graphic information to correct miscues in English than in their primary language, Spanish. In Spanish, readers show more confidence in their correcting by relying less on graphic information and more on semantic and syntactic information to self-correct.

Implications

The Office of English Language Acquisition (OLEA, 2005) reports a continued increase in the number of ELLs enrolled in U.S. schools. Between 1995 and 2005, the population of kindergarten through 12th-grade ELLs in this country grew by 61%, and the total K–12 enrollment grew by only 3%. In 1995, there were 3.2 million ELLs of the 47 million total students in

K–12 schools. By the 2004–2005 school year, the total enrollment had grown to 48.9 million, and the ELL population grew to 5.1 million, almost double what it was in 1991 (OLEA, 2005).

Of this rapidly increasing group of ELLs, 79.2% are from Spanish-speaking homes (Kindler, 2002). Traditionally, schools in the United States have not fared well in helping this population of students to succeed. In their publication, *Transforming Education for Hispanic Youth: Exemplary practices, programs, and schools*, Lockwood and Secada (1999) discuss the high dropout rate of Hispanic students in the United States. This includes "nearly one in three (30%) of the nation's Hispanic students between the ages of 16 and 24" (p. 1). Despite these discouraging statistics, however, the authors provide a list of recommendations for educators. Not surprisingly, the second recommendation is to help these students become good readers: "Hispanic students should receive high quality educations that guarantee that all students leave third grade able to read" (p. 3).

It is clear from these statistics that schools in America are faced with increasingly large numbers of ELLs whose native language is Spanish. Also, many of these students are not doing well in school, and helping these students develop the high levels of literacy needed for academic success is presented as part of a solution. Some of these students are taught to read in their primary language first; others are first taught to read in English. Regardless of which language is used, however, elementary teachers are encouraged to bring all their students to high levels of reading proficiency, even those students who are just beginning to learn English.

I began this chapter by discussing why I became interested in researching the reading process of bilinguals. The instructional methods I was encouraged to use while teaching reading in Spanish were different from those I used in English and would encourage students to focus on the graphophonic aspects of text in Spanish.

The findings of this study reveal that the four bilingual readers are knowledgeable about the relationships between letters and sounds in both English and Spanish. This is revealed in their high percentage of miscues with high and some graphic similarity in both languages. It is also revealed in the EMMA data, which show that when the readers cannot make sense of text, their strategy is to sample the graphic information provided by the text more often and for longer periods of time.

Instructional methods, such as the syllabic method I was encouraged to use, would lead students to focus even more on the graphophonic cueing system, a system these readers are effective in using but one they tend to overuse. Instructional methods that view reading as a meaning-making process prove more useful to readers. Readers should be provided with opportunities to integrate all three cueing systems as well as their background knowledge as they read.

The findings of this study also reveal that the strategies readers use in Spanish, their primary language, are the same strategies they use in English. These strategies include integrating their knowledge of the relationships between letters and sounds, syntax, semantics, and their background knowledge to make sense of text in both languages. This provides evidence that the reading process is universal. Those involved in reading instruction therefore should take this universality into account.

These findings are informative for both the reading and bilingual education fields in which teachers, such as those I described, are often overwhelmed, feeling that they have double work as they teach children to read one way in Spanish and another way in English. Because reading is a universal process, teachers can use the same holistic methods of teaching reading in each language. Such key reading strategies are described in detail in Paulson and Freeman's (2003) *Insight From the Eyes: The Science of Effective Reading Instruction.*

Also, because reading strategies transfer from one language to another (Cummins, 2000; Krashen, 1996), teachers can be assured that as readers become more proficient in one language, they will also become more proficient in the other. Cummins describes this as the *interdependence hypothesis.* Cummins (1981) originally stated the interdependence principle in this way:

> To the extent that instruction in Lx is effective in promoting proficiency in Lx, transfer of this proficiency to Ly will occur provided there is adequate exposure to Ly (either in school or environment) and adequate motivation to learn Ly. (p. 29)

What this means is that if students are effectively instructed in one language (Lx), the proficiency they develop in that language will transfer to a second language (Ly) as long as the student is exposed to the second language and is motivated to learn it. This interdependence is based on the idea that a common cognitive/academic proficiency underlies any two languages. Transfer can occur once a student has developed enough proficiency in the second language to be able to comprehend and express the concepts already learned in the first language.

Cummins (2000) has expanded his discussion of the interdependence hypothesis. He comments that the common underlying proficiency may be thought of as a central processing system consisting of cognitive and linguistic abilities like memory, auditory discrimination, and abstract reasoning as well as specific conceptual and linguistic knowledge derived from experience and learning, such as vocabulary knowledge. Cummins states that the positive relationship between two languages comes from three sources:

1. the application of the same cognitive and linguistic abilities and skills to literacy development in both languages;
2. transfer of general concepts and knowledge of the world across languages in the sense that the individual's prior knowledge (in L1) represents the foundation of schemata upon which L2 acquisition is built; and
3. to the extent that the languages are related, transfer of specific linguistic features and skills across languages. (p. 191)

This interdependence hypothesis helps explain why the bilingual students in this study are able to use the same strategies they use to read in Spanish to make sense of text in English. These readers know how to integrate their knowledge of the relationships between letters and sounds, syntax, semantics, and their background knowledge to make sense of text in Spanish, their primary language. Because they have this knowledge in Spanish, they can use the same process to read in English. However, because English is their second language, these readers may take longer to show the same levels of proficiency in the academic task of reading in English as they show in Spanish.

Conclusions

The present research could not have been carried out without the technological advances that allow accurate and authentic recordings of eye movements. New computer programs make it possible to overlay the eye-movement data on miscue data. Further advances may provide even more information. However, advances in technology cannot answer all our questions. Miscue analysis and eye-movement data provide windows on the reading process, but we must interpret the results because we cannot directly assess the psycholinguistic processes involved in reading. However, the research described in this study clearly supports a transactional, sociopsycholinguistic model of reading (see also Paulson & Goodman, chapter 2, this volume).

Because this research was carried out with bilingual readers reading in two languages, this research also supports the claim that reading is a unitary process. The four readers whose reading I analyzed here appear to use the same strategies to construct meaning in both Spanish and English. It is my hope that this research has opened the window just a bit wider on the process readers use in any language to construct meaning from texts.

References

Ada, A. (1993a). *Me llamo María Isabel.* New York: Simon and Schuster.

Ada, A. (1993b). *My name is María Isabel.* New York: Simon and Schuster.

Cattell, J. (1886). The time it takes to see and name objects. *Mind, 11,* 63–65.

Clarke, M. (1980, June). The short circuit hypothesis of ESL reading — Or when language competence interferes with reading performance. *Modern Language Journal, 64,* 203–209.

Crowell, C. (1995). Documenting the strengths of bilingual readers. *Primary Voices K–6, 3*(4), 32–37.

Cummins, J. (1981). The role of primary language development in promoting educational success for language minority students. In California State Department of Education (Ed.). *Schooling and language minority students: A theoretical framework* (pp. 3–49). Los Angeles: Evaluation, Dissemination, and Assessment Center, California State University.

Cummins, J. (2000). *Language, power and pedagogy: Bilingual children in the crossfire.* Buffalo, NY: Multilingual Matters.

Diaz, E., Moll, L., & Mehan, H. (1986). *Sociocultural resources in instruction: A context-specific approach. Beyond language: Social and cultural factors in schooling language minority students.* Los Angeles: Evaluation, Dissemination and Assessment Center, California State University.

Dodge, R. (1900). Visual perceptions during eye movement. *Psychological Review, 7,* 454–465.

Eaton, A. (1983). The oral reading miscues of field-dependent and field-independent Mexican American children. In T. H. Escobedo (Ed.), *Early childhood bilingual education: A Hispanic perspective* (pp. 222–238). New York: Teachers College Press.

Favreau, M., & Segalowitz, N. (1982). Second language reading in fluent bilinguals. *Applied Psycholinguistics, 3,* 329–341.

Freeman, D., & Freeman, Y. (1996). *Teaching reading and writing in Spanish in the bilingual classroom.* Portsmouth, NH: Heinemann.

Freeman, Y. S., & Serra, M. (1997). Alternativas positivas para la enseñaza tradicional de la lectura. *Lectura y vida, 18*(2), 17–26.

Goodman, K. (1984). Unity in reading. In A. Purves & O. Niles (Eds.), *Becoming readers in a complex society: 83rd yearbook of the National Society for the Study of Education* (pp. 79–114). Chicago: University of Chicago Press.

Goodman, Y., Watson, D., & Burke, C. (1987). *Reading miscue inventory.* Katonah, NY: Owen.

Hatch, E. (1974). Research on reading a second language. *Journal of Reading Behavior, 6,* 53–61.

Hodes, P. (1981). Reading: A universal process. A study of Yiddish-English bilingual readers. In S. Hudelson (Ed.), *Learning to read in different languages* (pp. 27–31). Washington, DC: Center for Applied Linguistics.

Hogaboam, T. (1983). Reading patterns in eye movement data. In K. Rayner (Ed.), *Eye movements in reading* (pp. 309–332). New York: Academic Press.

Huey, E. (1968). *The psychology and pedagogy of reading.* Cambridge, MA: MIT Press. (Original work published 1908)

Just, M., & Carpenter, P. (1987). *The psychology of reading and language comprehension.* Newton, MA: Allyn and Bacon.

Kindler, A. (2002). *Survey of the states' limited English proficient students and available educational programs and services 2000–2001 summary report.* Washington, DC: National Clearinghouse for English Language Acquisition and Language Instruction Educational Programs. Retrieved May 21, 2007 from http://www.ncela.gwu.edu/policy/states/reports/seareports/0001/sea0001.pdf

Krashen, S. (1996). *Under attack: The case against bilingual education.* Culver City, CA: Language Education Associates.

Lockwood, A., & Secada, W. (1999). *Transforming education for Hispanic youth: Exemplary practices, programs, and schools* No. (RC 022 112). Washington, DC: Office of Bilingual and Minority Languages Affairs.

MacNamara, J. (1970). Comparative studies of reading and problem solving in two languages. *TESOL Quarterly, 4,* 107–116.

Malik, A. (1990). A psycholinguistic analysis of the reading behavior of EFL-proficient readers using culturally familiar and culturally nonfamiliar expository texts. *American Educational Research Journal, 27,* 205–223.

Miramontes, O. (1987). Oral reading miscues of Hispanic good and learning disabled students: Implications for second language reading. In S. R. Goodman & H. T. Trueba (Eds.), *Becoming literate in English as a second language: Cognition and literacy* (pp. 127–154). Norwood, NJ: Ablex.

National Clearinghouse for English Language Acquisition (2005). *The growing number of limited English proficient students 2005-2005.* Retrieved May 21, 2007, from http://www.ncela.gwu.edu/policy/states/reports/statedata/2004LEP/GrowingLEP_0405_Nov06.pdf

Oller, J. (1972). Dictation as a test of ESL proficiency. In H. Allen and R. Campbell (Eds.), *Teaching English as a second language: A book of readings* (pp. 346–354). New York: McGraw-Hill.

Oller, J., & Tullius, J. (1973). Reading skills of non-native speakers of English. *International Review of Applied Linguistics in Language and Teaching, 11,* 69–79.

Paulson, E. J. (2000). *Adult readers' eye movements during the production of oral miscues.* Unpublished doctoral dissertation, University of Arizona, Tucson.

Paulson, E. J. (2002). Are oral reading word omissions and substitutions caused by careless eye movements? *Reading Psychology, 23,* 45–66.

Paulson, E. J., & Freeman, A. (2003). *Insight from the eyes: The science of effective reading instruction.* Portsmouth, NH: Heinemann.

Rigg, P. (1977a). Getting the message, decoding the message. *The Reading Teacher, 30,* 745–749.

Rigg, P. (1977b). The miscue-ESL project. In H. D. Brown, D. Yorio, & R. Crymes (Eds.), *Teaching and learning ESL: Trends in research and practice* (pp. 106–118). Washington, DC: Teachers of English to Speakers of Other Languages.

Rigg, P. (1986). *Children and ESL: Integrating perspectives.* Washington, DC: Teachers of English to Speakers of Other Languages.

Rodriguez-Brown, F., & Yirchott, L. (1983). *A comparative analysis of oral reading miscues made by monolingual versus bilingual students* (Bilingual Education Paper Series, Vol. 7, No. 5). Washington, DC: Office of Bilingual and Minority Languages Affairs.

Romatowski, J. (1981). A study of oral reading in Polish and English: A psycholinguistic perspective. In S. Hudelson (Ed.), *Learning to read in different languages* (pp. 21–26). Washington, DC: Center for Applied Linguistics.

Tucker, G. (1975). The development of reading skills within a bilingual program. In S. Smiley and J. Towner (Eds.), *Language and reading.* Bellingham, WA: Sixth Western Washington Symposium on Learning.

Wolverton, G., & Zola, D. (1983). The temporal characteristics of visual information extraction during reading. In K. Rayner (Ed.), *Eye movements in reading: Perceptual and language processes* (pp. 41–52). New York: Academic Press.

Zhang, J. (1988). Reading miscues and nine adult Chinese learners of English. *Journal of Reading, 32,* 34–41.

Section Four

STUDIES OF READING IN NONALPHABETIC ORTHOGRAPHIES
Syllabic Orthography

INTRODUCTION TO CHAPTER 7

*J*ASSEM AL-FAHID DESIGNED TWO related experiments to study how adult native speakers of Arabic make sense of written Arabic. His findings provide important support for our belief that there is a single process for making sense of print regardless of language and orthography. Although these are experimental studies, they support and extend the model of reading built on scientific realism. Scientific realism is hypothesis generating. Al-Fahid used his knowledge of Arabic linguistics and of the meaning-construction model of reading to study two unusual aspects of written Arabic.

Written Arabic and the related Semitic language Hebrew use a semialphabetic orthography that represents oral consonants but only minimally represents vowels. Both orthographies have a set of diacritical markings that can represent the vowels of oral language, but most written texts are not marked. Much of the inflectional system involves vowels, so that the syntactic system is also minimally represented. In Arabic, only the sacred Quran and old classic poetry usually use fully marked texts.

Al-Fahid confirmed in interviews with his adult readers that they were aware that making sense of Arabic required them to infer both the phonology and the syntax of Arabic from the context of the texts. He knew that they were skilled at doing so even though modern written Arabic is derived from classic Arabic and is not the home dialect of any modern Arabic speakers.

His first experiment involved two versions of the same text, one marked and the other unmarked. Most of his subjects read the unmarked form faster than the marked form. Those that read both forms about equally fast reported that they were quite religious and read marked texts relatively more often than the others did. His other subjects reported that they felt constrained to read the marked texts more carefully.

In his second experiment, he provided his subjects single, out-of-context sentences. Each of the sentences could be read a number of different ways with quite different meanings. He asked the subjects to mark the sentences with diacritics to represent as many possible readings as they could imagine. In some views of reading, readers are assumed to consider all possibilities when the text is ambiguous. Somewhat to Al-Fahid's surprise, his subjects could only think of a small number of possibilities for each sentence, and the ones they chose tended to be the ones others also could imagine. This suggests again the importance of context and the predictability of each possible reading.

The written forms of Hebrew and Arabic continue to be used for historical and cultural reasons, but they also work well for their language communities. These experiments demonstrate that written language does not have to be fully alphabetic to work well for written communication. Reading is a process of constructing meaning, not recoding print as speech; in fact, Arabic print represents no one's speech.

Ken Goodman

7

THE READING PROCESS IN ARABIC
Making Sense of Arabic Print*

Jassem Mohammad Al-Fahid and Kenneth S. Goodman

*A*LTHOUGH THERE IS A body of literature on teaching literacy in Arabic, there is little research on the process of reading Arabic. Yet, literacy in Arabic is unusual in several respects. First, modern written Arabic does not correspond to any modern spoken dialect of Arabic. There are many dialects of spoken Arabic, which vary considerably from each other. Modern Standard written Arabic is derived from Classic Arabic and is used across all dialects, so all Arab speakers learn to read a form of the language that is not their own. A second important feature of Arabic literacy is that, like Hebrew, the most common form of the orthography only minimally represents vowels and the syntactic markers of the oral language. There is a system of diacritics used to represent the vowels, but it is only used in the Quran and in classic poetry.

To investigate the reading process in Arabic, Al-Fahid (2000) designed a study of how readers of Arabic construct meaning. The main question of the study was as follows: How do readers make sense of written Arabic? To derive an answer, the linguistic study posed two subquestions:

1. How do Arabic readers assign phonology and inflectional features in reading unmarked (normal) texts?
2. How does the absence/presence of diacritics affect the readers' performance on the same reading task?

The study drew on the Goodman model of reading and was triggered by Goodman's claim that reading is a universal psycholinguistic process. Participants were 15 Saudi male undergraduate students enrolled at the University

---

* This chapter is based on the research of Jassem Mohammad Al-Fahid.

of Arizona in Tucson and who did not have majors in language or linguistics; their ages ranged between 19 and 25.

Because of the unique nature of Arabic orthography, which involves two interrelated tiers (i.e., a visible letter tier and a usually absent diacritic tier), a new methodology that would take both tiers into consideration was needed; thus, a new "multitier" methodology was designed. The methodology involved three tasks: (1) the diacritic placement task (DPT), (2) the Arabic text reading task (ATRT), and (3) recorded interviews. Both the DPT and the ATRT were developed by Al-Fahid for the purpose of this study.

The Diacritic Placement Task

In the DPT, each of the 15 readers was given 5 short written Arabic sentences. Each of these 5 sentences was a grammatical Arabic sentence consisting of two syntactic components (i.e., a verb phrase and a noun phrase) and was written in its usual form in Modern Standard Arabic with no diacritics. The readers were asked to provide (in writing) all the possible readings (interpretations) for each of the 5 sentences by placing the proper diacritics in their appropriate positions on the verb component only. The readers were given 15 minutes to complete this task, although most of them finished within 10 minutes. Because all the 15 readers had 12 years of formal instruction in reading Classical Arabic, it was hypothesized that they would provide most of the possible readings for each sentence, if not all of them.

However, the hypothesis does not hold. What follows is a detailed description and discussion of the readers' performance on each of the 5 sentences in the DPT. Readers' responses on each sentence are studied in terms of the number of possible readings provided by each reader for each of the 5 sentences. In an attempt to discover some generalizations, the responses are presented in tables and then compared for similarities and differences. The analysis is grounded in both linguistic theory and the readers' inputs from the playback interviews.

Findings

On Sentence 1, almost all subjects provided the two readings, katabtu alrisa:lah and kutibat alrisa:lah ['I wrote the letter' and 'The letter was written (by someone)', respectively]. Except for one reader (R1), none of the other 14 readers provided the reading kuttibtu alrisa:lah ('I was forced (by someone) to write the letter'). Four readers (R3, R10, R12, and R13) provided the reading katabat alrisa:lah ('She wrote the letter'). Only 1 of the 15 readers (R6) provided the reading kuttibat alrisa:lah ['She was forced (by someone) to write the letter']. Two readers (R6 and R13) provided the reading katabta alrisa:lah ['You (masc./sg.) wrote the letter']. Four readers (R2, R6, R11, and R13) provided the reading katabti alrisa:lah ['You (femin./sg.) wrote the letter']. None of the 15 readers provided any of the two readings kuttibta alrisa: lah and kuttibti alrisa:lah ['You (masc./sg.) were forced (by someone) to write the letter' and 'You (femin./sg.) were forced (by someone) to write the letter', respectively].

On Sentence 2, all 15 of the subjects provided the reading sharibtu alasi:r ('I drank the juice'). Three readers (R1, R4, and R5) provided the reading shurribtu alasi:r ['I was forced (by someone) to drink the juice']. Five readers (R3, R7, R10, R12, and R13) provided the reading sharibat alasi:r ('She drank the juice'). Four readers (R4, R6, R8, and R13) provided the reading sharibta alasi:r ['You (masc./sg.) drank the juice'], and four (R2, R6, R11, and R13) provided the reading sharibti alasi:r ['You (femin./sg.) drank the juice']. None of the 15 readers provided any of the three readings shurribat alasi:r, shurribta alasi:r, and shurribti alasi: r ['She was forced (by someone) to drink the juice', 'You (masc./sg.) were forced (by someone) to drink the juice', and 'You (femin./sg.) were forced (by someone) to drink the juice', respectively].

In response to Sentence 3, almost all subjects provided the two readings ʔakaltu altuffa:hah and ʔukilat altuffa:hah ['I ate the apple' and 'The apple was eaten (by someone)', respectively]. Of the 15 readers, only 3 (R1, R4, and R5) provided the reading ʔukkiltu altuffa:hah ['I was forced (by someone) to eat the apple']. Five readers (R3, R7, R10, R12, and R13) provided the reading ʔakalat altuffa:hah ('She ate the apple'), and only 1 reader (R6) provided the reading ʔukkilat altuffa:hah ['She was forced (by someone) to eat the apple']. Four readers (R4, R6, R8, and R13) provided the reading ʔakalta altuffa:hah ['You (masc./sg.) ate the apple'], and 4 (R2, R6, R11, and R13) provided the reading ʔakalti altuffa:hah ['You (femin./sg.) ate the apple']. None of the 15 readers provided any of the two readings ʔukkilta altuffa:hah and ʔukkilti altuffa:hah ['You (masc./sg.) were forced (by someone) to eat the apple' and 'You (femin./sg.) were forced (by someone) to eat the apple', respectively].

In response to Sentence 4, again, almost all subjects provided the two readings darabtu alqitah and duribat alqitah ['I hit the cat' and 'The cat was hit (by someone)', respectively]. Five readers (R3, R7, R10, R12, and R13) provided the reading darabat alqitah ('She hit the cat'), 4 (R4, R6, R8, and R13) provided the reading darabta alqitah ['You (masc./sg.) hit the cat'], and 4 (R2, R6, R11, and R13) provided the reading darabti alqitah ['You (femin./ sg.) hit the cat']. None of the 15 readers provided the reading durribat alqitah ['The cat was hit severely (by someone)'].

On Sentence 5, all 15 subjects provided the reading ʔakala alwalad ('The boy ate'). Except for five readers (R2, R3, R5, R14, and R15), all the other 10 readers provided the reading ʔukila alwalad ('The boy was eaten'). Five readers (R1, R4, R5, R6, and R13) provided the reading ʔukkila alwalad ['The boy was forced (by someone) to eat']. Three readers (R1, R7, and R12) provided the reading ʔakkala alwalad ('He forced the boy to eat'), and 3 (R7, R9, and R12) provided the reading ʔaklu alwalad ('The boy's way of eating'). Except for 1 reader (R9), none of the other 14 readers provided the reading ʔukulu alwalad ('The boy's food').

Discussion

Although the performance of the readers on the DPT and the responses they provided for each of the 5 sentences are different, they show the readers' preference for two readings: the first-person active sentence and the passive sentence (in which they are both grammatically acceptable). Table 7.1 shows these two readings (in which both are possible) for each of the 5 sentences and the number of readers who provided them.

Almost all readers who showed preference for these two readings provided them in the same order, with the first-person active reading preceding the

Table 7.1 Reading Speed on Two Versions of the Text

Reader	Version I	Version II	Difference
R1	60 s	70 s	10 s
R2	52 s	72 s	20 s
R3	61 s	59 s	−2 s
R4	68 s	90 s	22 s
R5	61 s	71 s	10 s
R6	61 s	65 s	4 s
R7	48 s	64 s	16 s
R8	58 s	69 s	11 s
R9	51 s	66 s	15 s
R10	50 s	61 s	11 s
R11	41 s	56 s	15 s
R12	49 s	57 s	8 s
R13	65 s	61 s	−4 s
R14	61 s	60 s	−1 s
R15	53 s	63 s	10 s

passive one. This observation holds for all the 5 sentences on the DPT. By asking the readers why they provided these two specific readings and why they did not provide many of the other possible readings, most of them said that these two readings are the most "common" and "frequent" ones they tend to hear and use all the time. Regarding their preference for the active reading of the sentence over the passive reading, some of them said that "it is easier to say." Also, many of the readers said that the active reading is more "natural" than the passive reading.

All these observations suggest that, when readers of Arabic are confronted with ambiguous written texts that are eligible for a number of readings or interpretations (i.e., as isolated sentences), a number of linguistic constraints seem to influence the choices that are to be made by these readers. One of these linguistic constraints has to do with the frequency of occurrence of a certain reading or interpretation (i.e., usage). That is, readings or interpretations that are used more frequently by most speakers seem to be more dominant than the ones that are not. This was clear in the readers' preference for the active and passive readings over the other readings and in their preference for the active reading over the passive one.

In Chomsky's (1972) model of transformational grammar, the passive sentence is merely a surface structure; the active sentence is what really constitutes the deep structure. In this sense, the passive is treated as an optional transformation of an active sentence.

Another linguistic constraint that seems to affect the readers' choices is phonological. When the readers said that they preferred the active reading of the sentence over the passive reading because it is easier to say, they were actually referring to the manner of articulation and the effort needed for reading. This observation holds for most languages in which there are certain phonological rules that are employed to simplify pronunciation. A common example of such rules is the process of assimilation in which a sound takes on the characteristics of a neighboring sound, especially in terms of the place of articulation (e.g., impossible, incorrect, illegal). It might be hypothesized, then, that the readers were following a universal tendency when they preferred the active reading that involves fewer vowel changes over the passive reading, which involves more vowel shifts.

The third linguistic constraint that seems to have an influence on the readers' choices has to do with the notion of markedness. When the readers said that they preferred the active reading over the passive reading because it is more natural, they were referring to the concept of markedness. The term *marked* is used to refer to the concept that some linguistic features or forms are "special" in relation to others, which are more "basic."

Ferguson (1984) points out that, although the concept of markedness refers to binary oppositions showing presence/absence of a certain linguistic feature, many instances involve a continuum of markedness in which there is a series showing a scale of naturalness of some type (e.g., implicational series: A > B > C > D > E, where E is the most unmarked form, and A is the most marked form in the series). It should be noted, however, that from a socio-linguistic perspective, and because of the complexity of the social world and the various variables affecting the social "context," determining the degree of markedness of any specific form is not an easy task. Although it is difficult to establish a continuum for the possible readings of the 5 sentences on the DPT, the readers' choices seem to suggest that the active reading of a sentence would precede the passive reading (if both are grammatically acceptable) if they were placed on a continuum of markedness. It is also clear that both the active and the passive readings would precede other readings.

Readers' responses on the DPT also revealed that the third-person (sg.) active reading is also dominant. In Sentence 5, in which the first-person (sg.) active reading is not possible, all the 15 readers provided the reading ?akala alwalad ('The boy ate'), with the verb inflected for the third-person (sg.) active reading, as their first reading. When the readers were asked why they provided this specific reading and why it was their first option, they replied using the same justifications they provided for the first-person active reading and the passive readings: frequency of occurrence (i.e., usage), ease of articulation, and markedness. As such, it might be hypothesized that if the third-person active reading is possible among other readings of a certain sentence, it would be placed at the beginning of the continuum of possibilities, which are arranged according to their degree of markedness. However, when both the first-person (sg.) active reading and the third-person (femin./sg.) reading are possible (Sentences 1–4), the first reading is likely to be more dominant over the second one.

This study shows that when readers encounter an ambiguous sequence in a written text, they do not consider all possible interpretations; rather, they go to the most likely or most marked form, which of course is much more efficient in terms of time and energy.

The Arabic Text Reading Task

In the ATRT, each of the 15 readers was asked to read orally two versions of a short Arabic story. The first version of the story (i.e., Version I) had no diacritics at all, whereas the second version (i.e., Version II) had all the diacritics. To investigate how the absence/presence of diacritics would affect the reading behavior, both readings for each reader were audiotaped and then transcribed. A detailed description and discussion of the readers' performance on the ATRT follows.

Rate of Reading

On completion of the ATRT, both readings for each reader were compared in terms of the time needed to be accomplished. Table 7.1 shows the rate of reading for each reader in both versions and the difference in time between the two readings. As the table shows, most readers needed relatively more time to read the version of the passage that had all the diacritics (Version II). The only exceptions to this observation were the three readers R3, R13, and R14, who were able to control the second version of the passage and read it slightly faster than the first one. The interviews revealed that all the three readers often read the Holy Quran and classical poetry.

Most of the other readers said they needed more time to read the second version because of the presence of diacritics. Because all the diacritics were there, the readers felt obliged to use most of them in reading. The readers thought that because all the diacritics were present, they had to use them in the most appropriate fashion. As they said, they had no excuse to ignore the diacritics.

This burden, so to speak, made the readers concentrate not only on the words but also on the many diacritics that accompanied those words. This double responsibility, along with the readers' desire to read the text as "it should be read," made them slower in reading the second version with all the diacritics. Many readers mentioned that they preferred reading the first version without diacritics because "it is more comfortable and easier." What they actually meant was that, in the first version, only the words of the text and their own intuitions as native speakers directed the reading and made it flow naturally. In contrast, when diacritics were there, the readers saw them as a controlling power that they had to follow to maintain both the grammaticality and the accuracy of the language.

The diacritics, or the controlling system as they might be called, made the readers focus too much on the graphic cues and pay less attention to the other cues. This practice might have some negative consequences on the reading process:

> If readers focus too much on any one cue or too many unrelated cues, they cannot hold them in short-term memory long enough to use them in constructing a conceptual unit. Reading them becomes merely a word-calling game in which the player obtains a high score by accurately reproducing a

string of expected but relatively meaningless sounds and sound sequences. (Goodman & Burke, 1980, p. 19)

It might be hypothesized then that the use of diacritics in Arabic written texts would make readers both less effective and less efficient, especially when they are reading long passages orally. Another factor related to diacritics that seems to play a role in determining the rate of reading and making it more time consuming are the many vowel shifts that are needed in reading texts with diacritics.

The three readers who read the version with full diacritics slightly faster demonstrate that at least some Arabic readers can learn to read either version with equal facility, although they were among the slower readers of the version with no diacritics, suggesting that they are more "careful" readers of either text form.

Manner of Reading

Regarding the miscues that were observed in the ATRT, most of them were related to the misuse of diacritics, especially those that are associated with the endings of the words. In reading the first version of the passage, although most of the readers were able to use the proper diacritics on verbs, many of them assigned inappropriate diacritics on nouns. Despite the fact that such miscues did not trigger significant shifts in the intended meaning, they did make the reading sound "unusual." In reading the second version, most of the miscues observed had to do with substituting some of the final diacritics on nouns with vowellessness, which is an acceptable reading strategy in Arabic, especially at the end of sentences or clauses.

Among those who assigned inappropriate diacritics on nouns were the readers R14 and R15, whose performances on the DPT were relatively low in terms of the number of possible readings they provided for each sentence. This observation might suggest that there is a relationship between the readers' competence/performance level in writing and their reading behavior. Another observation that would support this assumption is that the fewest miscues observed on the ATRT were for the readers R6 and R13, whose performances on the DPT were relatively high in terms of the number of possible readings they provided for each sentence.

One of the interesting miscues that was observed on the ATRT involved an insertion of a word that was not in the printed text. This insertion was observed in one of the readers' reading of the first version of the passage that had no diacritics. Figure 7.1 provides an English translation of the expected reading (ER) and the oral reading (OR) of R8 that involved the insertion.

ER: he gave him a precious gift and said to him: This gift is a reward for what you did...

OR: he gave him a precious gift and said to him: This precious gift is a reward for what you did...

Figure 7.1
An incident of insertion.

The incident shows that R8 inserted the adjective "precious" before the noun "gift" twice, although it was used only once in the printed text. The reader continued his reading; he did not stop, and he did not correct himself because the miscue was both semantically and syntactically acceptable. This incident also indicates that the reader was not decoding; rather, he was processing the language and making guesses that were determined by both the characteristics of the text and his own intuitions as a native speaker of the language.

Dialect Variation

Although all are Saudis, the subjects of this study spoke five regional dialects (i.e., Janobi, Shemali, Najdi, Sharqi, Hijazi). Even though they exhibit some differences in the phonology of consonants and vowels, except for one reader (R6), almost none of the other readers' performances reflected any influence of such differences at the letter stratum (no diacritical marks), which involves mostly consonants.

The performance of R6 on the ATRT reflected an interesting and clear influence of the consonant values he had over his reading. Although R6 spoke Shemali dialect, like R4, R11, and R15, he was raised in Kuwait. The Kuwaiti dialect influence on his phonology was clear at the consonant level. Many Kuwaiti speakers tend to replace the sound [q] with [ʔl], even when reading Classical Arabic texts. This alternation in the consonant value was clear in the two readings of R6 on the ATRT. When asked about this alternation, he said that the sound is dominant in his pronunciation, and that he always replaces the sound regardless of the context, whether formal or informal.

Most readers read the two versions abiding by the consonant values assigned by Classical Arabic. However, dialect variation was evident in some instances in the diacritic version. The influence of dialect on the reading behavior was clear in the assignment of some dialect vowel values to a number of words in the passage. For example, there was one word in the passage that was supposed to be read as assighar 'young'. Whereas R14, who spoke Hijazi dialect, read that word as assighar, replacing the vowel [i] with [u], most speakers of Najdi dialect (R8, R9, and R10) omitted the vowel [i] and read the same word as assghar. A point that is worth mentioning is that such differences do not usually affect the meanings of the words.

It seems that dialect variation among Saudi readers has a minor influence on their behavior when they read texts that are written either in Modern Standard Arabic or in Classical Arabic. The Saudi readers who participated in this study were consciously aware of the task at hand. When they spoke in the interviews, they always used their own dialects because the context called for it. However, when they read the two versions of the passage, they immediately shifted to Classical Arabic, also because this was the norm that was demanded by the context.

The hypothesis, however, cannot be generalized to include all speakers of Arabic. The dialect influence on reading Classical Arabic is evident in the case of Egyptian readers. Many Egyptian readers, including radio and television broadcasters, tend to transfer some of their dialect phonological features when they read Classical Arabic texts. For example, many Egyptian readers would usually replace the Classical Arabic voiced dental fricative sound with their own sound. It is not uncommon to hear an Egyptian radio or television broadcaster say haza for hatha 'this' (masc./sg.) or hazihi for hathihi 'this' (femin./sg.).

Conclusions and Implications

The readers' performance on both the DPT and the ATRT and their interviews revealed some significant insights into the reading process in Arabic. The DPT showed how readers tend to disambiguate unmarked sentences that are eligible for various interpretations or readings. Readers rely on their linguistic knowledge of the Arabic system in assigning phonology and inflectional features to such sentences. This process, however, is not random, and readers' choices seem to follow a regular pattern depending on their degree of markedness.

Choices or readings that are unmarked (i.e., active and passive readings) precede some other marked ones (i.e., causative readings). The two groups of choices could be classified into two categories, immediate readings and delayed readings, respectively. Whereas immediate readings are among the first choices to be made by readers, delayed readings are likely to come at the end and usually require a clear context to reveal them. The hypothesis that skillful readers are able to determine most of the possible readings for an ambiguous sentence does not hold. Most readers were not able to provide even half of the possible readings for the 5 sentences out of context on the DPT.

The ATRT showed how reading was relatively faster and more natural for most readers when they were inferring the diacritics that were absent. The presence of diacritics made reading relatively slower and less natural because readers saw it as a controlling system that they had to follow. This preoccupation of using all the diacritics distracted the readers' attention and made them focus more on the syntactic cues the markings provided and almost ignore the other cues. Both reading situations, however, revealed through miscues that readers were not simply decoding. They were constructing meaning from the text.

When readers were interviewed about their performance on both the DPT and the ATRT and the reasons behind it, most of them said that diacritics are used only in Classical Arabic, and that the form used in writing is Modern Standard Arabic, in which there are no diacritics. They also mentioned that there is no need to use diacritics in written texts because readers can construct the meaning from the context of the text itself. The readers were aware that context would usually determine the readers' predictions and guesses and hence reveal to them the meaning.

The readers' comments revealed their preference for reading texts with no diacritics unless they were to read in front of an audience. In the latter situation, they would prefer texts with diacritics. The presence of diacritics makes them feel more confident of their reading. As one of the readers said, "Diacritics make me feel more confident that I will not disrupt the language and sound uneducated." The readers also expressed their dissatisfaction with their performance in this study and insisted that the main reason behind this is not being able to use Classical Arabic in both their readings and their daily conversations. Goodman and Goodman (1990) state that, "Skills cannot be isolated from their use, in fact, they develop most easily in the context of their use" (p. 227). Reading is also a skill that cannot be isolated from its use.

All these observations suggest that Arabic reading is not a process of accurate word identification. If it were so, then reading in Arabic would have been almost impossible because most Arabic texts are written in Modern Standard Arabic, in which the phonology is not completely represented. Reading in Arabic must involve inference and guessing. It is a process of meaning construction that depends on both the characteristics encoded in the text (i.e., textual cues) and the reader's knowledge and expectations that he or she brings to the reading event. All these factors are involved in a dynamic transaction, and they are the real triggers of the guesses that are made by the reader. In reading, there is a simultaneous transaction between language and thought, and the active reader always tends to test his or her hypotheses throughout the reading event.

As such, instructional materials should not focus on isolated letters, words, or even larger units, which are not related to the readers' world. All these could be presented in coherent authentic texts that stem from the readers' world and hence give them the motivation to read. Goodman (1965) provides powerful evidence that children were able to read many English words in contexts (i.e., stories) that they could not read from lists. As Gollasch (1982) points out, the findings of the study supported the intuitive feeling of many teachers that children's reading of words out of context was very different from their reading of connected text; it was consistent with a large body of research that showed that whole meaningful language was easier to read, to learn, and to remember than were isolated sentences, lists of words, or nonsense syllables (p. 114).

Extending the Goodman Model of Reading English to Reading Semitic Languages

In discussing the process of meaning construction in English reading and the stages or the tasks that readers need to follow to construct meaning from printed texts, Goodman (1970) used the transformational-generative view of language. The underlying assumption of the model is that "meaning cannot be derived directly from the printed page" (p. 22). In this view, the writer starts with meaning and then assigns a deep underlying grammatical structure. The writer then uses transformational rules and generates a written surface structure. The writer utilizes the rules of English orthography (spelling, punctuation) and produces the graphic display (i.e., the printed text). The reader infers from that graphic display the rules that have produced it and its underlying deep structure so that he or she can construct his or her own message (i.e., comprehend the meaning). If the reader is reading orally, then the reader has to encode the message as oral output producing an oral surface structure.

This model provides an adequate explanation of how readers of English construct meaning, and it can also account for meaning construction in Arabic, in both oral and written communication. However, application to Arabic requires an adaptation of the model to explain how users of Arabic construct meaning.

The production of an Arabic message starts with meaning to which a deep structure is assigned. Through the application of transformational rules, the deep structure takes the form of an internal surface structure, which is neither oral nor written and carries all the syntactic and the semantic information. This internal surface structure is then transformed into the actual surface structure, which may be either oral or written. In the case of oral communication, the speaker's surface structure (i.e., an utterance) may take the shape of Classical Arabic, Modern Standard Arabic, or a colloquial dialect, depending on the context and the pragmatic cues that are involved. In written communication, the writer's surface structure (i.e., graphic display) may be in either Classical Arabic or Modern Standard Arabic, also depending on the context and the pragmatic cues that are involved.

Applying the model to Arabic reading, however, requires an extension; the extension and the modifications suggested here are needed to accommodate the multitier nature of Arabic orthography, which plays a major role in Arabic reading. This extension also stands as powerful evidence that the model is flexible, generative, and capable of accommodating features from other languages besides English.

The extended model provides a multitier account of Arabic reading to construct meaning from printed texts, which are usually written in Modern Standard Arabic with no diacritics. These tasks are summarized next.

The Arabic author starts with meaning and then assigns a deep structure. The author uses transformational rules and generates an internal surface structure (i.e., a multitier orthographic representation).

Following the convention of writing in Modern Standard Arabic (i.e., pragmatic cues), the author filters the diacritic tier and produces the surface structure represented by a unitier orthographic representation (i.e., the letter tier).

The author utilizes the rules of Arabic orthography (spelling, punctuation) and produces the graphic display (i.e., the printed text).

The reader infers from that graphic display the rules that have produced it and its underlying deep structure so that he or she can construct the meaning (i.e., comprehend the meaning). There are two possibilities here: Route 1 (R_1) and Route N (R_n).

If the printed text is provided within a clear context, then the reader would usually take one route (R_1), in which he or she constructs a meaning that is likely to be close to the author's intended meaning (i.e., deep structure). But, if the printed text is provided in isolation and without a context, exactly like the 5 sentences on the DPT, then the reader is likely to take a number of routes (R_n) by assigning the diacritics in various ways and thus creating a number of deep structures.

Readers of Arabic operate within a sociocultural context and use their own intuitions as native speakers to make predictions and guesses about the meaning of what they are reading. Their predictions, however, are not random and stem mainly from the context of the text and their acquaintance with the phonology, the syntax, and the semantics of the language as well as with some other situational and sociolinguistic factors such as usage and prestige.

This is what makes reading, including Arabic reading, fascinating. Reading enables us to see linguistic theory at work, with all the linguistic subsystems joining forces and teaming up in one system called *language*, which has a main goal to convey meaning. Indeed, the ultimate goal of language is meaning, and therefore, "We must see everything in language in its relationship to meaning" (Goodman, 1996, p. 12).

References

Al-Fahid, J. M. (2000). *The Goodman psycholinguistic model of English reading and its applicability to Semitic languages.* Unpublished doctoral dissertation, University of Arizona, Tucson.

Chomsky, N. (1972). *Syntactic structures.* The Hague, The Netherlands: Mouton.

Ferguson, C. (1984). Repertoire universals, markedness, and second language acquisition. In W. E. Rutherford (Ed.), *Language universals and second language acquisition* (pp. 247–258). Amsterdam: Benjamins.

Gollasch, F. V. (Ed.) (1982). *Language and literacy: The selected writings of Kenneth S. Goodman* (Vol. 1). Boston: Routledge and Kegan Paul.

Goodman, K. S. (1965). A linguistic study of cues and miscues in reading. In F. V. Gollasch (Ed.), *Language and literacy: The selected writings of Kenneth S. Goodman* (Vol. 1, pp. 115–120). Boston: Routledge and Kegan Paul.

Goodman, K. S. (1970). The reading process: Theory and practice. In F. V. Gollasch (Ed.), *Language and literacy: The selected writings of Kenneth S. Goodman* (Vol. 1, pp. 19–31). Boston: Routledge and Kegan Paul.

Goodman, K. S. (1996). *On reading.* Portsmouth, NH: Heinemann.

Goodman, K. S., & Goodman, Y. M. (1990). Vygotsky in a whole language perspective. In L. Moll (Ed.), *Vygotsky and education* (pp. 223–250). Cambridge, U.K.: Cambridge University Press.

Goodman, Y., & Burke, C. (1980). *Reading strategies: focus on comprehension.* New York: Holt, Rinehart and Winston.

Section Five

STUDIES OF READING IN NONALPHABETIC ORTHOGRAPHIES
Ideographic Orthography

INTRODUCTION TO CHAPTER 8

A KEY QUESTION for all types of research is the extent to which the findings can be generalized from the specific focus of a particular study or body of related studies to all related phenomena. In experimental research, that question is most often answered statistically through application of the laws of probability: What are the chances that a particular cause-effect relationship is or is not likely to be a true representation of the relationship under study?

But the focus of research from the perspective of scientific realism is on building a theory of the structures and processes in the aspect of reality under study. So, in this chapter, a much broader question is asked: Can a theory built through scientific realism of the structures and processes in reading English also explain how readers make sense of Chinese, a very different language with a very different orthography?

Before they can answer that question, the authors must deal with how the writing systems of English and Chinese are alike or different. In my own research, I found that before I could answer the question, How do readers make sense of print? I had to build knowledge of what it is that they are making sense of. I needed to develop thorough knowledge of the English language, in its multiple forms, and how the systems of language, symbol, syntax, and semantics related to each other. I found myself moving from the descriptive linguistics of Fries, to the generative grammar of Chomsky, and finally to the systemic-functional linguistics of Halliday to understand the data that my readers produced as they read English texts. My use of each view was my own. While benefiting from the understandings each view provided, I had to resist the temptation to make my data fit the theory rather than examining the theory in light of the data and modifying it to accommodate the actual reality my readers were showing me.

In this chapter, the authors have synthesized a wide range of the views of insiders and outsiders of the nature of the Chinese language and how it is written. In the course of Wang's research, she finds that concepts as basic as word and sentence have been forced onto Chinese by scholars who assumed that they were universals equally applicable to Indo-European and Chinese language. Wang demonstrates that these concepts do not fit Chinese. To achieve the synthesis, she has looked carefully at how the Chinese language and Chinese writing actually work, critiquing the views she uses from the vantage point of how they do or do not fit the reality of the written Chinese language.

Only when the authors are satisfied that she has a functional description of the nature of written Chinese can they then examine the applicability of the transactional sociopsycholinguistic theory of the reading process to the reading of Chinese. This they do in Chapter 10.

Ken Goodman

8

IDEOGRAPHIC ORTHOGRAPHY
A Linguistic Description of Written Chinese and Its Cueing Systems

Shaomei Wang and Yetta Goodman

*A*S THE OLDEST EXTANT writing system, Chinese writing has continuously and successfully served the needs of society for approximately 4,000 years (He, 2000). In spite of the dramatic differences among Chinese dialects, the written language that they all share has been a great unifying power, contributing to cultural continuity and cohesion.

In traditional Confucian culture, the written script was regarded and utilized as a tool to transform society and regulate social conduct. Since the flourishing of calligraphy in the Han dynasty (202 B.C. to 220 A.D.), the written script has become one of the most sublime Chinese arts, reflecting individuals' aesthetic tastes and spiritual pursuits (He, 2000). In a sense, the Chinese written script not only functions as the tool for social communication but also expresses Chinese culture, history, and philosophy.

Because of its pervasive influence on Southeast Asian culture, the Chinese writing system was never challenged during the golden age of Chinese civilization. Along with the decline of the Qing dynasty (1644–1912), however, the attitude toward Chinese writing subtly shifted. Domestically, during the New Cultural Revolution in the early 20th century, the Chinese script was considered as part of the "old" culture that should be reformed or even abandoned. To those early Chinese reformers, the old writing system stood in the way of modernization. Outside China, the view that the Chinese writing system was inferior emerged as the influence of the old civilization slowly began to fade. Having been used for thousands of years, the old Chinese writing system seemed to be gradually falling into an orthographic dilemma in the world's family of languages.

Having been tainted by evolutionary and ethnocentric beliefs about written languages, Chinese orthography has been labeled as "cumbersome," "primitive," and "illogical" in the Western world. Worse than that, though, is the perception that new or modern ideas or concepts cannot be expressed in the Chinese language because there is no new character for it. Regarding reading, some scholars claim that because Chinese characters are able to "function in different grammatical environments without overt changes to their forms, readers are less able to utilize this feature to predict what types of words can appear" (cited in Hannas, 1997, p. 185). Some of these misunderstandings about Chinese reading and writing persist.

Reading is a language process (Goodman, 1994, 1996, 2004). Misunderstandings about reading arise because of limited views concerning how language works. To understand how readers of Chinese transact with and thus make sense of Chinese texts, we examine written Chinese and its cueing systems in this chapter from the perspective of a transactional sociopsycholinguistic view of reading, writing, and written text (Goodman, 1994, 1996, 2004). Following Goodman's interpretations of the language cueing systems, we discuss written Chinese from three levels: graphomorphemic, syntactic and grammatical, and semantic-pragmatic.

The Graphomorphemic System

Goodman (1993) uses the term *graphophonic* to refer to the cues readers pick up at the graphic and phonological levels of English. In his own words, "Graphophonic represents a particular combination of cues that readers and writers use: the sound system (phonology), the graphic system (orthography), and the system that relates these two (phonics)" (p. 8). In contrast to alphabetic scripts, Chinese characters are nonalphabetic; each represents a morpheme. Thus, in this study we adopt the term *graphomorphemic* rather than graphophonic to describe the combination of the sound system, the graphic system, and the relationship between these two in Chinese.

Chinese Orthography

Characters   In English, words are equally separated by space in print. In Chinese, the smallest free occurring unit of writing is 字 (*zi* character) rather than the word. In linguistic circles, a variety of English terms have been used to refer to 字, including morpheme-syllables (Chao, 1968b; Hoosain, 1991); ideographs (Saussure, 1983); logographs (Halliday & Hasan, 1985; Sampson,

1985); morphosyllables (DeFrancis, 1984, 2002; Shu, 2004); and "meaning-plus-sound" syllables (DeFrancis, 1989). However, there is no universal agreement among linguists on which term best expresses 字.* In this chapter, for consistency we use the term *character* to refer to 字.

The Structure of Characters　To people who are not familiar with the Chinese writing system, in a visual sense Chinese characters might seem shockingly complicated. There is a common impression that characters are all very different from each other, and that each has to be memorized on its own. Actually, just as written English uses only 26 letters to write all the words, Chinese written scripts are also composed of components, which are further formed by strokes.

Chinese characters are traditionally constructed in a two-dimensional and square-based manner (He, 2000). There are two types of characters in written Chinese: noncomprised characters and comprised characters. Except for only several hundred noncomprised ones, all Chinese characters are comprised characters that are further composed of components. The combination of the components in any one character is not arbitrary. In many cases, components of characters are characters on their own. For example, 口 (*kou,* mouth) is a noncomprised character. It is also a component in the characters 喝 (*he,* drink), 唱 (*chang,* sing), 吹 (*chui,* blow), and 问 (*wen,* ask). The number of Chinese characters could exceed 60,000 if both classical and modern Chinese texts are taken into consideration (Zhou, 2003). However, there are only several hundred components in Chinese written scripts (Zhou, 2003).

The Formation of Characters　The first systematic study of Chinese scripts dates to 200 A.D., when Xu Shen created 说文解字 (*Shuowen jiezi*). Xu Shen classified Chinese characters into six categories according to their formation: (1) 象形 (*xiangxing,* pictographic); (2) 指事 (*zhishi,* ideographic); (3) 形声 (*xingsheng,* semantic-phonetic compound); (4) 会意 (*huiyi,* compound ideographic); (5) 转注 (*zhuanzhu,* mutually explaining); and (6) 假借 (*jiajie,* phonetic borrowing). While creating the potential for some ambiguities (Chen, 1956; Qiu, 1988), Xu Shen's classification is still widely used. Of the six types of characters, we discuss only semantic-phonetic compound characters for two reasons: (a) they compose the majority (81%) of Chinese characters (Gong, 2002), and (b) they cause the greatest controversy among researchers regarding the function of phonetic components in the process of reading Chinese.

---

* Both DeFrancis (1984) and Hung (2000) discuss in detail some of the concepts listed.

Traditionally, a semantic-phonetic compound character contains two components: a phonetic one that represents the pronunciation and a semantic one that implies the meaning of the derived character. For instance, the character 妈 (*ma*, mom) is composed of 女 (*nü*, female) and 马 (*ma*, horse). The left component 女 suggests that the character is "female"-related; the right component 马 gives the sound of the character. In The Form of Frequently-used Characters in Modern Chinese (现代汉语通用字表), 81% of the 7,000 simplified characters are semantic-phonetic compound characters (Gong, 2002).

The importance of semantic-phonetic compounds lies in the fact that, in comparison with the other categories, they most directly represent the orthography-phonology relationship in Chinese (Qiu, 1988). In the following sections, we look at the reliability of the semantic and phonetic components in indicating the meaning and sound of a character.

Reliability of the Semantic Component   The semantic component of a semantic-phonetic compound character often signifies the general meaning of the character. Table 8.1 shows the percentage of semantic components that are semantically related to the derived characters. The table indicates that the majority of the semantic components still have the function of signifying the general meaning of the derived characters (Gong, 2002). In other words, the Chinese script itself provides important cues for readers to make sense of it. On the other hand, because of historical meaning changes, some characters in modern Chinese are no longer related to their semantic components. For instance, most of the characters with the semantic component 女 (*nü*, female) are related to women (*nü*, woman), but 如 (*ru*, like, if, or for example) has no semantic relationship with the

Table 8.1   Percentage of Semantic Components That Are Semantically Related to the Derived Characters

Number of Characters Examined	Semantic-Phonetic Compound Characters	Semantic Component	Semantically Related to the Derived Characters	Semantically Unrelated to the Derived Characters
7,000 frequently used characters	5,631 (80.5%)	246	4,885 (87%)	746 (13%)
3,500 high frequently used characters	2,522 (72%)	167	2,082 (83%)	440 (17%)

Note: Adapted from 汉字汉语汉文化论集 [Character, language, and culture], by J. Gong, 2002, Bashushushe, Chengdu, China.

semantic female component even though the character has the component 女. Moreover, because the semantic component only gives some clues to the meaning of a character, it is unlikely to ascertain an accurate meaning of a character solely based on the semantic component it carries. For example, 湖 (*hu*, lake), 海 (*hai*, ocean), 游 (*you*, swim), and 洗 (*xi*, wash) all share the "three-drop water" radical 氵, but it is difficult to guess their meanings in isolation. Therefore, the context in which a character is involved plays a more crucial role than the semantic component of the character in making sense of it.

Reliability of the Phonetic Component　　There is no doubt that the phonetic component of a character provides useful information about the pronunciation of the character, just as the semantic component provides useful information about the meaning of the character. However, because of historical sound changes, many phonetic components of semantic-phonetic compound characters have lost their function in specifying the pronunciations of the derived characters (Gong, 2002). In some cases, phonetic components are not at all related to the pronunciations of the characters they compose. So, to what degree does the phonetic component of a character accurately indicate the pronunciation of the derived character? Table 8.2 presents the percentage of phonetic components that specify the sounds of the derived characters.

Based on the studies shown in Table 8.2, less than 40% of the semantic-phonetic compound characters inherit the pronunciations from their phonetic components. If tones are taken into consideration, less than 20% of the semantic-phonetic compound characters have exactly the same pronunciations as their phonetic components (Gong, 2002; Ye, 1965; Zhou, 1978).

Table 8.2　Percentage of Semantic-Phonetic Compound Characters That Inherit the Sounds From Their Phonetic Components

Number of Characters Examined	Percentage	Study
8,000 simplified characters in the *New Chinese Dictionary*	39% (excludes tones)	
	Less than 20% (includes tones)	Zhou, 1978
7,504 simplified characters in the *Modern Chinese Dictionary*	10% (exclude tones)	
	4.7% (include tones)	Ye, 1965
7,000 simplified characters in the *Form of Commonly-used Characters*	18% (includes tones)	Gong, 2002

In summary, the semantic and phonetic components were traditionally created to indicate the meaning and sound of a semantic-phonetic compound character, respectively. Although the majority of the semantic components still have the function of signifying the general meaning of the derived characters, the phonetic components have lost much of their original function because of the historical changes of sounds in Chinese. Therefore, it is inappropriate to exaggerate the reliability of the phonetic component of a character in reading Chinese.

The Phonology of Mandarin Chinese

Syllables   According to Li and Thompson (1982), Mandarin Chinese has more than 400 segmentally distinct syllables, which make up about 1,600 phonetically distinct syllables when the four tones are taken into consideration. However, because not all the syllables have four tones, Mandarin has only about 1,300 tone syllables. The Chinese syllable is composed of an initial, a final, and a tone. *Initials* are consonants (\b\ and \p\); *finals* are comprised mainly of vowels (e.g., \a\ and \ai\). A few syllables, such as *ao* (袄, coat) and *ai* (爱, love), do not have an initial. The only two consonants that occur in a final are the velar nasal and the alveolar nasal, which are represented by *ng* and *n* in *pinyin*, respectively (Li & Thompson, 1989).

There are four tones in Mandarin: high level, high rising, low dipping, and high falling (Chao, 1968a). In addition, there is a neutral tone in Mandarin. Neutral tone morphemes include those that do not have any one of the four tones, such as suffixes and particles, and those that are not stressed or have a weak stress in certain compounds (e.g., the second 妈 *ma* in 妈妈 *mama*, mom).

Romanized Spelling System for Chinese   Unlike alphabetic languages, there is no script-sound correspondence in Chinese. The same character can be pronounced very differently in various dialects. Also, the gap between the spoken and written forms of Chinese is so enormous that written Chinese is very different from the spoken varieties. This is most obvious in classical Chinese.

Because of these reasons as well as other social and political influences, the Chinese writing system has encountered several challenges from alphabetic systems through its long history. When the old Qing (1644–1912) empire was awakened by the boom of cannons and modern industrial machines from the West, much effort was undertaken to develop an alphabet for Chinese to promote education for national self-preservation (DeFrancis, 1950). A variety of phonetic scripts were developed for Chinese, such as the Phonetic Symbols or Sound Annotating Graphs (*zhuyin fuhao,* 注音符号), Latinized New

Script (*lading xinwenzi*, 拉丁新文字), and National Romanization Script (*guoyu luomazi*, 国语罗马字) (Ingulsrud & Allen, 1999). However, none of the scripts achieved nationwide popularity.

Pinyin (拼音, Romanized Spelling of Chinese) was promulgated in mainland China in 1958. Based on the Latinized New Script initiated in the late 1920s, the *pinyin* system uses 25 letters of the English alphabet (letter *v* is deleted, and letter *ü* is added) and tone markers to write the sounds of Mandarin Chinese. According to Premier Zhou Enlai's speech at the National Political Consultative Conference in 1958, the purpose of the use of *pinyin* was not to substitute a phonetic writing system for Chinese characters but to (a) indicate the pronunciation of characters, (b) to spread the use of *Putonghua* (Mandarin), (c) to help Chinese minorities to create or reform their scripts, and (d) to help foreigners to study Chinese (Zhou, 1980). Despite these government-supported purposes, the use of *pinyin* has evoked great controversies among Chinese intellectuals. Xu Mumin was among those who were strongly against Romanization:

> The Latin alphabet is not our national product; it is a stranger to the people in general in our country. As Chairman Mao has said, we have our nation forms. We should use our national form of writing. … If we do Latinize Chinese writing, then we will be fighting the world for Latin writing! If we do, we will not be able to face our ancestors and we will not be able to face our descendants; our ancestors will berate us for not being "sons who bring honor to the family" and our descendants will berate us for having surrendered our teachers! (cited in Ingulsrud & Allen, 1999, p. 37)

Despite the decades of debates and controversies, *pinyin* is used today to teach children the sounds of Chinese characters. However, debates on the use of *pinyin* as well as Romanization are ongoing. One thing for sure is that Romanization scripts can never replace characters because of the characteristics of the Chinese language. He (2000) discusses this issue through the story 漪姨 (*yiyi*), which was created by Chao Yuenren. For the purpose of clarification, the story is cited next:

> 漪姨倚椅，悒悒，疑异颐，宜诣医。医以宜以蚁胰医姨。医以亿弋弋亿蚁。亿蚁殪，蚁胰溢。医以亿蚁溢胰医姨，姨疫以医。姨怡怡，以夷衣贻医，医衣夷衣，亦怡怡。噫！医以蚁胰医姨疫，亦异矣；姨以夷衣贻医，亦益异已矣！ (p. 276)

The story tells how a patient shows his gratitude to his doctor after recovering from a disease. The text contains 82 characters. Excluding the repeated characters, there are 27 homophones *yi*. If the 82 characters are changed into *pinyin*, with the numbers 1, 2, 3, and 4 used to mark the tones, the text would be as follows:

> Yi1yi2yi3yi3, yi4yi4, yi2yi4yi4, yi2yi4yi1, yi1yi3yi2yi3yi3yi2yi1yi2。 yi1yi3yi4yi4yi4yi3。yi4yi3yi4, yi3yi2yi4。yi1yi3yi4yi3yi4yi2yi1yi2, yi2y-i4yi3yi1。yi2yi2yi2, yi3yi2yi1yi2yi1。yi1yi4yi2yi1, yi4yi2yi2。 yi1! Yi1y-i3yi3yi2yi1yi2yi4, yi4yi4yi4yi3; yi2yi3yi2yi1yi2yi1, yi4yi4yi4yi4yi3! (p. 277)

By no means can one construct the meaning of the *pinyin* version of the story. He (2000) further concludes that because of the significance influence of homophones in the Chinese language, Chinese characters have to be highly semantic rather than phonological.

The Relationship Between Chinese Orthography and Phonology

Morpheme, Syllable, and Character   In Chinese, a morpheme does not necessarily correspond to a character. In most instances, one morpheme is one character. However, in some cases, one morpheme refers to the combination of two or more characters. Some examples are 蝴蝶 (*hudie*, butterfly), 踟蹰 (*chichu*, hesitation), and 琵琶 (*pipa*, a type of Chinese musical instrument). Characters and syllables also do not have a one-to-one correspondence. A character may have different meanings and pronunciations, which produces many homographs. On the other hand, a syllable may correspond to multiple characters with different meanings, which also produces many homophones. Such a relationship between characters and syllables results in much ambiguity in Chinese. This requires readers to make increased use of the semantic or meaning context cues.

Homophone/Homograph Ambiguities   Chinese contains an extraordinarily large number of homophones. Gong (2002) examines 7,000 characters in the Form of Frequently-used Characters in Modern Chinese (现代汉语通用字表) and concludes that one character has 20 homophones on average. In an extreme case, one character has 118 homophones.

Besides homophones, homographs also cause ambiguities in the Chinese language. As a "highly semantic" language, Chinese shows the change of a character's meaning and grammatical function through the change in its pronunciation (He, 2000). In other words, as the pronunciation of a character changes, its grammatical function and meaning may change accordingly, although the graphic features of the character remain the same. He discusses this issue by taking a famous Chinese couplet as an example. For illustration, the couplet is as follows:

海 水 朝 朝 朝 朝 朝 朝 落

hai shui chao zhao zhao chao zhao chao zhao luo

'As for the tide of the sea, it has a morning tide which rises and falls'

浮 云 长 长 长 长 长 长 长 消

fu yun zhang chang chang zhang chang zhang chang xiao

"As for the rising of the clouds, often when they rise they also disappear"

Among the seven 朝 characters in the first line of the couplet, four are read as *zhao,* a noun meaning "morning." The other three are read as *chao,* a verb meaning "tide rise." Similarly, in the second line, four of seven 长 characters are read as *chang,* an adverb meaning "often." The other three are read as *zhang,* a verb meaning "rise." He (2000) concludes that the example clearly demonstrates an important characteristic of Chinese; that is, the change in the function of a character may lead to a change in its pronunciation.

Morphophonemic Ambiguities   In Chinese, "a syllable has one of the [four] tones when it stands alone, but the same syllable may take on a different tone without a change in meaning when it is followed by another syllable" (Li & Thompson, 1989, p. 8). This is known as *tone sandhi.* For example, a third-tone syllable changes into a low-tone syllable when it is followed by a syllable with a first, second, or fourth tone, but it changes into a second tone when it is followed by another third-tone syllable. Sometimes ambiguities occur when *tone sandhi* is involved. For example, 美好 (*mei3hao3,* good) and 没好 (*mei2hao3,* not ready) are homophonous because the third tone character 美 changes to a second tone in 美好 according to the rule of *tone sandhi.*

For most of the reduplication character compounds (Xu, 2002), the second character of a two-syllable unit and the last two characters of a four-syllable unit are read neutrally (Chao, 1968a). For example, the second 试 (*shi,* try) in 试试 (*shishi,* have a try) changes to the neutral tone from the fourth tone. In 漂漂亮亮 (*piaopiaoliangliang,* beautiful), both *liang* lose their original tones when read. However, this is not a general rule, and there are exceptions. For example, no tone changes happen in reading the second character in 本本 (*benben,* every volume) or 天天 (*tiantian,* every day).

Some morphemes show tonal changes only in certain contexts. For example, in the character compound 地道 (*di4dao4*, tunnel), 道 (*dao*) has the fourth tone. However, when 地道 takes the meaning of "authentic," it is read as *di4dao*, where 道 *dao* changes into the neutral tone.

There are two particular morphemes, 一 (*yi*, one) and 不 (*bu*, no), that exhibit *tone sandhi* alternations as well (Chao, 1968a). The basic rule is that when "*yi*" or "*bu*" appears before morphemes with a first, second, or third tone, it changes into a fourth tone. When followed by a fourth tone, it changes into a second tone. Examples include 一生 (*yi4sheng1*, the whole life), 一起 (*yi4qi3*, together), and 一半 (*yi2ban4*, half).

Dialect Ambiguities   The Chinese language family includes seven major dialects (Beifanghua/Mandarin, Wu, Yue/Cantonese, Xiang, Min, Kejia/Hakka, and Gan), which are dramatically different from each other (Norman, 1988). The lack of some phonemes in the reader's dialect may bring up ambiguities in reading Mandarin. For example, 男人 (*nanren*, male-person/man) would be articulated as "*lanren*" by Gan dialect speakers because the two syllables "*nan*" and "*lan*" are indistinguishable in the Gan dialect. For Cantonese speakers, they would pronounce 花钱 (*huaqian*, spend-money) as "*faqian*" because of the lack of the \h\ sound in Cantonese.

How to Resolve Ambiguities   Every oral language is pervasively ambiguous. Every written language is also pervasively ambiguous. However, there is no problem for speakers and readers to resolve ambiguities because human beings have "a set for ambiguity" (Goodman, 1996, p. 73). The meaning of a single character may be ambiguous. But, in authentic texts or speech, no character will show up without a context for readers or listeners to use to make sense of it. In fact, meaning is in the context rather than in a single character or word.

Syntactic and Grammatical System

Unlike English grammatical relationships that are shown by affixes or by internal changes in the word itself, Chinese grammar is reflected either by change of order of characters and character compounds (Xu, 2001) or by use of independent grammatical particles. In other words, grammar markers are not overtly realized in Chinese sentences. In the following sections, we discuss the relationship between characters and character compounds to show the features of the Chinese lexicon. We also examine Chinese sentences that are characteristic of "idea-joining" (Shen, 1992). To understand the semantic effects of the order of characters and character compounds, at the end of the sections we provide several examples of Chinese sentences that are full of ambiguities.

The Relationship Between Characters and Character Compounds

For over a century, the Chinese language has been studied under a grammatical model designed for Indo-European languages (Shen, 1992; Tsao, 1990; Xu, 2001). Therefore, it is not surprising that the word has long been considered as the basic grammatical unit in Chinese. Although it might be useful to identify words and segment word boundaries in Chinese under a Western grammatical model, we believe that studying the relationship between characters and character compounds reveals far more of the dynamic nature of the Chinese lexicon.

The Chinese lexicon is an interdependent and intergenerated system (Hoosain, 1992; Liu, 1992). On the one hand, a large group of individual characters can be used as a separate unit in texts. On the other hand, a character can be combined with other characters to form character compounds. Thus, the meaning of a Chinese character is highly context based. Each individual character has its own core meaning, but this core meaning can generate new meanings when the character is compounded with other characters to form new units. Remember, though, that in print all characters are equally spaced so readers must perceive a character as free or part of a compound.

Just as the majority of the characters that share the same radical are semantically related to each other, in most of the instances the character compounds sharing the same characters also have close semantic relationships with each other. For example, the following three compounds 火车 (huoche, fire-car/train), 电车 (dianche, electricity-car/trolley), and 马车 (mache, horse-car/carriage) are semantically related because they all share the character 车 (che, vehicle). In these cases, the character 车 can be treated as a semantic component, suggesting the meaning of the character compound of which it is a constituent part.

Many character compounds are formed on the basis of two characters that have a close semantic relationship. For instance, in the character compound 宝贝 (baobei, treasure-treasure/treasure), the two components have a similar meaning in modern Chinese. At the same time, the compound has high semantic similarity with the two components. The prevalence of this category of character compounds in Chinese shows that the Chinese language is pervasively redundant, as all languages are. Although some character compounds are composed of two characters that have similar meanings, some are formed by two characters that have opposite meanings. For example, 好

(*hao*, like) and 恶 (*wu*, dislike) are combined together to refer to "the attitude toward people or things."

In addition to the above examples, Chinese is also rich in reversal character compounds. There are many two-character compounds that are formed from the same characters, yet in reverse order. For example, 语言 (*yuyan*, language) and 言语 (*yanyu*, speech) are two compounds that share the same characters and are closely related to one another regarding meaning.

In summary, although the components of character compounds suggest the meaning of the derived compounds to some degree, character compounds should not be studied or explained simply through the characters they contain but through the context in which they are applied. In fact, semantic and syntactic information of a text is not carried by individual characters or character compounds. Rather, it is contained in the context of a whole written text.

Chinese Sentences

In the last few decades, Chinese grammarians have been studying and defining the sentence in Chinese through the functional approach, suggesting that the basic structure of Chinese sentences is topic-comment (Li & Thompson, 1976, 1989). Applying the discourse grammar approach, some scholars claim that the sentence in Chinese is a discourse unit rather than a syntactic category. For example, Tsao (1990) suggests the following:

> A sentence in Chinese can be roughly defined as a topic chain, which is a stretch of discourse composed of one or more comment clauses sharing a common topic, which heads the chain. (p. 63)

To distinguish the Chinese sentence from the sentence that is largely determined by syntax, such as the English sentence, Chu (1998) labels the former as a *discourse sentence* and defines it as a structural unit that mediates between syntax and discourse:

> A Mandarin Chinese SENTENCE consists of one or more clauses that are related by formal devices identifiable by overt signals. ... The formal devices include, though not limited to, topic chain, conjunction, adverb, verb form, mode of presentation, clause order and end of discourse. The overt signals are zero-anaphor, conjunctions, adverbs, verbal affix, type of verb, unmarked clause order, and sentence-final particles, respectively. (p. 370)

Here, we discuss a unique type of Chinese sentence, the 流水句 (*liushuiju*, flowing-water sentence), which greatly reflects the characteristics of Chinese sentences. Physically, Chinese sentences are often quite long. That is not to say that an average Chinese sentence generally constitutes more characters or "words" than a sentence in other languages but suggests that the former has more independent "small sentences" or clauses that are conjoined together by commas. Shen (1992) examines the sentences in a contemporary Chinese novel 井 (*jing*) and concludes that among the sentences he has investigated, 90% contain two to eight independent clauses. Native Chinese linguists usually call this type of sentence 流水句 (*liushuiju*) or "flowing-water sentence," in which the metaphor 流水 (*liushui*) "flowing water" vividly describes the physical feature and the logical relationships of the syntactic constructions of the sentence. This metaphor also reveals the fact that the syntactic constructions of the sentence in Chinese are to a great extent iconically motivated (Tai, 1993), which is largely different from the English sentence pattern featured by "form-agreement."

Take the following sentence as an example:

孔乙己 刚 用 指 甲 蘸 了 酒 想 在 柜 上 写

Kong Yiji just use finger dip particle wine want at bar top write

字，见 我 毫 不 热 心，便 又 叹一口气，显出 极 惋惜

character, see me indifference then again sign show very pity

的 样 子。

particle appearance

"Kong Yiji just dipped his finger in wine; [he] wanted to write the characters on the bar; [he] saw my utter indifference; [he] sighed; [he] looked sad." (X. Lu, 1981)

Descriptively, the five small sentences in these sentences share the same topic, Kong Yiji. The topic and each of the five small sentences form topic-comment constructions of their own in isolation. As an entire unit, the sentence is long but not tedious because the topic chain is logically linked together with the change of the time and space as well as the sequence of the event. In this sense, whether a sentence is grammatically acceptable depends largely on whether it is logical and meaningful in a specific context (Shen, 1992).

Sentence Boundary Ambiguities

Compared with English sentences, the boundaries of Chinese sentences are "larger." An American student once commented on this by stating that there are so many commas in a Chinese sentence, and that they never seem to stop. The boundaries of Chinese sentences are also ambiguous. Many native Chinese speakers point out that sometimes it is difficult to make a choice between a comma and a period in writing. This is not because they lack knowledge of punctuation. It is because commas and periods are exchangeable in many Chinese sentences. Tsao (1990) conducted a study of Chinese and English sentences by asking 18 Chinese college students to segment sentences in two Chinese and two English texts, respectively. The results show that the Chinese readers have vague as well as different ideas about how to segment Chinese sentences. However, their segmentation of the English sentences proved to be similar to that in the original English texts, even though they were not considered proficient in English. This suggests that Chinese syntax is more likely governed by meaning than form (Li & Thompson, 1989; Shen, 1992), and hence the segmentation of Chinese sentences varies with individuals.

Zero-Anaphora Ambiguities

In Chinese sentences, noun phrases do not need to be specified when there is no ambiguity in meaning. It is possible for a single subject to take several verb phrases without using any conjunctions in a sentence (Li & Thompson, 1989). In the sentence used as an example in the last section, Kong Yiji is referred to only once, at the beginning of the sentence. However, he is the "agent" of all those actions. In addition to zero-pronoun in the above example, Chinese syntax tolerates the omission of several subjects at the discourse level as long as the sentences are within the same topic chain (Tsao, 1990). The issue here is that people may have different understandings concerning the appropriateness of the omission of a noun phrase at the sentence level or a subject at the discourse level. Because of the zero-anaphora phenomenon, readers of Chinese are perhaps required to focus more on larger linguistic units than characters or character compounds in a Chinese text.

Semantic Effects of Ambiguities

As are all other cultures, Chinese culture is rich in stories, jokes, and humorous anecdotes that are good examples to use to discuss the ambiguities in the language. The following text is a well-known joke that illustrates the characteristics of Chinese syntax:

A person visits his friend on a rainy day. He prefers to stay rather than to leave. So he writes a note saying: 下雨天留客 (The rainy day [is the day to] host guests.). However, his friend doesn't want to host him and writes back on the note: 天留人不留 (The rain keeps [guests], [but] the host doesn't want [to do it].). The smart guest modifies the two sentences by segmenting them as: 下雨天。留客天。留人不？留。 ([It's a] raining day. [It's a] day to treat guests. [To] treat guests or not? Sure. [I will treat them]). The meaning of the whole sentence is that the host invites the guest to stay at his place. (Translated from the Chinese version in S. Lü, 1980, p. 48)

In this case, the order of the characters stays the same, but the meaning of the sentence is completely changed because of the different segmentations by different persons. This text demonstrates that the meanings of the sentence are in both the writer and the reader rather than in the sentence itself (Goodman, 1996).

Here is another text that reveals the ambiguity as well as the flexibility of the Chinese lexico-grammatical system. In Chinese teahouses, you can often see some teapots engraved with the following five characters:

可

也　　　　　以

心　　清

If starting with a different character each time and reading the text in a clockwise direction, then you will have a five-line poem as follows:

可以清心也 [Tea] can purify the heart.

以清心也可 [To use tea] to purify the heart is fine.

清心也可以 [To] purify the heart [with tea] is fine.

心也可以清 Heart can be purified [by tea.]

也可以清心 [It's fine] to [use tea] to purify the heart.

In this case, the five characters can be arranged in various ways to generate different sentences that are absolutely meaningful in the context. Perhaps this is only one extreme case of Chinese writing, but this type of ambiguity is not at all rare in Chinese texts, especially in classical Chinese texts. While reflecting the writer's remarkable skills in creatively applying the language, this text also reveals the uniqueness of the lexico-grammatical system of Chinese.

Semantic-Pragmatic System

The reading of a text is a "literacy event," involving the writer, the text, and the reader (Goodman, 1996). For writers, how to use the language to express their own attitudes toward the world not only is related to their linguistic knowledge, but also depends on their social and cultural experiences (Rosenblatt, 1989). For readers, how to construct meaning of a text is determined by their use of the linguistic cues in the language, personal reading experiences, sociocultural backgrounds, text features, and so forth (Goodman, Watson, & Burke, 2005). The reader is transformed as new knowledge is assimilated and accommodated (Goodman, 1994). To make reading comprehension possible, the text simultaneously presents the reader with three types of meaning: experiential, interpersonal, and textual (Halliday & Hasan, 1985).

Three Meaning Systems

Goodman (1996) suggests that among the three meaning systems in a text, the experiential meaning is the most obvious one that represents the experiences or ideas shared by both the writer and the readers. In contrast, the interpersonal meaning is the sociocultural values, attitudes, and feelings underlying the text for the reader to experience and respond. Both the experiential and interpersonal meaning systems of the text are represented by the rhetorical considerations of the text, such as the arrangement of discourse, the choice of words, and matters of rhythm. The third type of meaning is textual meaning, which is represented by the structure of the text. To construct meaning, the reader needs not only to have sufficient linguistic knowledge of the language, but also to know how ideas are embodied in the text and customized into contexts.

What follows is an excerpt from a reader's reading of the story "A Gold Axe" (Wang, 1979) in a miscue study. The reader's miscues clearly illustrate how the text provides the reader with the three meaning systems she uses to construct its meaning.

shake his head
什么 什么

张有金一看不是金的, 马上 摇　摇 头 说： "老先生, 这不是我的。"
老人也不点头也不笑了。

axe
他说："河里边儿只有这一把 斧 头，不是你的，我没办法了。"

The excerpt can be translated as follows: As soon as Zhang Youjin found it was not a gold axe, he immediately shook his head. "This one is not mine." This time the God didn't laugh. He said, "This is the only axe in the river. If this one is not yours, I can't help you."

After reading the sentence "老先生, 这不是我的" (This one is not mine), the reader gives comments about the main character's behavior in the story: "That is not right." Her response to the story shows that she has understood the dialogue between the old man and Zhang Youjin, and also knows that Zhang Youjin is lying. Her English substitution "shake his head" for 摇摇 头 (*yao yao tou*, shake-head) demonstrates effective use of strategies to deal with unfamiliar characters and reveals her interaction with the three types of meaning of the paragraph.

Three Meaning Systems as a Whole

Goodman (1996) divides the meaning level of the text into three systems when looking at how the text provides the reader with the semantic and pragmatic cues to make sense of it. Meanwhile, he suggests that the text represents the three meaning systems simultaneously. In the example in the preceding section, the Chinese story "A Gold Axe" is comprehensible to the reader because the reader shares all three types of meaning in the text while making sense of it. By sharing the experiences with the writer, the reader knows that the old man is benevolent, and Zhang Youjin is greedy. The reader reads the dialogue between the old man and Zhang Youjin in an appropriate way because language is used to share not only experiences but also attitudes, emotions, and social values. The English substitution of "shake his head" for 摇摇头 (*yao yao tou*, shake-head) shows the reader's use of context cues to build up meaning. As shown in the reader's miscues, the text brings together the experiential, interpersonal, and textual meanings and provides cues for the reader to construct the meaning of it.

Conclusion

As a form of communication, each written language functions well as a part of life in the society that creates it. Different languages may have different symbol systems to represent meaning and sound. However, all written languages provide readers with information, in the form of cues, to make sense of the text (Goodman, 1994, 1996, 2004).

If we understand that reading, regardless of language and orthography, is making sense, constructing meaning, then we can see that there is a single reading process. Although the three levels of cueing systems work differently in English and Chinese, our discussions of the three cueing systems in written Chinese show that Chinese texts provide readers with information at different linguistic levels to allow them to construct meaning. Chinese texts require readers to focus more on the context cues than on the graphic and phonemic cues because of the highly semantic characteristic of the Chinese language, but it is the construction of meaning that is central to all reading.

References

Chao, Y.-R. (1968a). *A grammar of spoken Chinese.* Berkeley: University of California Press.

Chao, Y.-R. (1968b). *Language and symbolic systems* Cambridge, U.K.: Cambridge University Press.

Chen, M. (1956). 殷墟卜辞综述 [On Oracle-bone script]. Beijing, China: Zhonghua shuju.

Chu, C. C. (1998). *A discourse grammar of Mandarin Chinese.* New York: Lang.

DeFrancis, J. (1950). *Nationalism and language reform.* Princeton, NJ: Princeton University Press.

DeFrancis, J. (1984). Phonetic versus semantic predictability in Chinese characters. *Journal of Chinese Language Teachers Association, 31*, 1–12.

DeFrancis, J. (1989). *Visible speech: The diverse oneness of writing systems.* Honolulu: University of Hawaii Press.

DeFrancis, J. (2002). The ideographic myth. In M. Erbaugh (Ed.), *Difficult characters: Interdisciplinary studies of Chinese and Japanese writing* (pp. 1–20). Columbus, OH: National East Asian Languages Resource Center, The Ohio State University.

Gong, J. (2002). 汉字汉语汉文化论集 [Character, language, and culture]. Chengdu, China: Bashushushe.

Goodman, K. (1993). *Phonics phacts*. Richmond Hill, Ontario: Scholastic Canada.

Goodman, K. (1994). Reading, writing, and written texts: A transactional sociopsycholinguistic view. In A. Flurkey & J. Xu (Eds.), *On the revolution of reading: The selected writings of Kenneth S. Goodman* (pp. 3–45). Portsmouth, NH: Heinemann.

Goodman, K. (1996). *On reading*. Portsmouth, NH: Heinemann.

Goodman, K. (2004). Reading, writing, and written texts: A transactional sociopsycholinguistic view. In R. Ruddell & J. Norman (Eds.) *Theoretical models and processes of reading* (5th ed., pp. 1093–1130). Newark, DE: International Reading Association.

Goodman, Y., Watson, D. & Burke, C. (2005). *Reading miscue inventory*. Katonah, NY: Owen.

Halliday, M. A. K., & Hasan, R. (1985). *Language, context, and text: Aspects of language in the social semiotic perspective*. Victoria, Australia: Deakin University.

Hannas, W. C. (1997). *Asia's orthographic dilemma*. Honolulu: University of Hawaii.

He, J. (2000). 汉字文化学 [A sociocultural study on Chinese characters]. Shenyang, China: Liaoning renmin chubanshe.

Hoosain, R. (1991). *Psycholinguistic implications for linguistic relativity: A case study of Chinese*. Hillsdale, NJ: Erlbaum.

Hoosain, R. (1992). Psychological reality of the word in Chinese. In H.-C. Chen & O. J. L. Tzeng (Eds.), *Language processing in Chinese* (pp. 111–130). Amsterdam: North-Holland.

Hung, Y. (2000). *What is writing and what is Chinese writing: A historical, linguistic, and social literacies perspective*. Unpublished doctoral dissertation, University of Arizona, Tucson.

Ingulsrud, J. E., & Allen, K. (1999). *Learning to read in China: Sociolinguistic perspective on the acquisition of literacy*. Lewiston, NY: Mellen Press.

Li, C., & Thompson, S. A. (1976). Subject and topic: A new typology of language. In C. N. Li (Ed.), *Subject and topic* (pp. 458–489). New York: Academic Press.

Li, C., & Thompson, S. A. (1982). The gulf between spoken and written language: A case study in Chinese. In D. Tannen (Ed.), *Spoken and written language: Exploring orality and literacy* (pp. 77–88). Norwood, NJ: Ablex.

Li, C., & Thompson, S. A. (1989). *Mandarin Chinese: A functional reference grammar*. Berkeley: University of California Press.

Liu, J. (1992). Bridging language and culture: A cognitive approach to the study of Chinese compounds. *Journal of Chinese Language Teachers' Association, 3*, 1–19.

Lü, S. (1980). 语文常谈 [On Chinese]. Beijing, China: Sanlian Shudian.

Lu, X. (1981). 呐喊 [Call to arms]. Beijing, China: Foreign Languages Press.

Norman, J. (1988). *Chinese.* Cambridge, U.K.: Cambridge University Press.

Qiu, X. (1988). 文字学概要 [Chinese writing]. Beijing, China: Shangwu yinshuguan.

Rosenblatt, L. (1989). Writing and reading: The transactional theory. In J. Mason (Ed.), *Reading and writing connections* (pp. 153–176). Needham Heights, MA: Allyn and Bacon.

Sampson, G. (1985). *Writing systems: A linguistic introduction.* London: Hutchinson Education.

Saussure, F. de. 1983. *Course in general linguistics* (R. Harris, Trans.). London: Duckworth.

Shen, X. (1992). 语文的阐释 [On Chinese]. Shenyang, China: Liaoning jiaoyu chubanshe.

Shu, H. (2004). International reports on literacy research: China. *Reading Research Quarterly, 39*(1) 114–115.

Tai, J. H.-Y. (1993). Iconicity: Motivations in Chinese grammar. In M. Eld & G. Iverson (Eds.), *Principles and predication: The analysis of natural languages* (pp. 153–174). Amsterdam: Benjamins.

Tsao, F.-F. (1990). *Sentence and clause structure in Chinese: A functional perspective.* Taibei, Taiwan: Student Book.

Wang, P. (1978). *Stories in modern Chinese.* Columbus, OH: National East Asian Languages Resource Center. The Ohio State University.

Xu, T. (2001). 基础语言学教程 [Fundamentals of linguistics]. Beijing, China: Beijing University Press.

Ye, C. (1965). Statistics relating to the pronunciation of current Chinese characters in general use. *Zhongguo yuwen, 3*, 201–205.

Zhou, Y. (1978). To what degree are the phonetics of present-day Chinese characters still phonetic? *Zhongguo yuwen, 146*, 172–77.

Zhou, Y. (1980). 拼音化问题 [Issues on Romanization]. Beijing, China: Wenzi gaige chubanshe.

Zhou, Y. (2003). *The historical evolution of Chinese language and scripts.* Columbus, OH: National East Asian Languages and Resource Center. The Ohio State University.

INTRODUCTION TO CHAPTER 9

*B*ECAUSE SCIENTIFIC REALISM deals with actual reality, it is possible to use the procedures of the research to help people understand the nature of reality. As my transactional theory of the reading process has become more robust, I have been constructing what I call protocols — samples of texts — to use in involving my students and audiences in examining their own reading. My intent is to move them away from the commonsense notion that reading is a process of sequential word recognition.

One such protocol I constructed was a one-paragraph story in which I deliberately embedded errors. It involved a common folk theme: someone builds a boat in the basement forgetting that it will be too big to get out when it is finished. The exercise worked well, in fact better than I had originally expected it would. In every audience, there were several readers who were unaware that there were any errors. They made sense of the text and did not perceive the errors. No one ever saw all the errors. In fact, when I asked for a show of hands for the number of errors of which they were aware, the mean was always less than half. An embedded error involving two successive *thes* turned out to be the hardest error to detect. Rarely, more than one or two in a large group detected it. The rich discussion of their own reading helped them to see the difference between vision and perception in reading and to realize the constructive nature of reading comprehension. Each time I used the protocol, I was conducting an informal experiment with highly predictable results.

One way to look at miscue research and other research based in scientific realism is that it is hypothesis generating rather than hypothesis testing. Because the goal is to provide an explanatory theory of the structures and processes, that theory can be used to predict what would happen in particular conditions. So, it is possible to construct experiments to test the predictive power of the theory. The experiments refine the theory by showing how the actual responses of subjects conform to theoretically based predictions.

This chapter brings together two experimental research studies based on my protocol. The authors compare the similarities and differences of the findings of the two studies.

Fred Gollasch turned my informal experiments into a formal one. He modified the story a bit and added a sixth embedded error. The basic results were highly predictable in view of the less-formal experiments I had been doing for years. The experimental findings supported the theory: Although older readers were somewhat more successful than younger readers, their patterns of error detection were similar. The fact they were told to look for errors did not detract those readers from making sense of the text or make them much more successful in detecting errors. Even with unlimited time, few subjects could detect all the errors.

Jingguo Xu replicated the Gollasch study. His intent was to test the applicability to Chinese of the constructivist model of reading. He reasoned that if the process is essentially the same, then the patterns of error detection would be much the same. He used the Gollasch design, but he chose a somewhat longer story and embedded eight errors similar in variety to those in the Gollasch study. His reason for making the task somewhat more difficult was a sense he had that Chinese readers might read more carefully than English readers. What he found was a virtually identical pattern to the one that Gollasch found. Chinese readers were slightly less likely to detect errors than English readers. This study certainly extended the theory because it demonstrated that reading in Chinese is no more a matter of accurate sequential character recognition than English reading is accurate sequential word recognition.

Comparing the results of the two studies, the authors highlight a single reading process but one responsive to the differences of the two languages and their orthographies.

These studies demonstrate that experimental research certainly has value. It has the most value when it is rooted in a well-articulated theory of what is studied. The theory not only makes for a strong experimental design but also makes the findings of the experiments more useful in checking the limits of the theory and refining it.

Ken Goodman

9

CHINESE AND ENGLISH READINGS
OF EMBEDDED ANOMALIES
IN WRITTEN TEXTS

Koomi Kim, Yetta Goodman, Jingguo Xu, and Fredrick Gollasch

> Reading isn't simply recognizing words in succession. Something propels you forward as you read, helps you to anticipate so well what's coming that you simply use cues from the print to move constantly toward meaning.

> Goodman, 1996, p. 40

*T*HIS CHAPTER ADDRESSES CONCEPTS of universality in the reading process, specifically whether a range of English-speaking readers and Chinese-speaking readers display similar reading processes when negotiating a text with multiple types of embedded errors. Two separate studies are discussed, based on adaptations of a text, "The Boat in the Basement," an error-detection exercise originally written by Ken Goodman (1996). These studies conducted by Fredrick Gollasch (1980), an Australian researcher, and Jingguo Xu (1998), a Chinese researcher, were designed to replicate Goodman's original error detection experiment.

History of "The Boat in the Basement"

"The Boat in the Basement" was originally created by Goodman as part of his work with preservice and in-service teachers. He was interested in developing experiences that would allow teachers to inquire into the nature of the reading process and to examine what readers (including themselves) do when they are engaged in reading. Goodman wanted to provide ways for teachers and researchers to consider how they construct their own meanings and, at the same time, to

The Boat in the Basement

A man was building a boat in his basement.

When the boat was finished he couldn't get the

boot out of the basement because it was

too wide to go though the door. So he had to

take the boat a part to get it out. He should

of planned ahead.

Figure 9.1
"The Boat in the Basement" by Ken Goodman.

dispel the commonsense notion that reading is a process of accurate, sequential, identification of words. He wrote a number of protocols for groups of readers to examine the ways in which they respond to errors in a text and how they use their language knowledge in their reading. One of these protocols is "The Boat in the Basement," illustrated in Figure 9.1 (Goodman, 1996, p. 38).

Goodman wrote this original short story in 1972 while writing about his developing model. It has been used by hundreds of teacher educators and speakers with audiences wanting to learn about the reading process. There are five anomalies or "errors" embedded in the story. The embedded errors illustrate different aspects of the selective and perceptual nature of reading, the strategies readers use, and readers' knowledge of the language cueing systems (each error and its purpose in the written text is discussed in this chapter).

For purposes of in-service and conference presentations, the audience is told that they will read a short story from an overhead projector. The directions go something like the following:

> The story you'll be reading has a problem in it. Read to see if you can discover what the problem is. Read it once and once only and then write down everything you remember reading. I will read it slowly twice and then turn off the projector. Ready? Begin (the projector is turned on).

After the reading and with the projector left off, the audience is engaged in a discussion of what they have read, what they wrote, and how the experience informs them about the reading process. Someone usually announces a noticed error in the passage. The presenter asks who else saw errors and how many there were. They are asked not to call out the specific error yet. Most readers detect two to three errors the first time through. If there are readers who do not see any errors or only one, then they are asked to read out loud as they would if they were reading a story to a group of children. The audience watches as that reader often discovers another error but still does not see them all. In almost no case does any single member in the audience discover all the errors by themselves during their first reading. The presenter involves the audience in discussing how they responded to the experience: when they decided to self-correct, when they decided not to reread because they were told not to, how they responded to the specific errors, and what their responses meant regarding the reading process. The discussion often involves readers in considering their emotional responses and how they wrote in a form different from the one they read. Readers who believe they read slowly or who believe they are accurate readers with high comprehension are often surprised at their responses and begin to reconsider what they know about reading.

This engagement works well in reading classes and with parents. It is a powerful tool to begin a discussion about how people read. The many graduate students who have worked with Ken Goodman continue to use this engagement with adaptations in their teacher education work with undergraduate and graduate classes because it leads to dynamic discussions about the reading process. Gollasch and Xu, graduate students who worked with Goodman at different times, decided to develop experimental research studies on readers' responses to errors embedded in a short story to test the efficacy of Goodman's reading model.

Experimental Studies by Gollasch and Xu

Gollasch (1980) and Xu (1998) asked university students and junior high school students to read a short story with embedded errors. Gollasch conducted his study using an English text adapted from the original "The Boat in the Basement." Xu replicated Gollasch's study using a Chinese text. In each study, the participants were divided into four groups:

- University students with the focus on meaning
- University students with the focus on error detection
- Junior high school students with the focus on meaning
- Junior high school students with the focus on error detection

Sample Size

Gollasch (1980) randomly selected 240 participants in the United States (Tucson, AZ) to read an English text. Of these, 120 were university students,

The Boat in the Basement

A woman was building a boat in her

basement. When she had finished the

the boot, she discovered that it was

too big to go though the door. So he

had to take the boat a part to get

it out. She should of planned ahead.

Figure 9.2
"The Boat in the Basement" as modified by Fredrick Gollasch.

and 120 were junior high school students. Of the 120 university students, 60 were in the meaning-focused group, and 60 were in the error-focused group. Each group was given different directions to establish their purpose for reading: reading for meaning or reading for error detection. The 120 junior high school students were divided in the same manner as the university students.

Xu's (1998) Chinese readers were 100 university and 100 junior high school students in Shanghai, China. Of the 100 university students, 50 were in the meaning-focused group, and 50 were in the error-focused group. The 100 junior high school students were divided in the same manner, with 50 in the meaning-focused group and 50 in the error-focused group. After the participants in each study were given limited time to follow the directions (limited time exposure), they were told that there were errors and that they had unlimited time (unlimited time exposure) to look for them.

Texts

Gollasch (1980) used an adaptation of "The Boat in the Basement." His alterations to the original text are discussed later. His text has a total of six embedded errors, including two content words and four function words (Figure 9.2).

Xu (1998) used a Chinese text, "Min Jian Wen Xue," written by Wu (1993) (Figure 9.3). Xu embedded eight errors in the text for his experimental study: five content words and three function words (see Figure 9.4).

朱二打猎

朱二见村里天天有人猎获野味，很眼红，也买了杆猎枪去打猎，却从未打到野味。

冬季的一天，老婆叫喊无柴煮饭了。他只得放下猎枪上山去打柴。当他走到溪边时，忽然发现一只山兔睡在树边晒太阳，就悄悄地扑上去，捉住了它。他很高兴。突然，他灵机一动，取出草绳，将兔子的一只后脚系着，倒挂在树上。然后飞奔回家去取枪，边跑边叫："今天不打回只兔子，我就不叫朱二！"他赶回来，见吊着的兔子仍不停挣扎，就在一两丈远的地方站住，举起枪来。一声枪响，打中了系兔子脚的那根草绳，兔子落到地上就逃之夭夭了。

他气得呆若木鸡，只听背后跟来看热闹的人哄然大笑。

Figure 9.3

Chinese text without embedded errors.

朱二打猎

朱二见村里天天有人猎获野味，很眼红，也买了杆猎枪去打猎，却从末*打到野味。

冬季的一天，老婆叫喊无柴煮饭了，他只得放下猎枪上山去打柴。当她*走到溪边时，忽然发现一只山兔睡在树边晒太阳，就悄悄得*扑上去，捉住了它。他很高兴。突然，他灵机一动，取出绳草*，将兔子的一只后脚系着，倒挂在树上。然后飞奔回家去取枪，边跑边叫："今天不打回只兔子，我就不叫朱二！"他赶回来，见吊着的兔子仍不停争扎*，就在一两丈远的的*地方站住，举起枪来。一声枪响，打中了系兔子脚的那根草绳，兔子落到地上就逃之夭夭了。

他气得呆如*木鸡，只听背后跟来看热闹的人轰*然大笑。

Figure 9.4

Chinese text with embedded errors.

The embedded errors in both texts were created by using linguistic insights similar to those Goodman used in the development of the original short story. Errors included function words, content words, spelling, and repetition errors. The texts satisfy the criteria for material selection. Both are self-contained short stories containing meaningful and predictable contexts with a beginning, events, and a conclusion.

Linguistic Rationales for Embedded Errors for "The Boat in the Basement"

The text "The Boat in the Basement" is a paragraph that contains 53 words, four sentences, and 197 letters. It contains six anomalies. Each error is constructed considering the three cueing systems' linguistic aspects.

The error *boot* for *boat* involves words with high graphic similarity. Syntactically, both words are nouns, so substituting one for the other does not involve syntactic change. However, in terms of the semantic cueing system, there is considerable meaning change. The error *he* for *she* has high graphic and sound similarity. Syntactically, there is no change because they are both pronouns. Semantically, there is a considerable change because *he* and *she* refer to different genders. The error *a part* for *apart* has high graphic similarity, although one is two words, and the other is one word. Phonologically the two are pronounced the same in context. Syntactically, there is a significant difference, with *a part* a noun phrase and *apart* an adverb. Semantically, there is a considerable meaning change as well because one is an action, and the other one has a noun-related function. The error *though* for *through* has a significant phonological difference, yet graphically they share high similarities. Syntactically, there is a significant difference because *though* is a conjunction, and *through* is a preposition. Semantically, *though* and *through* have different meanings. *Should of* for *should've* are graphically different. However, phonologically they are homophones unless *should have* is articulated carefully, and it is considered the only correct form. *Should of* is not an acceptable syntactic or semantic form. The error *the the* for *the* has a considerable change graphically because the word *the* is repeated. In this sentence context, the pattern is neither semantically nor syntactically acceptable.

Gollasch's Findings For Each Error

Errors "he" and "boot": Content Words   Figure 9.2 shows the text with all the embedded errors. One of the significant findings by Gollasch (1980) is that the meaning-focused group detected the error *he* to a greater extent than he had expected. In relation to this finding, Gollasch's experimental study reveals that subjects from both focused groups detected the errors *he* and *boot* at a similarly high rate (see Table 9.1). Gollasch's study shows that the error-focused group performed less well than the meaning-focused group on finding *he* and *boot*. Gollasch suggests that readers pay more attention to content words than function words. This factor probably affected the high rate of error detections of these two content words. *Boat* and *she* are key words in the meaning of this passage. This result supports Goodman's reading model (Goodman, 1967, 1996), which theorizes that readers read for meaning construction (Table 9.1).

Errors "a part" and "should of": Function Words   More of Gollasch's (1980) university readers detected these two errors *a part* and *should of* than his junior high school readers. The junior high school readers seldom found these two

Table 9.1 Categories of Errors and Percentage Detected

| | | Percentage Detected (Entire Population) | | | | | |
| | | Limited Exposure | | | Unlimited Exposure | | |
Type	Error	College (120), %	Junior High (120), %	Overall Detection, %	College (120), %	Junior High (120), %	Overall Detection, %
Function words	though	10	12.5	11.3	56.7	57.5	57.1
	should of	7.5	1.7	4.6	51.7	8.3	30
	the the	2.5	1.7	2.1	20.8	24.2	22.5
Content words	boot	80	70.8	75.4	95.8	99.2	97.5
	he	73.3	59.2	66.3	96.7	95.8	96.26
	a part	49.2	24.2	36.7	95.8	62.5	79.2

Note: From *Readers' Perception in Detecting and Processing Embedded Errors in Meaningful Text*, F. Gollasch, 1980, unpublished doctoral dissertation, University of Arizona, Tucson.

errors, even with unlimited time exposure. Gollasch suggests that university students were able to detect the errors more easily than the junior high students because of their richer experience. He also suggests that the similarities of these words phonologically might have affected the low detection rates among the junior high readers.

Error "though" (Syntactic and Spelling): Function Word   Gollasch's (1980) finding indicates a consistent rate of detectability across all groups and levels under unlimited exposure for *though*. Less than 60% of all the readers detected the error in this condition. It also suggests the power of syntactic knowledge and prediction. *Though* could never fit into the linguistic slot ___ the door. *Through* is highly constrained in this setting and therefore highly predictable. This finding also supports Goodman's reading model, which posits that readers do not decode one letter at a time in a text.

Error "the the": Function Word   The error *the the* has the lowest detection rate across all groups and educational levels. Gollasch (1980) was surprised to find that only 3 of 120 experienced university readers, whether in the meaning-focused or error-focused group, detected the error under limited time exposure. Even under unlimited time exposure, only 25 university readers (of 120) detected the error despite the fact that they were deliberately told to look for the errors.

Eye-movement research has shown that many readers actually fixate on the two *thes* but orally read only one (Paulson & Freeman, 2003, pp. 18–21). The constraint of the syntactic system is so strong that readers rarely orally read the two *thes* or even orally report that they saw them.

Linguistic Rationales for Embedded Errors for 朱二打猪, "Min Jian Wen Zue"

The Chinese text 朱二打猪, "Min Jian Wen Zue" contains 229 Chinese characters (Figure 9.3). The story contains 10 sentences. This text is longer than the English text "The Boat in the Basement" by 4 sentences and has two more embedded errors (a total of eight). This story is a folk tale. Xu (1998) reports that he used a longer text, "thus proportionately increasing the number of errors was reasonable" (p. 156).

The Chinese characters 末 *mo* (end) for 未 (*wei*, not), share high graphic similarity; however, phonetically they share no similarity. Syntactically, there is some similarity; semantically there is a significant difference. The error 她 (*tal*, female pronoun) for 他 (*tal*, male pronoun) is graphically similar. Phonetically, these words are homophones, but syntactically they are both pronouns. Semantically, there is a significant difference because they refer to a different gender. The error 得 (*de*, particle) for 地 (*de*) are graphically not similar; however, phonetically they are homophones. Syntactically, there is a significant difference because one indicates relationship between verb and adjective, and the other indicates a relationship between attributive and noun. The error 绳草 (*sheng-cao*, rope-straw) for 草绳 (*cao-sheng*, straw-rope) is a reversal. Graphically, the two characters are somewhat similar, but each is reversed. Semantically, there is a significant difference. The error indicates "straw for a rope," and the written text indicates "a kind of rope that is made of straw." The error was included in the text based on findings related to reversal miscue in miscue studies (Xu, 1998). The error 争 (*zheng*, contend) for 挣 (*zheng*, struggle) is a homophone. Homophones often occur in Chinese. However, there is a significant difference syntactically as well as semantically. Adjectives in Chinese are marked by the particle 的 (*de*). Here, the particle 的 (*de*) is repeated, which is syntactically not acceptable in Chinese. This error is parallel to the error "the the" in "The Boat in the Basement," in which a function word is repeated. As for the error 如 (*ru*, like) for 若 (*ruo*, like), semantically they both have the same meaning, "like." Phonologically, there is a tonal difference. Graphically, these two characters are not similar except that they both contain a square. The last error is 轰 (*hong*, bang) for 哄 (*hong*). These two characters are semantically similar; however, their configurations (graphic representations) are different. Tables 9.1 and 9.2 summarize the errors and their types as well as percentages of detections for Gollasch's (1980) and Xu's (1998) studies, respectively.

Xu's Findings for Each Error

Xu (1998) indicates that his readers detected the embedded content word errors easier than the function word errors.

The Errors 她 *(tal, pronoun),* 争 *(zheng, verb): Content Words*   The content word-related errors 她 (*tal*) and 争 (*zheng*) were detected at a higher rate than other errors in the limited time condition. Xu (1998) points out that "the direct relationship between radicals and word meanings in these two words facilitated the subjects to notice the errors in meaning construction" (p. 237).

The Error 末 *(mo, orthographic): Function Word*   The error 末 (*mo*) was detected by 34% of the participants in the limited time condition. Xu (1998) notes that 末 (*mo*) was not as easily detected as the errors 她 (*tal*) and 争 (*zheng*) because of the change within component strokes of the character. This stroke change was unnoticed by a majority of the participants. Xu suggests, "The subjects constructed the meaning of the sentence with syntactic and semantic knowledge as well as the context of the text. Once the meaning was acceptable, there was no need to confirm the graphic input" (p. 272).

The Errors 绳草 *(sheng-cao, noun reversal) and* 轰 *(hong, onomatopoeia): Content Words*   The two content words 绳草 (*sheng-cao*, noun reversal) and 轰 (*hong*, onomatopoeia) were not as easily detected as other content words. Of the participants, 18.5% detected the error *sheng-cao*. The majority of the participants failed to detect the reversal of the expression, which demonstrates that Chinese reading is not processed in a linear manner or in an accurate order; this is also demonstrated in Gollasch's (1980) study in English reading. The error 轰 (*hong*), which is an onomatopoeia representing an explosive sound, was detected by 17.5% of the participants. According to Xu (1998), the meaning generated by the onomatopoeia could bring to mind the sound of laughter and hinder the detection of the error because the constructed meaning was acceptable.

Table 9.2   Categories of Errors and Percentage Detected

| | | Percentage Detected | | | | | |
| | | Limited Exposure | | | Unlimited Exposure | | |
Type	Error	College (100), %	Middle School (100), %	Overall Detection, %	College (100), %	Middle School (100), %	Overall Detection, %
Function words	得 (*de*, wrong type of particle)	27	10	18.5	66	49	57.5
	如 (*ru*, "like" wrong in the idiomatic expression)	15	6	10.5	41	33	37
	的的 (*dede*, particle, repeated)	0	0	0	6	18	12
Content words	轰 (*hong*, "loud crashing sound" semantics same as replacement but configuration different)	24	11	17.5	44	29	36.5
	争 (*zheng*, two characters that by themselves have meaning but not when combined as they are here)	56	42	49	95	85	90
	绳草 (*shengcao*, "rope-straw" inversion error)	30	7	18.5	58	35	46.5
	她 (*tal*, "she" pronoun; sounds identical to "human being")	39	55	47	82	91	86.5
	末 (*mo*, "end" similar to replacement and acceptable morpheme in other context)	40	28	34	75	67	71

Note: From *A Study of the Reading Process in Chinese Through Detecting Errors in a Meaningful Text,* J. Xu, 1998, unpublished doctoral dissertation, University of Arizona, Tucson.

The Errors 如 *(ru, preposition),* 得 *(de, particle), and* 的的 *(dede, repeated adjectives): Function Words*   Only a small number of participants detected the function word errors 如 (*ru*, preposition), 得 (*de*, particle), and 的的 (*dede*, repeated adjectives). Under limited time exposure, 10.5% of readers detected the error 如 (*ru*), and 18.5% of the participants detected the error 得 (*de*). As for the error 的的 (*dede*) none of the participants detected the error. Table 9.2 summarizes the types of errors and percentages of error detections.

Both studies (Gollasch, 1980; Xu, 1998) indicate that the error detection order is similar across all groups in Chinese and in English. This is discussed in greater detail in the following section (see Tables 9.1 and 9.2).

Results of the Studies

Gollasch's Results

Gollasch's (1980) study shows that his 240 English readers detected 33% of total errors during the limited reading time. The participants in the error-focused groups detected 37% of the total errors, and meaning-focused participants detected 28% of the total errors. The error detection rate for the university students was 37%, and for the junior high school students it was 28%. Although these differences are statistically significant, they show the same processes at work as readers of various ages and abilities detect errors in similar ways and in a similar order.

Xu's Results

Xu's (1998) study found that 24% of the total errors were detected by his 200 Chinese readers during the limited reading time. The meaning-focused group detected 16% of the errors, and the error-focused group detected 33% of the errors. The error detection rate for the university students was 29%, and it was 20% for the junior high students. The English groups each detected more errors than their comparison group reading in Chinese. This may reflect that, although both orthographies represent meaning, Chinese does it more directly. For example, Chinese characters have the same meaning even when used in Japanese and Korean (except for Chinese function words, which cannot be understood easily by Japanese or Korean readers). Characters do not represent oral language; they represent meanings.

Similarities Between the Two Studies

The similarities of results of the two studies (Gollasch, 1980; Xu, 1998) that involve English and Chinese readers include the following:

1. Limited time exposure versus unlimited time exposure:
   - None of the participants in either study was able to detect half of the errors under limited time exposure (Table 9.3).
   - Readers focused on constructing meaning. So, when they were instructed to detect errors even during unlimited time exposure, none of the participants were able to detect every error (Table 9.4).
2. Function words versus content words:
   - Overall, for all groups and in all conditions, errors on content words were detected more frequently than errors on function words (Tables 9.1 and 9.2).
3. Meaning-focused versus error-focused groups:
   - Meaning-focused groups scored higher in story recall than the error-focused groups.
   - Meaning-focused groups had lower rates of error detection than the error-focused groups.
4. University students versus junior high students:
   - The university students scored higher in story recall than the junior high students.
   - The university students had higher rates of error detection (Tables 9.3 and 9.4).
5. Order of error detection:
   - Patterns of the order in which errors were detected were similar across all groups in both languages, Chinese and English (Table 9.5).

As Tables 9.1 and 9.2 indicate, the order of detections is parallel to word categories. The content word-related errors were detected by more readers than the function word-related errors. At the same time, the order of detections is similar in both the English and Chinese texts. Table 9.5 summarizes the order of detection for both texts. In both studies, the readers detected the content word errors more easily than the function word errors. For example, pronoun errors in both English and Chinese texts were detected easily. On the other hand, repeated determiners, "the the" in the English text and repeated particles 的的 (*dede*) in the Chinese text were the most difficult errors to detect. Under limited time exposure, only 2.1% of the English readers detected the "the the" embedded error. As for Chinese readers, 0%

Table 9.3 Percentage of Errors Detected by Chinese Readers and English Readers Under Limited Time Exposure to the Text

Participants	Educational Levels, %		Focus Groups, %		Overall, %
	Junior High	College	Meaning Focus	Error Focus	
Chinese (*N* = 200)	20	29	16	33	24
English (*N* = 240)	28	37	28	37	33

Table 9.4 Percentage of Errors Detected by Chinese Readers and English Readers Under Unlimited Time Exposure to the Text

Participants	Educational Levels, %		Focus Groups, %		Overall, %
	Junior High	College	Meaning Focus	Error Focus	
Chinese (*N* = 200)	51	59	56	54	55
English (*N* = 240)	58	70	63	64	64

Table 9.5 Order of Detections

Order of the Detections	"The Boat in the Basement" (English Text)	Order of the Detections	朱二打猪, "Min Jian Wen Xue" (Chinese Text)
1	boot (noun — content word)	1	争 (*zheng*, content word)
2	he (pronoun — content word)	2	她 (*tal*, pronoun — content word)
3	a part (spacing — content word)	3	末 (*mo*, orthographic — content word)
4	through (spelling — function word)	4	得 (*de*, homophones — function word
5	should of (homophones — function word)	5	绳草 (*shengcao*, inversion — content word)
6	the the (repeated function word)	6	轰 (*hong*, onomatopoeia — content word)
		7	如 (*ru*, idiomatically not acceptable)
		8	的的 (*dede*, repeated particle)

of them detected the *dede* error under limited time exposure. Even under unlimited time exposure, only 22.5% of the English readers detected the repeated determiner error, as did only 12% of the Chinese readers for the repeated particle (see Tables 9.1 and 9.2).

Gollasch (1980) points out that the inability to detect the "the the" error is one of the most powerful findings in his study and provides support for Goodman's reading model. He concludes that

1. Readers do not process text letter by letter or even word by word.
2. Cognitive processes influence perception.
3. Readers bring their grammatical knowledge to the reading process. They know that only one determiner is permissible prior to a noun in English.
4. Readers tentatively move through visual, perceptual, and syntactic cycles as they efficiently process text for meaning.
5. Absolute accuracy in reading is a misnomer. (p. 158)

The conclusions apply to Chinese reading as well. Both studies show the Chinese and English readers read for meaning, not for accuracy, even when instructed to find errors.

Differences Between the Two Studies

Although most aspects of the Gollasch (1980) and Xu (1998) studies show similar results, there were differences between the Chinese and English studies that are important to take into consideration. Chinese readers detected fewer errors than English readers in both limited and unlimited reading time exposures. Xu speculates regarding the reason:

> The difference might be due to the configurational compactness as well as the direct association of form and meaning in Chinese characters. Certainly, there is no evidence here to show that Chinese reading is less efficient than English reading. In fact, it appears that Chinese writing may make access to meaning somewhat more efficient. (p. 266)

This suggests that because Chinese characters are meaning based and do not involve as much phonological processing as English does, Chinese readers learn not to depend on this cueing system to the degree that they use the other cueing systems. However, they still are influenced by the orthography and, to some degree, its relation to phonology.

Xu (1998) also suggests that the compactness of Chinese characters in configuration might have some impact on sampling language elements in large chunks. Xu's conclusions suggest that Chinese readers may not be focused on surface text features to the same extent that English readers are. In the Chinese context, the role of accuracy relates more to meaning and comprehension than it does to accurate oral reading. "Accurate" oral reading is not the focus of instruction in the reading of Chinese because once the meaning of characters is acceptable, there is no need to confirm the graphic input.

These differences suggest that although the underlying reading process is the same across languages, there are differences among readers. The differences in the groups represented by language, age, ability, the content and length of the material, and the purposes of the reading have an impact on the reader in many ways. Yet, the underlying process that readers use to make sense of their world by engaging in a cyclical and integrated transaction with the language cueing systems (graphophonic, semantic, syntactic, and pragmatic) and the reading strategies (predicting, inferencing, etc.) is the same for all readers. Evidence in support of this process is shown by the errors that are detected in a similar order and similar percentages in two different languages.

Perception, Not Recognition

Taken together, the studies by Gollasch (1980) and Xu (1998) support Goodman's view that "perception and not recognition is the key process involved in making sense in reading" (Goodman, 1996, p. 95). Perception is one of the four reading cycles, along with visual, syntactic, and semantic cycles:

> It's true that we use visual information to form perceptions, assign syntax and wording on the basis of our perceptions, and can get to meaning only after we've decided on the language structures and wording we're dealing with. But reading isn't a linear process — we have all kinds of information available all the time. And the information is sufficiently ambiguous that we are constantly leaping to conclusions while, at the same time, being tentative enough to look out for conflicting information." (Goodman, 1996, p. 93)

Conclusion

The error detection task, compared with reading comprehension, was neither natural nor easy to do while reading the texts in the Gollasch (1980) and Xu (1998) studies. Yet, the results support the universality of Goodman's (1996) theory of reading:

> Because our perceptions are so strongly influenced by our expectations, we may have a strong sense that we saw something different from what we actually saw. But unless we have some problem with making sense of the text, we are unlikely to know that our perceptions don't match reality. (p. 97)

Both Gollasch and Xu conclude from their experimental studies that reading is a meaning-construction process for all readers at various ages and who read different languages and different orthographies. Although readers who are asked to search for errors in reading detect more errors than readers asked to read to solve a problem, both groups read for meaning and are able to talk about the meanings of what they read. In this way, Gollasch and Xu's experimental studies give support to the universality of Goodman's transactional sociopsycholinguistic reading model for reading in both English and Chinese.

Reading in both languages demonstrates the ways readers make use of the language cueing systems simultaneously. The brain, as a result of the reader's search for meaning, predicts what it expects to find in a particular text based on the reader's knowledge of language and level of sophistication in using reading strategies. Perception based on knowledge is at the heart of reading.

The results from these studies support our view that reading instruction based on the word recognition model underestimates and ignores the significance of the role of context, syntax, flexible use of reading strategies, and the transaction between the reader and the writer's text. The issue of accuracy is overrated in such reading instruction, and the concept of word or character recognition is promoted. Reading becomes an end in itself, set aside from the world of literacy through worksheets and direct instruction.

As readers become engaged in a text, they bring their own knowledge about the world to the reading experience. This is what Freire and Macedo (1987) help us understand in their powerful metaphor of "reading the word and the world." Classroom teachers should encourage students to utilize various aspects of their lives and backgrounds to construct meaning of what they read.

The studies we have examined not only support the transactional view of the reading process but also suggest that engaging readers and preservice and in-service teachers in reading experiences with similar passages provides them with opportunities for rich discussions about the reading process. Using a short story with carefully selected embedded errors gives readers with a range of backgrounds the opportunity to verify the reality of the reading process. The text is contrived to highlight readers' responses, and the manipulation of the text is done to reveal the underlying process of meaning construction. It involves readers in a real act of reading in a situation that does not control the reader's response. Through the opportunity to discuss active reading, readers often come to conclusions similar to those of Ken Goodman's:

> Simply stated, the common sense notion I seek here to refute is this: "Reading is a precise process. It involves exact, detailed, sequential perception and identification of letters, words, spelling patterns and large language units." … In place of this misconception, I offer this: reading is a selective process. It involves partial use of available minimal language cues selected from perceptual input on the basis of the reader's expectation. As this partial information is processed, tentative decisions are made to be confirmed, rejected, or refined as reading progresses. (1967, p. 126)

References

Freire, P., & Macedo, D. (1987). *Literacy: Reading the word and the world.* South Hadley, MA: Bergin and Garvey.

Gollasch, F. (1980). *Readers' perception in detecting and processing embedded errors in meaningful text.* Unpublished doctoral dissertation, University of Arizona, Tucson.

Goodman, K. (1967). Reading: A psycholinguistic guessing game, *Journal of the Reading Specialist, 6,* 126–135.

Goodman, K. (1996). *On reading: A common-sense look at the nature of language and the science of reading.* Portsmouth, NH: Heinemann.

Paulson, E. J., & Freeman, A. E. (2003). *Insight from the eyes: The science of effective reading instruction.* Portsmouth, NH: Heinemann.

Wu, Y. J. (1993). Zhu Er went hunting. *Folk Literature, 9*(4), 153–155.

Xu, J. (1998). *A study of the reading process in Chinese through detecting errors in a meaningful text.* Unpublished doctoral dissertation, University of Arizona, Tucson.

INTRODUCTION TO CHAPTER 10

*T*HIS CHAPTER REPORTS WANG'S analysis of the miscues of her second-year American students reading a story in Chinese. She used the methodology—miscue analysis—that I developed in miscue research in English that is consistent with scientific realism. Her intent is to see whether the theory of the reading process built on that research also explains reading in Chinese. She concludes that it does:

> As suggested by K. Goodman (1994, 1996, 2003), reading is a transactional sociopsycholinguistic process by which readers make use of the language cueing systems, their existing linguistic and conceptual schemata, and a variety of strategies to get to meaning. Regardless of differences in orthography and grammatical patterns and rules, each written language carries information at three levels (graphophonic, lexico-grammatical, and semantic-pragmatic) to help readers make sense of it. Due to its social-cultural and psycholinguistic nature, the reading process is much the same for all languages, with minor variations to accommodate the specific characteristics of the language.

This is an excellent example of how a theory built on scientific examination of the structures and processes of one aspect of reality can be expanded to include a related aspect. So, the theory of reading English shows the same structures and processes at work in Chinese. Wang is able to refine the theory of reading so that is consistent with the characteristics of the Chinese language and its writing systems (discussed in Chapter 8) and the reading of her students. And, she modifies miscue analysis to fit the character-based nature of Chinese writing and the differences in syntax between Indo-European languages and Chinese. The miscues her readers produce provide actual evidence (as scientific realists would describe it) of the readers' transactions with the text. She interprets their miscues in light of the theory and of the features of Chinese writing to which they are responding. An example is that readers of English sometimes produce "nonwords" based on attempts to sound out words based on how they are spelled. Her readers of Chinese produce no nonword miscues because there is no way to produce an artificial Chinese word from the components of the character.

Wang's study has made a major contribution to understanding reading in Chinese. At the same time, it is has expanded and refined the transactional theory of the reading process.

Ken Goodman

10

MAKING SENSE OF WRITTEN CHINESE
A Study of L2 Chinese Readers' Miscues

Shaomei Wang and Yetta Goodman

*I*N THE PAST FEW years, a great deal of research has been undertaken to examine Chinese readers' reading behavior (Chen, Anderson, Li, Hao, Wu, & Shu, 2004; Huang & Wang, 1992; Li, Anderson, Nagy, & Zhang, 2002; Perfetti & Zhang, 1995; Shu & Anderson, 1999; Taylor, 2002). These studies have predominantly focused on the lexical processing in relation to character recognition, such as the role of phonological and visual-orthographic information in character identification and the orthographic effect on character recognition. However, there is a dearth of research on the analysis of the Chinese reading process, the actual way readers transact with an authentic written Chinese text to make sense of it.

Shaomei Wang conducted a study to explore the nature of Chinese reading in relation to Ken Goodman's transactional sociopsycholinguistic model and theory of reading (1996, 2003, 2004). By means of miscue analysis, she examined the oral reading of a Chinese text by 12 American adults, using the Wang Taxonomy of Chinese Reading Miscues adapted for the study by Wang from the Goodman Taxonomy of Reading Miscues (Goodman & Burke, 1973).

We present and discuss the following issues in this chapter: (a) All readers of different writing systems construct meaning, making use of cues from graphophonic (or graphomorphemic), lexico-grammatical, and semantic-pragmatic levels of language; (b) the selection of linguistic cues and use of reading strategies vary to different degrees as required by the writing system; and (c) readers of Chinese have a stronger reliance on the syntactic and semantic context cues than on the graphic and phonemic cues, which is demanded by the "highly semantic" characteristic of the Chinese writing system.

Data Collection

The subjects in this study are 12 undergraduate students enrolled in a second-year Chinese language course at a large Western university. They are all young adults, native English speakers who have studied Chinese as a second language for three and a half semesters. Five of them are of Chinese heritage, and 7 are of European backgrounds. To facilitate comparison, all the readers read the same Chinese story that they had not read before, 金斧头 ("Jinfutou," "A Gold Axe," a total of 653 characters) from *Stories in Modern Chinese* (Wang, 1978).* We selected this reading material based on the length and approximate difficulty.

Following Reading Miscue Inventory procedures (Goodman, Watson, & Burke, 2005), each tape-recorded data collection session is comprised of an interview, an uninterrupted reading of a whole real text, and a retelling. All the reading interviews in this study were conducted in English, with the assumption that readers are more comfortable in sharing their reading experiences in their native language. The interview questions are adopted from the Burke Interview Modified for Older Readers (BIMOR) (Burke, 2005) with slight modifications. The oral reading starts after the interview. Following the reading, readers retell the story orally in their own words. Because L2 readers sometimes comprehend much more of what they read in the L2 than what they can express in the L2 (Goodman, Goodman, & Flores, 1979), the retelling is done in either English or Chinese, depending on each reader's preference.

The Wang Chinese Taxonomy of Reading Miscues

The Goodman Taxonomy was originally developed for the analysis of miscues generated by readers in English. As a diagnostic and evaluative tool, it provides researchers with much information about the reading process. Since 1967, hundreds of miscue studies have used the Goodman Taxonomy to study readers with wide ranges of abilities and cultural and linguistic backgrounds (Brown, Goodman, & Marek, 1996). Most of these studies do not require modifications to the Goodman Taxonomy because they are dealing with languages that share an alphabetic system similar to English. Chinese, as a logographic language, differs greatly from English in many aspects, such as graphs, sounds, syntactic structures, and so forth. Therefore, a number of modifications are needed to make the Goodman Taxonomy more applicable to reading in Chinese.

---

* There are several versions of the folk story "A Gold Axe" in Chinese literature. The version used in this study is reproduced based on Appendix "Jinfutou" in Sergent (1990).

While coding the Chinese reading miscues produced by the readers in this study, Wang developed the Chinese Taxonomy of Reading Miscues for analysis of Chinese reading, building on the Goodman Taxonomy of Reading Miscues. The following is a summary of several major modifications.

First, characters are considered as the coding unit for graphic and phonemic proximity rather than words because characters are the smallest free-occurring unit in Chinese. Second, the *clause*, defined as the Theme-Rheme structure by Fang, McDonald, and Cheng (1995), is used as the coding unit for syntactic and semantic acceptability in consideration of the fact that the Chinese sentence differs greatly from the English sentence in both grammatical levels and inner structures (Chu, 1998). Finally, to accommodate the features of the Chinese writing system, Wang added to, modified, or deleted some miscue categories from the Goodman Taxonomy (see the appendix); these categories are described in the Data Analysis section.

General Findings

Using the Wang Taxonomy, a total of 643 miscues produced by the readers were coded in this study. The readers' miscues per hundred characters (MPHC) ranged from 3.5 to 11, and their comprehension or retelling scores ranged from a low of 31% to a high of 98%. When comprehension scores are compared to MPHC, a slight trend emerges: As MPHC increases, there tends to be a decrease in comprehension. Of the total miscues counted, 80% are substitutions, 13% are omissions, and 1% are reversals. Insertions and complex miscues are each 3% of the miscues among all the readers. When comprehension scores are taken into consideration, there is no correlation between the miscue types and reading proficiency.

The fact that Chinese readers make miscues as do readers of alphabetic languages is itself an important finding of this study. The data show that Chinese reading is no more or less accurate than English reading; Chinese readers make miscues like readers of other written languages and in similar proportions. In the following sections, we present general miscue patterns evidenced in our data.

Graphic Proximity and Phonemic Proximity

Graphic proximity and phonemic proximity measure the graphic and sound similarity between a substitution and the expected response (ER) at the character level. As illustrated in Table 10.1, of the miscues coded under

Table 10.1 Graphic and Phonemic Proximity of Character-Level Substitution Miscues

	Graphic Proximity, %				Phonemic Proximity, %				
								Homophone	
								Different Tones	Same Tone
	No	Some	High	Homograph	No	Some	High		
All	48	30	14	8	70	18	6	3	2
Group 1	62	27	5	5	74	16	5	3	1
Group 2	37	33	22	8	72	19	7	1	1

graphic proximity, 48% have no graphic similarity, and 30% show some graphic similarity; 14% show high graphic similarity to the ERs.

The percentages of phonemic proximity for the miscues coded under this category follow a similar pattern: 70% for no similarity, 18% for some similarity, and 6% for high similarity. Overall, the phonemic mean is consistently lower than the graphic mean. This indicates that the readers have stronger reliance on the graphic cues than on the phonemic ones because reading begins with the readers responding to graphic symbols and because Chinese characters do not represent sounds in any consistent way.

To understand the effect that level of proficiency has on the use of language cueing systems, we divided the readers into two groups of six according to their comprehension or retelling scores. The comprehension means for Groups 1 and 2 are 91% and 44%, respectively. Table 10.1 summarizes the mean percentages of graphic and phonemic proximity of the miscues produced by the two groups. The findings show a definite pattern: Group 2 has higher graphic and sound similarity than Group 1. This suggests that the readers with lower comprehension scores have stronger reliance on the graphic and sound cues than the readers with higher comprehension scores. The result is consistent with the finding on English readers that when proficiency, as indicated by retellings, increases, the reliance on the graphic and phonemic cueing systems decreases (Devine, 1981).

Syntactic Acceptability and Semantic Acceptability

Syntactic and semantic acceptability are concerned with whether a miscue that occurs in a structure is syntactically or semantically acceptable in the reading of the whole text and in the reader's dialect. All the readers in this study produced some proportion of syntactically and semantically acceptable miscues, although their abilities vary. Of all miscues produced by 12 readers, 40% are syntactically acceptable, and 23% are semantically acceptable within the whole text (see Table 10.2).

Table 10.2   Syntactic and Semantic Acceptability

	Completely Unacceptable	Acceptable With the Prior Portion	Acceptability With the Following Portion	Acceptable Within the Clause	Acceptable Within the Clause Complex	Acceptable Within the Whole Text
Syntactic Acceptability, %						
All	36	16	5	3	0	40
Group 1	23	12	4	4	0	57
Group 2	50	19	5	3	1	22
Semantic Acceptability, %						
All	38	16	5	11	8	23
Group 1	24	14	4	13	10	35
Group 2	51	19	5	8	5	11

Because semantic acceptability is not coded higher than syntactic acceptability in miscue studies, it is reasonable that the readers have higher syntactic acceptability than semantic acceptability. Table 10.2 also shows that Group 1 (the more proficient readers) has slightly higher syntactic and semantic acceptability than Group 2 (the less-proficient readers). This suggests that the degree of syntactic and semantic acceptability is linked to reading proficiency. The results offered here have also been found in research on readers of English; as readers improve their proficiency, they move toward greater and more stable semantic and syntactic acceptability of miscues (Devine, 1981; Goodman & Burke, 1973; Goodman & Goodman, 1978).

Syntactic Change and Semantic Change

Syntactic change and semantic change measure the extent to which the reader's miscue has altered the grammatical structure and meaning of a clause within the context of the entire story. We judge these variables only for miscues that are syntactically or semantically acceptable within the clause, clause complex, or whole text. Table 10.3 summarizes the mean percentages of syntactic change and semantic change of the text.

What Table 10.3 shows is that 83% (changes scored as a minor change, a function word/minor change, or unchanged) of the miscues coded have a similar grammatical function to the ER, and 75% (changes scored as a

Table 10.3 Syntactic Change and Semantic Change

	Syntactic Change, %								Semantic Change, %								
	Unrelated	Single element in Common	Key Element in Common	Major Change in the OR	Minor Change in the OR	Change in Function Word/Minor Change	Unchanged Syntax	Completely Anomalous	Major Anomalies	Changed Key Aspects	Inconsistency With Major Character	Inconsistency With Minor Character	Significant Loss With No Inconsistencies	Change Unimportant Detail	Change in Person/Numeral	Slight Change	No Change
All	4	0	1	12	14	2	67	2	6	2	6	1	2	19	1	14	41
Group 1	0	0	0	11	13	4	72	0	2	1	8	3	4	16	1	12	48
Group 2	7	0	1	13	15	0	63	4	10	3	3	0	0	22	1	16	34

change of unimportant details, a slight change, a change of person/numeral, or unchanged) have a close meaning to the text. Thus, for all the readers in this study, the syntactically and semantically acceptable miscues only slightly alter the structure and meaning of the text.

If a miscue is acceptable, then it is unlikely for it to result in much syntactic or semantic change to the text. In this case, both groups show a high percentage of acceptable miscues causing no syntactic change to the story. Table 10.3 also presents the mean percentages of syntactic and semantic change in the two groups. For Group 1 (the more proficient readers), the mean percentage of miscues causing no syntactic change is 72%, and for Group 2 (the less-proficient readers), the mean reaches 63%. In terms of no semantic change, Group 1 has 48%, and Group 2 has 34%. The results suggest that there is an important relationship between syntactic and semantic change and proficiency.

Correction and Graphic and Phonemic Proximity

Correction is an important part of the reading process because it shows that the reader is aware of miscues that may have disrupted the reading.

The readers in this study did not demonstrate a great tendency to correct their miscues. The mean percentage of correction is 18%, with the lowest level only 4%. The readers' low correction might be tied to silent correction. It is also possible that they just did not see the need to correct a miscue as they may produce a miscue and still make sense of the text. For example, a reader substituted a person's name 诚实 (*chengshi*, honesty) in the story with the English word *Bob* in his reading. Superficially, it seems that he could not articulate the two Chinese characters correctly, but actually he was clear that the Chinese characters represent a boy's name.

To study which cues interact with correction in Chinese reading, we examine the graphic proximity and phonemic proximity of corrected and uncorrected miscues. If the graphic and phonemic cues are important factors in correction, then miscues with no graphic or sound similarity to the ERs would be more likely to be corrected, and high graphic or sound proximity miscues would be less likely to be corrected. However, expectations such as these are not upheld in this study. Table 10.4 shows the graphic proximity of corrected and uncorrected miscues.

As can be seen in Table 10.4, the readers have 17% correction on miscues that have no graphic proximity and 12% correction on miscues that have high graphic proximity to the ER. For phonemic proximity, the readers have 13% correction on no proximity, 44% on some proximity, and 16% on high proximity (see Table 10.5).

Table 10.4 Graphic Proximity and Correction

	No Correction	Correction	Original One Abandoned	Unsuccessful Correction
No Graphic Proximity				
No. of Miscues 110				
%	71	17	0	12
Some Graphic Proximity				
No. of Miscues 34				
%	71	15	0	15
High Graphic Proximity				
No. of Miscues 73				
%	77	12	3	8
Homograph				
No. of Miscues 16				
%	81	6	6	6

Table 10.5   Phonemic Proximity and Correction

	No Correction	Correction	Original One Abandoned	Unsuccessful Correction
No Phonemic Proximity				
Number	182			
%	75	13	0	12
Some Phonemic Proximity				
Number	18			
%	50	44	0	6
High Phonemic Proximity				
Number	44			
%	77	16	5	2
Homophone				
Number	7			
%	72	0	14	14

Taking both the graphic proximity and phonemic proximity of the corrected miscues into consideration, it is clear that the readers in this study do not have great reliance on the graphic and phonemic cues for correction.

Correction and Syntactic and Semantic Acceptability

Because the graphic and phonemic cues are not primary sources of information for correction, the syntactic and semantic cueing systems were examined to determine if they play important roles in correction. As illustrated in Table 10.6, the mean percentages of corrections on syntactically and semantically unacceptable miscues are very low.

Furthermore, the highest correction is not on the miscues that are syntactically or semantically unacceptable, but on those that are acceptable with the following portion of the clause or within the clause (17% each). Thus, there is a notable tendency for the partially syntactically and semantically acceptable miscues to be corrected more often than the unacceptable ones. The factors involved in correction are complex. One possible reason for this phenomenon is that the readers had more control over the meaning of the text in situations in which they made completely or partially acceptable miscues. Another possible reason is tied to the linguistic knowledge of the L2 Chinese readers. In some cases, the sentence produced by the L2 reader is syntactically unacceptable, but the meaning of the sentence may be clear to

Table 10.6 Correction and Syntactic and Semantic Acceptability

	No Correction	Correction	Original One Abandoned	Unsuccessful Correction
Completely Unacceptable				
Syntactic, %	91	5	1	4
Semantic, %	91	5	1	3
Acceptable With the Prior Portion				
Syntactic, %	84	12	0	4
Semantic, %	83	13	0	4
Acceptability With the Following Portion				
Syntactic, %	83	17	0	0
Semantic, %	83	17	0	0
Acceptable Within the Clause				
Syntactic, %	83	17	0	0
Semantic, %	85	9	2	5
Acceptable Within the Clause Complex				
Syntactic, %	50	0	50	0
Semantic, %	71	12	0	17
Acceptable Within the Whole Text				
Syntactic, %	78	11	0	11
Semantic, %	77	11	1	11

the reader or become clearer as meaning construction continues. The results about correction and the cueing systems are similar to the results in other miscue studies on L2 English readers (e.g., Freeman, 1986).

Graphic Proximity and Syntactic and Semantic Acceptability

Table 10.7 summarizes the graphic proximity of both syntactically and semantically acceptable and unacceptable substitution miscues. It shows that 46% of no graphic proximity, 33% of some graphic proximity, and 31% of high graphic proximity miscues are syntactically acceptable within the story. Because of the close relationship between syntactic acceptability and semantic acceptability, it is not surprising that graphic proximity is related to both in similar fashion. For semantic acceptability, 24% of no graphic proximity, 6% of some graphic proximity, and 4% of high graphic proximity miscues are

Table 10.7   Graphic Proximity and Syntactic and Semantic Acceptability

	Completely Unacceptable	Acceptable Within the Prior Portion	Acceptability Within the Following Portion	Acceptable Within the Clause	Acceptable Within the Clause Complex	Acceptable Within the Whole Text
No Graphic Proximity						
Syntactic, %	27	19	3	5	0	46
Semantic, %	29	19	3	19	7	24
Some Graphic Proximity						
Syntactic, %	25	33	6	3	0	33
Semantic, %	28	31	6	11	19	6
High Graphic Proximity						
Syntactic, %	43	13	7	3	1	31
Semantic, %	46	15	7	10	16	4
Homograph						
Syntactic, %	93	7	0	0	0	0
Semantic, %	93	7	0	0	0	0

completely acceptable within the story. This indicates that high graphic similarity miscues are more likely to be syntactically unacceptable within the
structure than are low graphic similarity miscues because heavily focusing
on the graphic and phonemic cues is disruptive to reading comprehension.

The results presented here are consistent with Devine's (1981) study of
L2 English readers: The lower the graphic proximity is, the higher the syntactic and semantic acceptability will be. However, they differ from those
described in Tien's (1983) study of L1 Chinese readers. Tien suggests that
the miscues sharing high graphic similarity with the ERs tend to have high
semantic acceptability scores among the readers in her study. Because Tien
does not explicitly state which criterion was used to judge graphic similarity,
it is difficult to make any comparison here.

To summarize, there are six general findings in this study:

1. There is a tendency that indicates that the higher the MPHC is, the
    lower the comprehension scores will be, but no individual judg-
    ment can be based on general tendencies.
2. There is no clear relationship between miscue types and reading
    proficiency.

3. The phonemic similarity mean is consistently lower than the graphic similarity mean, and the difference is strong.
4. The group with higher comprehension scores has higher syntactic and semantic acceptability than the group with lower comprehension scores.
5. The readers have a tendency to correct miscues that are syntactically or semantically acceptable with the following portion of the clause or within the story.
6. The higher the graphic similarity is, the lower the syntactic and semantic acceptability scores will be.

Therefore, we conclude that, similar to miscue studies of readers of other languages, readers of Chinese are active language users who make use of their knowledge of the language cueing systems, as well as a variety of strategies, to construct meaning. They do not process what they read in a linear fashion, character by character. Instead, they select from the input the eyes provide, predict what is coming, confirm/disconfirm their prediction, and focus on language units that are larger than individual characters in the reading. Despite the differences in the writing systems, there is no significant difference between the reading process in Chinese and in other languages.

Findings Related to Language-Specific Effects on Reading in Chinese

The analyses suggest that the general miscue patterns of the readers in this study are strikingly similar to those of English readers in other miscue studies (Brown et al., 1996). In addition, the data show distinct differences between the L2 Chinese readers and the English readers in terms of the selection of reading strategies and linguistic cues. In the following sections, we discuss several interesting linguistic constraints on reading in Chinese.

Absence of Nonsense Character Substitutions

When a reader of English produces a miscue that is not recognizable as a known word in the language of the reader, the miscue is identified as a non-word substitution. Accordingly, in Chinese, miscues that are not recognizable as known characters could be called nonsense character substitutions. During the data collection process, we encountered a couple of instances when we were not clear which character the readers were intending to produce as the articulation could correspond to a couple of different characters. However, nonsense character substitutions did not occur in any reader's reading in this study. The reason for this is clearly expressed in one subject's explanation of the differences in his reading of Chinese and English texts: "If I don't know a word in English, I still can say it in English. But for Chinese, if I don't know a character, I don't know how to pronounce it."

Here, the reader actually points out one important characteristic of Chinese; that is, the language does not have a script-sound correspondence. For this reason, it has been suggested that each Chinese character represents a semantic unit and can be considered as a logograph.

The lack of correspondence between print and speech in Chinese raises an interesting question: How do Chinese readers cope with unfamiliar characters in their reading? Our data show some common strategies used by readers when they could not assign "conventional" pronunciations to the characters. For instance, sometimes the readers read aloud a component of a character as the derived character. At other times, they read a character as another one that shares the same component. A listener who does not share the same strategies as these readers might simply classify these types of miscues as nonsense characters. However, examining these miscues closely makes clear the readers' concern for constructing meaning and the influence of context in the reading process. The following excerpt from a subject's reading of the story "A Gold Axe" illustrates this point clearly:*

> 成 something. (The reader said, "Maybe shi or something. It looks like shi.")

0101 从前有个孩子　叫　诚　实，

0102 在地主张有金家做小工，

> 这个人

0103 有一天，诚实　上山去 砍柴，

> something.

0104 把斧头　掉　到河里去了，

---

* The English translation of the excerpt is provided here (it is deliberately literal to reflect the grammatical style of the original sentence). 0101: Once upon a time there was a boy called Chengshi (the name means "honesty"). 0102: He worked for his boss Zhang Youjin (the name means "having money"). 0103: One day Chengshi went to a mountain to cut trees. 0104: He accidentally dropped his axe into a river. 0105: Chengshi lost his axe and couldn't do his work.

这个孩子　*verb*　　　　　*do his work*

0105 诚实　　掉　了斧头不能上山　砍柴　了。

In the text, the character compound 诚实 (*chengshi*, honesty/a name) occurs three times (0101, 0103, and 0105). In the first instance, the reader substituted 诚 (*cheng*, sincerely) with 成 (*cheng*, become) and 实 (*shi*, truly) with "something," respectively. After reading the compound, she self-corrected, "Maybe *shi* or something. It looks like *shi*." Apparently, from the reader's think-aloud protocol we can see her active interaction with the text. Here, the observed response (OR) 成 is the phonetic component of the ER 诚, and the OR "something" is an English placeholder. The reader read the same compound as 这个人 (*zhe ge ren*, this person) in Line 0103 and substituted it with 这个孩子 (*zhe ge hai zi*, this child) in Line 0105. Although the reader did not know how to pronounce the two characters in the compound, she learned from the context that the compound refers to a person. Her second and third miscues on the compound not only are syntactically acceptable but also are semantically acceptable within the context of the story.

From the perspective of a traditional view of reading, the reader seemed to have great difficulty reading the passage as she could not pronounce the characters "correctly," and her Chinese reading process was "interrupted" by her native language. In a meaning-centered view, however, the reader was making sense of the text and learning from the text, and she was doing so quite successfully. She demonstrated effective use of strategies to deal with unfamiliar characters rather than simply producing nonsense character substitutions for them.

Another category of miscues that occurred in our data is the code-switched form. For instance, one reader read the character 神 (*shen*, God) as "kami" (a Japanese pronunciation of the character) when he encountered it the first time. The second time he saw it, he substituted it with "God" in English. When asked why he read the character as "kami," he explained that he learned the character in Japanese, but he did not know how to say it in Chinese. This case is similar to different Chinese dialect speakers' readings of the same Chinese text, in which characters are articulated differently in various dialects, but the meanings of the characters are shared by the speakers of different dialects. Although Chinese oral dialects differ dramatically from one another, they all share the same written language (see Wang & Goodman, chapter 8, this volume). This phenomenon has become a great unifying power, contributing to cultural continuity and cohesion. In this sense, the "unconventional" pronunciation of a character should never be considered as an indication of meaning loss without a careful analysis of the influence of the miscues on the comprehension of the text.

Low Graphic and Phonemic Similarity

As described, of the character-level substitutions, 48% show no graphic similarity to the ERs, and 70% have no sound similarity (see Table 10.1). Taking the readers' Chinese proficiency and the difficulty of the story into consideration, their high percentages of no graphic similarity and no sound similarity are truly noticeable. When the results are compared with the results of research on readers of L1 Chinese and readers of L1 and L2 English, differences between readers of Chinese and readers of English become apparent.

Tien (1983) examined the oral reading miscues of 10 highly proficient adult L1 Chinese readers as they read a short Chinese novel. Her study shows that the L1 Chinese readers produce 62.8% of miscues with no graphic similarity and 79.6% of miscues with no phonemic similarity to the words in the text. By comparison, it is obvious that both the L1 and L2 readers of Chinese have a large proportion of miscues that have no graphic or sound similarity to the ERs, although in the case of the L1 readers this tendency is higher. Because the first language of these subjects is English, they tend to rely more on the graphic and sound cues than the L1 Chinese readers do.

Goodman and Burke (1973) investigated the oral reading miscues of 94 American children with different language proficiencies. The results show that the percentages of no graphic and no phonemic similarity for the high proficient group are 10.8% and 18.0%, respectively. Devine's (1981) study of 14 L2 English readers presents a similar pattern to Goodman and Burke's: 1.3% for no graphic similarity and 8% for no phonemic similarity (high proficient group).

A comparison of these numbers illustrates the fact that the Chinese readers and English readers in all the studies we compare have similar miscue patterns in their use of the graphic and phonemic cueing systems. For example, the percentage of no graphic similarity is lower than the percentage of no phonemic similarity, and the percentages of no graphic and phonemic similarity for the proficient readers are higher than those for less-proficient readers. More important, the results also reveal that the L1 and L2 Chinese readers have a much lower degree of graphic and phonemic similarity than the L1 and L2 English readers do. This shows that, in general, readers of Chinese make less use of the graphic and phonemic cues than the syntactic and semantic cues, which is a result of differences in the orthographies.

No Notable Relationship Between Phonemic Similarity and Proficiency

The two groups of readers with different comprehension scores in this study produced almost the same proportion of miscues that have no phonemic proximity to the ERs. Their differences in some similarity and high similarity are also slight. In Tien's (1983) study, the percentage of no sound similarity for adult L1 Chinese readers is 76.9%, which is only slightly higher than that for the L2 readers in the present study. Considering their varied language backgrounds, the L1 and L2 groups' slight differences in the use of the phonemic cues is negligible. According to miscue research on readers of alphabetic languages (Goodman & Burke, 1973), proficient readers have a lower phonemic mean than less-proficient readers because they rely less on the phonemic cues than the latter. However, our findings show that the readers' miscues in this study do not follow this pattern in the same way readers of alphabetic readers do. We believe that the reason lies in the meaning-based characteristic of Chinese characters.

Every written script is a combination of graph, sound, syntax, and meaning. However, for social, historical, and cultural reasons, Chinese characters are more semantically based than phonologically grounded. To ensure cultural continuity and social unification and to cope with the dramatic phonological variations in Chinese dialects, Chinese characters have to be highly semantic, rather than phonological, to allow users to make sense of them over time and space (Gong, 2002; He, 2000). In this sense, Chinese characters do not represent sound as directly as letters in alphabetic languages do and thus require readers to focus more on cues other than the phonemic cues in the reading process.

To stress this point more clearly, we now discuss a type of miscue that is related to the phonetic component of a semantic-phonetic compound character. In Chinese, more than 80% of the characters are formed by a semantic component and a phonetic component. Traditionally, the radical, or semantic component, gives a rough indication of the meaning of a character, and the phonetic component serves as a sound indicator. For instance, in the character 妈 (*ma*, mom), the left component 女 (*nü*, woman) suggests that the character is "female"-related; the right component 马 (*ma*, horse) suggests the sound of the character. Although 80% of the semantic components still have the function of signifying the general meaning of the derived characters, more than 60% of the phonetic components have lost their original function to a large extent because of the historical changes of sounds in Chinese (Gong, 2002).

When readers of Chinese encounter an unfamiliar character, a common strategy they use is to substitute the whole character with its phonetic part or pronounce one character as another that shares the same phonetic component. For example, a reader in this study substituted 诚 (*cheng*, sincerely) with 城 (*cheng*, city), a character that shares the same phonetic component 成 (*cheng*, become). Miscues such as these have led some researchers to argue that phonological recoding is involved in reading Chinese because Chinese readers can make successful guesses concerning how to pronounce a character based on its phonetic component (Tzeng, 2002).

To examine the phonetic myth of characters, we looked at the sound similarity of all the phonetic component-related miscues produced by the readers. The results show that, of the 35 phonetic component-related miscues, only 12% are homophones of the ERs. If tones are considered as well, then only 6% have exactly the same pronunciation as the ERs. The results show that the majority of the phonetic component-related miscues do not share the same sound as the derived characters. Hence, the reader's reliance on the phonemic cueing system should not be exaggerated in the discussion of Chinese reading.

On the other hand, even if a reader articulates a character correctly through its phonetic component, it does not necessarily indicate that the reader has constructed the meaning of the character. In our data, 63% of the cases show that the phonetic-driven miscues are completely syntactically unacceptable, and that 69% of the miscues are completely semantically unacceptable within the text. These results indicate that focusing on the sounds of characters is actually disruptive to reading comprehension, and the ability to read a character correctly is not an indication of the ability to successfully construct the meaning of it.

High Syntactic and Semantic Acceptability of Radical-Related Miscues

The term *radical-driven miscue* refers to a miscue that is the radical or semantic component of the ER or shares the same radical with the ER. For example, the miscue 鱼 (*yü*, fish) is the semantic component of the ER 鲤 (*li*, carp) and thus is considered a radical-related miscue. As mentioned, the semantic part of a character conveys the meaning of the character to a great extent. Gong's (2002) study suggests that, in modern Chinese, approximately 87% of the semantic components signify the meaning of the derived characters. To see how reliable the radicals are in Chinese reading, we examine the syntactic and semantic acceptability of the radical-related miscues produced by the readers in this study. The results show that, of a total of 33 miscues related to the radicals of the ERs, 52% are syntactically and semantically acceptable within the clause, clause complex, or whole text, and 12% are syntactically and semantically acceptable with the prior or following portion of the clause.

So, the Chinese script itself provides important cues for readers to make sense of it. However, this does not say that the readers achieve comprehension solely through the radicals. Actually, without the context, the readers are not able to make sense of unfamiliar characters even if they know the radicals. Here is an example to illustrate this point:. A reader substituted 河 (*he,* river) with 湖 (*hu,* lake), a character that shares the same "water" radical with the ER, in his reading. In Chinese, hundreds of characters contain the radical 氵 and are semantically related to "water." The question arising here is why the reader read the target character as 湖 but not as any one of the others with the same radical in his vocabulary. The reader answered, "At the beginning of the paragraph, it was mentioned that the boy went to a mountain to do something. If there is a mountain, probably there is a lake. So I guess that character is 'lake.'" And I know that radical means 'water' and that character is a noun."

This example strongly suggests that the semantic component of a character does help a reader gain some clues to the meaning, but meaning construction is more successfully accomplished in context. As suggested by Goodman (1996), "In the process of making sense of print, *we* decide what the words are, using not only their graphophonic characteristics (what they look and might sound like), but also a full set of syntactic cues and a full semantic setting" (p. 102).

High Percentage of Miscues Related to Context Cues

To better understand the dynamics of substitution miscues, we examine a total of 209 character-level substitutions categorized as graphic alternatives.* Unlike graphic similarity, which measures how much the miscue looks like the ER, graphic alternatives are concerned with the relationship between the miscue and the ER from the perspectives of the formation of characters and "character compounds" (Xu, 2001).

Specifically, Subcategory 1 of graphic alternatives deals with the cases in which both the ER and OR are noncomprised characters. Subcategories 2–7 register those involving semantic-phonetic compound characters (see Table 10.8). For illustration, both 成 (*cheng,* become) and 湖 (*hu,* lake) should be coded under these subcategories. The reasons are that (1) 成 is the phonetic component of the character 诚, which is comprised of a semantic part 讠 and a phonetic part 成; and (2) 湖 (*hu,* lake) shares the same semantic component 氵 with the ER 河 (*he,* lake).

---

* Subcategories 2, 3, 6, 7, 9, and 10 under graphic alternative are similar to the six error types (phonetic-derivation, phonetic analogy, radical-related, word-related, and semantic-related errors) listed in the error-classification system in Ho and Bryant's (1997) and Ho and Ma's (1999) studies. The difference is that Subcategories 9 and 10 in graphic alternative deal with both noncomprised and comprised characters, but the word-related and semantic-related types in the error-classification system are only for semantic-phonetic comprised characters.

Subcategories 8 and 9 are set up for the cases involving character compounds. Take the following miscue as an example:

OR 由　　(1)

ER 于是他快乐地唱着歌回家了。

The character 于 (*yu*) was read as 由 (*you*). Although the OR 由 is not syntactically and semantically acceptable within the sentence, it is one constituent of the character compound 由于 (*youyu*, because). The ER 于 is the other constituent. In this case, the OR 由 is neither syntactically nor semantically acceptable within the sentence, but it is related to the ER through the character compound 由于.

Subcategory 10 is also concerned with the case involving character compounds. However, the miscue coded under this subcategory not only is one constituent of a character compound, of which the ER is the other, but also is a synonym of the ER.

OR　　　　音 (2)

ER 他的哭声

In the case of Example 2, the OR 音 (*yin*, sound) and the ER 声 (*sheng*, sound), which are two synonyms, are compounded to form the character compound 声音 (*shengyin*, sound). In other words, the miscue not only is related to the ER through the character compound 声音 but also is syntactically and semantically acceptable within the sentence.

In Subcategories 11, 12, and 13, the ER is read either as the OR in a character compound or as a structure in which the characters preceding, following, or surrounding the ER are the constituent characters of the compound or structure:

OR　好　　(3)

ER 最后他的

In Example 3, the OR 好 (*hao*, good) is one constituent of the character compound 最好 (*zuihao*, would better), and the character preceding the ER 后 (*hou*, behind) is the other constituent. In this case, the OR is syntactically and semantically acceptable within the sentence.

Table 10.8 provides the number and percentage of miscues for each subcategory coded under graphic alternative. Among those miscues driven by

Table 10.8 Number and Percentage of Miscues Involving Graphic Alternatives

Subcategory	1	2	3	4	5	6	7	8	9	10	11	12	13	14
Number	26	12	7	7	2	16	24	6	7	1	13	30	37	21
%	12	6	3	3	0	8	11	3	3	0	6	14	18	10

Note: Subcategories are described as follows:

1. The OR and ER share the key unit and configuration (both the ER and OR are noncomprised characters).

2. The OR is the phonetic component of the ER, or the OR is a part of the phonetic component of the ER.

3. The OR is the semantic component of the ER, or the OR is part of the semantic component of the ER.

4. The ER is the phonetic component of the OR.

5. The ER is the semantic component of the OR.

6. The OR has the identical or a similar phonetic component to the ER.

7. The OR has the identical or a similar semantic component to the ER.

8. The ER is read as the other character in a character compound in which the ER is the homograph of one of the constituent characters of the compound.

9. The ER is read as the other character in a character compound in which the ER is one of the constituent characters of the compound.

10. The ER is one constituent of a character compound in which the OR is the other. Also, the ER is the synonym of the OR.

11. The OR is one constituent of a character compound in which the character preceding the ER is the other constituent.

12. The OR is one constituent of a character compound in which the character following the ER is the other constituent.

13. The ER is read as the OR in a structure in which the character(s) preceding, following, or surrounding the ER is/are the constituent character(s) of the structure.

14. Others.

the phonetic or semantic component of the ER, 35 are either the phonetic component of the ER or share the same phonetic component with the ER (Subcategories 2, 4, and 6), and 33 are either related to the semantic component of the ER or share the same semantic component with the ER (Subcategories 3, 5, and 7). Of these 68 miscues, the most frequently produced are those sharing the same semantic component with the ER (11%).

Table 10.8 also shows that 6% of the miscues are related to the ER through character compounds (Subcategories 8 and 9), and 38% are mostly driven by the syntactic and semantic contexts of the sentence (Subcategories 10–13). Although the miscues coded under Subcategories 8 and 9 are neither syntactically nor semantically acceptable within the sentence, they definitely reflect the readers' concerns for the meaning of the ER.

A reader usually makes use of the three cueing systems simultaneously during the reading process, so it is problematic to say that a miscue is solely driven by one of the linguistic cues of language. However, readers are likely to focus more on some cues than on others at specific moments during the reading process. Under graphic alternatives, the readers produced the highest percentage of miscues that are mainly driven by the syntactic and semantic context cues of the text (38%). The data illustrate that the syntactic and semantic contexts are crucial for the perception and interpretation of language. Considering their first language backgrounds, the readers' high reliance on the syntactic and semantic cueing systems is truly remarkable.

The phenomenon demonstrates that Chinese readers do focus more on larger language units than individual characters in the reading process because "perception and not recognition is the key process involved in making sense in reading" (Goodman, 1996, p. 95). On the other hand, it reveals an important feature of the Chinese language as well as traditional art forms: "essence," "meaning," or "spirit" (意, 神) is more essential than the "form," "format," or "rule" (形, 法). As one system among a set of interrelated semiotic systems (Halliday & Hasan, 1985), the Chinese language is governed to a large extent by considerations of "idea-joining," rather than "form-agreement" (Shen, 1992). For this reason, it is logical that readers of Chinese focus heavily on context cues in the reading process.

Gap Between Meaning Construction and Grammatical Relationship Scores and Comprehension Scores

As suggested in the Reading Miscue Inventory (RMI) In-Depth Procedure (Goodman et al., 2005), meaning construction and grammatical relationship examine the reader's concern for making sense of the text and the reader's ability to integrate concern for producing syntactically and semantically acceptable sentences, respectively. Of all the miscues coded, 63% involve "no meaning loss" or "partial loss," and 41% show the readers' "strength" or "partial strength" for producing sentences that are syntactically and semantically acceptable. The results indicate that readers are capable of constructing the meaning of the text by using the linguistic cues of the language. When comparing each reader's meaning construction and grammatical relationship scores with the reader's comprehension score, we observed that the gap between the variables is considerably wide among all the readers. That is, the percentages of no loss and strength are relatively low even for the readers who had fairly high comprehension scores.

One possible reason for this phenomenon is tied to the correction of miscues. The readers might have corrected some miscues mentally without bothering to correct them in their oral readings, or they corrected miscues as they continued to read. The second reason lies in the limitation of the coding itself. While comparing the reader's meaning with what we infer to be the author's intended meaning, we were introducing our own interpretation of the text as the basis for comparison. Besides, the semantic acceptability score may not completely reflect the readers' proficiency, although it does reflect the comprehending process. The third reason is related to the characteristics of the Chinese writing system, which we discuss in detail next.

No Script-Sound Correspondence As discussed, there is no correspondence between sound and characters in Chinese. In our data, in many instances the readers substitute the English word "something" for characters unfamiliar to them. These substitutions could easily be considered as syntactically and semantically unacceptable miscues. However, their retellings indicate that these characters are not always unknown to them. In many cases, the readers correctly predict the meaning of the unfamiliar characters through the syntactic and semantic contexts and even through the radicals.

No One-to-One Character-Syllable Correspondence Characters and syllables in Chinese do not always have a one-to-one correspondence. Gong's (2002) study points out that, in Chinese, one character has 20 homophones on average, and 8.9% of the characters have more than one pronunciation.

Although the readers in our data sometimes had problems articulating homographs, they were actually clear concerning the meaning and even the function of the homographs. For example, the character 地 has two pronunciations: *di* (ground, land) and *de* (particle). In the story used in this research, 地 (*de*) appears three times. A reader misarticulated 地 (*de*) as 地 (*di*) throughout his reading. However, his retelling shows that he was clear about the meaning of the character. The example shows that even if homographs are a hurdle in oral articulation for readers, they are not necessarily a problem in terms of comprehension. We encountered a similar example while listening to a native adult Chinese reader's reading of the story "A Gold Axe." Just like the L2 reader example in this paragraph, the L1 Chinese reader read every 地 (*de*) in the story as 地 (*di4*) and insisted that he was using the correct pronunciation. Interesting enough, the reader never mispronounced 地 (*de*) as 地 (*di4*) in his daily life oral use of Chinese. In this case, 地 (*de*) is not a miscue. It is really an indication of the reader's idiolect when reading orally.

Influence of the Lexico-Grammatical System   In Chinese, many individual characters can be independently used in texts and can also be combined with other characters to form character compounds. Similar to a generic molecular net, an active character that has strong generative ability can form a group or a clan of new compounds with meanings that are closely related to the meaning of the salient character (Hoosain, 1992; Liu, 1992). In reading, as long as the reader can make sense of the salient character, he or she will probably get the meaning of the whole compound. For example, a reader in this study constructed the meaning of the character compound 河神 (*heshen*, the God of the River) through the salient character 神 (*shen*, God), although he made a semantically unacceptable miscue on 河 (*he*, river).

In many cases, components of a character compound have a close semantic relationship to each other. Thus, readers are able to construct the meaning of a character compound even though they only know one of the characters in the given compound. For example, in the character compound 灾难 (*zainan*, disaster-trouble), the two characters have a high semantic similarity that allows readers to get the meaning of the compound from either of the characters with which they are familiar. They do not need both to develop an appropriate meaning in this segment of the text.

The complexity of the formation of a character compound is also reinforced by reversal compounds. In Chinese, there are a large number of two-character compounds that are formed from the same characters, yet in reverse order. For example, 面前 (*mianqian*, in front of) and 前面 (*qianmian*, in front of) are two compounds that share the same characters and are highly semantically similar. Sometimes, even if a two-character compound sounds unconventional when read in reverse, the reversal is still meaningful to the reader.

Language is pervasively ambiguous and redundant (Goodman, 1996). The Chinese language is no exception. In the reading process, sometimes even if readers produce a miscue that is syntactically unacceptable, they are still able to make sense of the text by using the linguistic redundancies available to them. Take the following sentence as an example:

诚实回答说 … (Chengshi answered...)

In this sentence, the three characters 回 (*hui*, reply), 答 (*da*, answer), and 说 (*shuo*, say) are semantically related to each other. In his reading, one reader omitted the character 答, making the miscue syntactically unacceptable in modern Chinese. However, his retelling revealed that this did not affect his understanding of the clause.

Influence of Tones   In Chinese, tones are used to distinguish meanings of a syllable. For L2 Chinese readers, especially in the case of those whose native languages are not tonal languages, tones often cause problems in their readings. In some cases, L2 readers articulate a character with a different tone because of their incomplete mastery of the pronunciation system of Chinese, which in turn changes the syntax and meaning of the sentence from the listener's perspective. However, this change may not interfere at all with the readers' full comprehension of the sentence.

In the previous sections, we describe some scenarios in which the readers make sense of the text without knowing the correct pronunciation of some of the characters in it. On the other hand, there are some cases for which the readers read characters correctly but cannot make any sense of them. For example, a reader pronounced the compound /ʃʋ̩Ĺ̩ (*xiaoxin*, carefully) with correct pronunciation and tones in his reading, implying that he was clear about the meaning of the compound. However, during the follow-up discussion, he said that the compound did not make sense in the sentence because /ʃʋ̩Ĺ̩ means "little heart" to him (literally, *xiao* means little, and *xin* means heart).

In short, the data offered here strongly indicate that an individual reader's proficiency should not be determined only by oral reading performance. As a matter of fact, "bilingual readers may gain more information than they show in oral reading because they may process the information and correct silently, and they may 'tune into alternative communication systems in their search for meaning, and … seek information from each and every alternative source'" (as cited in Ewoldt, 1977, p. 47).

Conclusions

As suggested by Goodman (1994, 1996, 2003), reading is a transactional sociopsycholinguistic process by which readers make use of the language cueing systems, their existing linguistic and conceptual schemata, and a variety of strategies to obtain to meaning. Regardless of differences in orthography and grammatical patterns and rules, each written language carries information at three levels (graphophonic, lexico-grammatical, and semantic-pragmatic) to help readers make sense of it. Because of its social-cultural and psycholinguistic nature, the reading process is much the same for all languages, with minor variations to accommodate the specific characteristics of the language.

Like other written languages, Chinese texts provide readers with information at different linguistic levels to allow them to construct meaning.

As illustrated in the following excerpt from a subject's reading of the story "A Gold Axe," readers of Chinese make use of the language cueing systems (graphomorphemic, lexico-grammatical, and semantic-pragmatic) simultaneously to transact with texts:

这个孩子

"老先生， 我的斧头掉到河里去了， 我怕主人打我。" 诚实　回答说。

担　　　　　拎

"孩子， 别 伤 心了， 我下去给你 捞 上来。" 老人说完就跳进河里去。*

When reading "孩子，别伤心了" (Child, don't be so sad), the reader articulated it in a passionate way, the way that one might say it to a child who needs care and warmth. Her tone shows that she has understood the relationship between the old man and the child and is aware of the child's pitiful situation. The substitutions of 担心 (worry) for 伤心 (sad) and 拎 (lin, pick up/carry) for 捞 (lao, pick up) show the reader's use of the text features and strategies (e.g., prediction and confirmation) to build up meaning.

As shown in the ways they transact with authentic written Chinese texts, readers of Chinese share great similarities with readers of alphabetic languages. First, all readers of Chinese make miscues. Second, in the reading process, readers of Chinese do not merely focus on accurately and quickly recognizing a string of characters. Instead, they actively make use of the linguistic cues, as well a variety of reading strategies (sampling, prediction, confirming, correction, etc.), to make sense of texts. Finally, in contrast to less-proficient readers who focus more on graphic input, proficient readers rely more on syntactic and semantic cues of language to construct meaning.

At the same time, the three cueing systems in written Chinese suggest that the language activates reading strategies that rely more on context and less on individual characters or character compounds because it is governed to a large extent by considerations of 意 meaning (Shen, 1992). This study reveals that readers of Chinese demonstrate stronger reliance on the syntactic and semantic cues than on the graphic and phonemic cues. Also, they do not make use of the phonemic cues in the same way that readers of alphabetic languages do because there is no direct correspondence between orthography and phonology in Chinese.

---

* Translation of the excerpt is provided here: "Mister, I lost my axe. I am afraid that my boss will beat me," said Chengshi. "Child, don't be so sad. I will go to pick it up for you." The old man jumped into the river after he said this.

In conclusion, this study supports the transactional sociopsycholinguistic theory and model of reading in its claim that the reading process is universal for all languages, and that the purpose of reading is to construct meaning. This study also demonstrates that there are language-specific effects on reading in Chinese regarding the selection of linguistic cues and use of reading strategies.

Appendix: Wang Chinese Taxonomy of Reading Miscues (Short Form)

(1) Correction
(2) Dialect
(3) Graphic proximity
(4) Phonemic proximity
(5) Graphic alternative
(6) Allologs
(7) Retroflex suffix (-*er* suffix)
(8) Code-switched form
(9) Syntactic acceptability
(10) Semantic acceptability
(11) Syntactic change
(12) Semantic change
(13) Segmentation
(14) Tone

References

Brown, J., Goodman, K., & Marek, A. (Eds.). (1996). *Studies in miscue analysis: An annotated bibliography*. Newark, DE: International Reading Association.

Burke, C. L. (2005). The reading interview. In Y. Goodman, D. Watson, & C. Burke (Eds.). *Reading miscue inventory* (pp. 275–276). Katonah, NY: Richard C. Owen.

Chen, X., Anderson, R., Li, W., Hao, M., Wu, X., & Shu, H. (2004). Phonological awareness of bilingual and monolingual Chinese children. *Journal of Education Psychology, 96*, 142–151.

Chu, C. C. (1998). *A discourse grammar of mandarin Chinese*. New York: Lang.

Devine, J. (1981). Developmental patterns in native and non-native reading acquisition. In S. Hudelson (Ed.), *Learning to read in different languages* (pp. 103–114). Washington, DC: Center for Applied Linguistics.

Ewoldt, C. (1977). *A psycholinguistic description of selected deaf children reading in sign language*. Unpublished doctoral dissertation, Wayne State University, Detroit, MI.

Fang, Y., McDonald, E., & M. Cheng. (1995). Subject and theme in Chinese: From clause to discourse. In R. Husan & P. Fries (Eds.), *Subject and theme: A discourse functional perspective* (pp. 235–273). Amsterdam: Benjamins.

Freeman, D. (1986). *Use of pragmatic cohesion cues to resolve degrees of pronoun reference ambiguity in reading*. Unpublished doctoral dissertation, University of Arizona, Tucson.

Gong, J. (2002). 汉字汉语汉文化论集 [Character, language, and culture]. Chengdu, China: Bashushushe.

Goodman, K. (1994). Reading, writing, and written texts: A transactional sociopsycholinguistic view. In A. Flurkey & J. Xu (Eds.), *On the revolution of reading: The selected writings of Kenneth S. Goodman* (pp. 3–45). Portsmouth, NH: Heinemann.

Goodman, K. (1996). *On reading*. Portsmouth, NH: Heinemann.

Goodman, K. (2003). What's universal about the reading process. In A. Flurkey & J. Xu (Eds.), *On the revolution of reading: The selected writings of Kenneth S. Goodman* (pp. 87–93). Portsmouth, NH: Heinemann.

Goodman, K. (2004). Reading , writing, and written texts: A transactional sociopsycholinguistic view. In R. Ruddell & J. Norman (Eds.), *Theoretical models and processes of reading* (5th ed., pp. 1093–1130). Newark, DE: International Reading Association.

Goodman, K., & Burke, C. (1973). *Theoretically based studies of patterns of miscues in oral reading performance, final report*. Detroit, MI: Wayne State University. (Eric Document Reproduction Service No. ED179708).

Goodman, K., & Goodman, Y. (1978). *Reading of American children whose reading is a stable, rural dialect of English or language other than English*. Washington, DC: National Institute of Education, U.S. Department of Health, Education, and Welfare.

Goodman, K., Goodman, Y., & Flores, B. (1979). *Reading in the bilingual classroom: Literacy and biliteracy*. Rosslyn, VA: National Clearinghouse for Bilingual Education.

Goodman, Y., Watson, D., & Burke, C. (2005). *Reading miscue inventory*. Katonah, NY: Richard C. Owen.

Halliday, M. A. K., & Hasan, R. (1985). *Language, context, and text: Aspects of language in the social semiotic perspective*. Victoria, Australia: Deakin University.

He, J. (2000). 汉字文化学 [A sociocultural study on Chinese characters]. Shenyang, China: Liaoning renmin chubanshe.

Ho, C. S.-H., & Bryant, P. (1997). Learning to read Chinese beyond the logographic phase. *Reading Research Quarterly, 32,* 276–290.

Ho, C. S.-H., & Ma, N. L. (1999). Training in phonological strategies improves Chinese dyslexic children's character reading skills. *Journal of Research in Reading, 22,* 131–142.

Hoosain, R. (1992). Psychological reality of the word in Chinese. In H.-C. Chen & O. J. L. Tzeng (Eds.), *Language processing in Chinese* (pp. 111–130). Amsterdam: North-Holland.

Huang, J., & Wang, M. (1992). From unit to gestalt: Perceptual dynamics in recognizing Chinese characters. In H.-C. Chen & O. J. L. Tzeng (Eds.), *Language processing in Chinese* (pp. 3–36). Amsterdam: North-Holland.

Li, W., Anderson, R., Nagy, W., & Zhang, H. (2002). Facets of metalinguistic awareness that contribute to Chinese literacy. In W. Li, J. Gaffiney, & J. L. Packard (Eds.), *Chinese children's reading acquisition* (pp. 87–106). Dordrecht, The Netherlands: Kluwer Academic.

Liu, J. (1992). Bridging language and culture: A cognitive approach to the study of Chinese compounds. *Journal of Chinese Language Teachers' Association, 3,* 1–19.

Perfetti, C., & Zhang, S. (1995). Very early phonological activation in Chinese reading. *Journal of Experimental Psychology, 21,* 24–33.

Sergent, W., Jr. (1990). *A study of the oral reading strategies of advanced and highly advanced second language readers of Chinese.* Unpublished doctoral dissertation, The Ohio State University, Columbus, OH.

Shen, X. (1992). 语文的阐释 [On Chinese]. Shenyang, China: Liaoning jiaoyu chubanshe.

Shu, H., & Anderson, R. C. (1999). Learning to read in Chinese: The development of metalinguistic awareness. In J. Wang, A. W. Inhoff, & H. C. Chen (Eds.), *Reading Chinese script: A cognitive approach* (pp. 1–18). Mahwah, NJ: Erlbaum.

Taylor, I. (2002). Phonological awareness in Chinese reading. In W. Li, J. Gaffiney, & J. L. Packard (Eds.), *Chinese children's reading acquisition* (pp. 39–58). Dordrecht, The Netherlands: Kluwer Academic.

Tien, S. (1983). *Chinese adult readers: A psycholinguistics and transactional study of the reading process in Chinese, with comparison to English.* Unpublished doctoral dissertation, Michigan State University, East Lansing.

Tzeng, O. J. L. (2002). Current issues in learning to read Chinese. In W. Li, J. Gaffiney, & J. L. Packard (Eds.), *Chinese children's reading acquisition* (pp. 3–16). Dordrecht, The Netherlands: Kluwer Academic.

Wang, P. (1978). *Stories in modern Chinese.* San Francisco: East-West.

Xu, T. (2001). 基础语言学教程 [Lectures on linguistics]. Beijing, China: Beijing University Press.

Section Six

STUDIES OF READING
THAT RECONCEPTUALIZE
"ERRORS" AND "FLUENCY"

INTRODUCTION TO CHAPTER 11

*A*MAJOR PROBLEM WITH EXPERIMENTAL research is that it requires control of reality, which leads to research that highly constrains the phenomena it studies. In reading, that has meant designing studies that involve readers responding to small pieces of language: letters, sounds, syllables, and words. Even when the study involves connected texts, the texts are often artificial and minimal to avoid too many uncontrolled variables. This leads to minitheories that fit the findings of such reductionist research. Particularly, it has led to a dominant paradigm of reading as involving accurate rapid identification of words.

More than a century of research on eye movements has produced a remarkably consistent understanding of the eye as an optical instrument with a lens that must stop and focus to provide useful visual information to the brain. Only a few letters in a text are in sharp focus, although the visual field includes areas of fuzzy input. Eye-movement research has sought to explore and explain where and why the reader looks at different aspects of the text.

The underlying question in eye-movement research has usually been an example of the type of questions scientific realism generates: What does the eye do during reading? What structures and processes can we understand from observing the movements of the eye during reading? And, the findings must be integrated into a more general theory of how readers make sense of print, as is the focus of my transactional model of reading.

In this study, Eric Paulson employs the eye movement/miscue analysis research tool that he developed to examine visual causes of miscues — whether miscues are a result of faulty eye movements, like skipping the miscued word or not looking at it for a long enough period of time. This question could potentially be pursued within a narrow, word-level experimental paradigm. But, because Paulson is interested in how reading works in the real world, this study took place within the context of readers reading real, complete texts, with no "task" to do besides read the texts.

When eye-tracking studies have asked similar-yet-different questions such as, How does the eye function in identifying words?" experiments have been designed that focus on word identification rather than meaning. Even with these limitations, the researchers keep finding that the eye is acting under the intelligent control of the brain. The researchers have been led to question the role of context and predictability in eye movements and fixations. When they do, the results are consistent with studies that use more natural texts — like this study.

In this study, Paulson discovers that, instead of visually skipping over miscued words, they are fixated — looked directly at — the majority of the time. Miscues are evidence of the power of the reader's expectations and predictions to take precedence over the visual information they find in the text. In addition, Paulson points out that many words that are skipped over visually are not miscued. As this study illustrates, reading is clearly more than recognizing a series of one-to-one text correspondences; Paulson's research demonstrates that reading is a nonlinear process of transaction with the text.

Ken Goodman

11

MISCUES AND EYE MOVEMENTS
Functions of Comprehension*

Eric J. Paulson

*T*HIS CHAPTER FOCUSES ON two observable aspects of reading processes: that readers will omit or substitute words when reading
aloud and that readers will skip over words visually while reading. The
first is researchable through miscue analysis, the second through eye-
movement analysis; this chapter combines the two types of analyses to
examine what readers are looking at while they make oral reading omissions or substitutions. Intuitively, the two phenomena should intersect;
the words that readers visually skip should be the ones that are orally
omitted or substituted. This chapter reports the results of a research
study that explores this assumption.

As other chapters in this volume explain, miscues are unexpected responses
to the text that readers produce when reading a text aloud. Miscue researchers agree that miscues are produced for a host of psycholinguistic reasons
that involve cues from semantic, syntactic, graphic, or pragmatic aspects
of the text (Goodman & Goodman, 1994). For example, in Figure 11.1, an
excerpt from a reading done by a college undergraduate, the word *with* is
omitted, indicated by the circled word; *the* is repeated, indicated by the symbol ® and the underlined word; the reader's word *trotting* is substituted for
the text word *tottering*, indicated by the reader's word appearing above the
text item.

A miscue analysis explanation would include the awkward syntactic construction of the lengthy prepositional phrase that, instead of following the
verb *fell* as a reader might expect, is instead found at the beginning of the

---

* This chapter is based on and updated from the article "Are oral reading word omissions and substitutions caused by careless eye movements? in *Reading Psychology*, 23(1),
45–66, 2002.

The lights contin-

ued showing right up until the day when, (with) a muffled

crash and a cloud of dry dust, [the] sagging roof finally fell in

trotting
and the tottering walls collapsed into the cellar hole.

Figure 11.1
Omission of *with*.

subordinate clause after *when*. The reader's assignment of syntax is consistent with a prediction of a prepositional phrase following *fell*, as an independent clause + subordinate WH-clause syntax, beginning with a noun phrase (*a muffled crash*).

In addition to these psycholinguistic explanations, however, many readers and reading researchers intuitively believe that visual factors also play a role in explaining how miscues are made possible, and some believe that visual factors alone explain miscues. For example, Marek (1996) describes one of her adult student's views about why she makes oral reading errors as literally not seeing some words: "In response to the question 'Why do you think you made the miscue?' Marlene frequently stated that she was 'trying to rush through,' or that she was 'skipping words'" (p. 75).

This view is not limited to readers; reading researchers imbue visual processes with similar explanatory power. For example, Smith (1994) explains miscues in general as the by-products of a focus on meaning: "The prior use of meaning ensures that when individual words must be identified, for example, in order to read aloud, a minimum of visual information will be used. And as a consequence, mistakes will occur" (p. 154). While an early eye-movement study (Fairbanks, 1937) done before the formalization of miscue analysis procedures did not find support for oral reading miscues as caused by a lack of visual input, this view is nevertheless not uncommon, has intuitive appeal, and provides the purpose of this study. To investigate whether miscues have visual explanations, eye-movement analysis is used to examine where readers look while they produce two common types of miscues: substitutions and omissions. The question addressed here is, Are miscues caused by the reader not looking at the miscued word?

Research Traditions: Miscue Analysis and Eye-Movement Recording

Miscue Analysis

Miscue data collection procedures are important as they are designed to provide as close to an authentic reading experience for the reader as possible: A complete text is used, and there is no additional task aside from retelling the story after it is read. Analysis of the miscues the reader made involves coding the linguistic systems of the text and of the reader and the nature of miscue patterns across texts and across readers. Each miscue is examined in terms of the relationship between it and the sentence in which it is embedded and the entire text. Areas of examination include syntactic acceptability, semantic acceptability, meaning change, correction, graphic similarity, and sound similarity (Goodman, Watson, & Burke, 1987). Miscue analysis has been undertaken with readers from a variety of ages, backgrounds, and reading levels (Brown, Goodman, & Marek, 1996).

Although procedures for miscue analysis are designed to be as authentic as possible, the necessity for readers to read aloud has generated criticism based on perceived differences between oral and silent reading (Leu, 1982). However, there is evidence that similarities between oral and silent reading outweigh their differences. Goodman and Goodman (1982) explained that "a single process underlies all reading. The cycles, phases, and strategies of oral and silent reading are essentially the same" (p. 160). Levin (1979) constructed a persuasive argument for the similarities of oral and silent reading that includes evidence that:

> Those who read well in one mode do so in the other. Comprehension is similar as is the development of the skills. Anderson and Dearborn conclude that silent and oral reading may be implicit and overt expressions, respectively, of the same underlying processes. (p. 20)

In addition, Beebe (1980) concluded that "analysis of oral reading miscues is an effective way of inferring what kinds of miscues may occur during silent reading" (p. 335).

Classic eye-movement research has come to similar conclusions; in 1920, Buswell found that the eye movements relative to ambiguous words were the same in oral and silent reading, which "shows that eye movements in both oral and silent reading are largely controlled by the recognition of meaning" (in Levin, 1979, p. 31). In addition, Anderson and Swanson (1937) compared the eye movements of readers reading orally and silently and found that the difference in eye movements between oral and silent reading is one of degree, not kind: "Correlations between each measure of eye-movements in silent reading and the same measure in oral reading were uniformly positive and rather high for all groups" (p. 68). These early studies, in addition to the large body of research supporting miscue analysis (see Brown et al., 1996), allow consideration of oral reading, although superficially different from silent reading, as proceeding from the same central reading process and able to generate reliable inferences about silent reading. Perhaps even more important than the validity of miscue analysis, however, is the pragmatic understanding of the fact that miscues do indeed happen—and the study reported here is an attempt to understand whether miscues have a visual explanation.

Eye Movements

Information gained from the analysis of readers' eye movements has had an impact on reading theory for over a century (e.g., Huey, 1908/1968; Rayner, 1997). During reading, the eye must pause, or fixate, on a word to provide usable visual information to the brain as no information is gained while the eye is in motion (Rayner, 1997), and a very small amount of text information is in focus during each fixation (see Paulson & Goodman, chapter 2, this volume, for a thorough description). Because of these *physical* limitations of the eyes' ability to present visual information to the brain, reading researchers and theorists have been able to learn more about reading as a *perceptual* process: what the brain does with the visual information provided by the eyes. These perceptual processes are inferred from two main types of data provided by eye-movement recording: where the eye stops (fixations) and for how long it stops there (fixation duration).

Evidence from eye-movement studies demonstrates that anywhere from 25% to 40%—or more—of the words in a given text are not fixated (Duckett, 2001; Fisher & Shebilske, 1985; Freeman, 2001; Hogaboam, 1983; Just & Carpenter, 1987; Rayner, 1997); in normal reading, about two thirds of the words are fixated, a finding replicated here, as readers fixated 67.36% of the words in the text. The extent to which readers skip words, yet perceive themselves as reading every word, depends on contextual constraint (Rayner & Well, 1996): how their a priori predictions interact with the a posteriori information they find in the text, a continually updated, flowing process. This same process also affects fixation duration; how long a reader spends in a certain area of the text depends on how closely the text matched the reader's prediction (Rayner & Pollatsek, 1987).

In general, eye movements are useful in reading research because readers' eye movements indicate the part of the text to which they are attending (Just & Carpenter, 1987), providing a window to perceptual and comprehension processes during reading. More in-depth reviews of eye-movement research can be found in Paulson and Goodman's chapter 2 of this volume; Paulson and Goodman, 1999; and Rayner 1998, 1997.

Methodology

Purpose

At the beginning of this chapter, I noted that the focus is on two observable aspects of reading processes: readers will omit or substitute words when reading aloud, and readers will skip over words visually while reading. This is often understood to be a causal relationship. That is, the well-known phenomenon that readers omit or substitute words when reading aloud is often assumed to be caused by readers skipping over those words visually. Figure 11.2 illustrates this relationship.

Because approximately 20–40% of the words in a given text are not looked at, it stands to reason that it is those words that are miscued by the reader. The purpose of this study is to test that assumption, to present a view of the behavior of these readers' eyes relative to the oral reading omissions and substitutions they made. Specifically at issue is whether oral reading omissions and substitutions are caused by readers failing to fixate substituted and omitted words or fixating them for such a short time that perception was hindered.

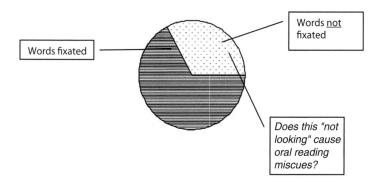

Figure 11.2
Percentage of words fixated during reading.

Approach: Eye Movement/Miscue Analysis

Although the analysis of eye movements is a useful investigative tool, to better understand the reasons behind a particular series of eye movements it is important to supplement those data with another comprehension measure (Just & Carpenter, 1984). For that reason, eye-movement analysis has been combined with miscue analysis in this study. This combination of eye-movement records and oral reading records has been termed eye movement/miscue analysis (EMMA) in several publications (Duckett, 2001, 2002; Freeman, 2001; Paulson, 2000, 2002, 2005; Paulson & Freeman, 2003). The usefulness of looking at both eye movements and miscues is based on the perspective that they each provide information the other cannot; both verbal and visual data are available to provide information about a reading.

As an example of the information available through EMMA, Figure 11.3 reintroduces the miscues shown at the beginning of this article with the reader's eye movements added. In this example, the reader omits a preposition that demonstrates his prediction of the syntax. In this and all eye-movement overlays, the dot signifies the position of the fixation on the word directly above it, and the number below the dot signifies the order of fixations. Thus, in the second line, the first fixation is on the *h* of *showing*, the second on the *gh* of *right*, the third on the *p* of *up*, and the fourth is a regression back near the *r* of *right*. In this passage, as was pointed out at the beginning of this chapter, a lengthy prepositional phrase has been moved by the author from the verb *fell* to the beginning of the subordinate clause after *when*. Assignment of syntax predicts the verb but not this unexpected interruption of the syntactic flow — the sentence might have been more predictable if the prepositional phrase followed *fell*. Note that the reader fixates on *with*, then on *a* and *muffled*, at which time he has subconsciously rejected the

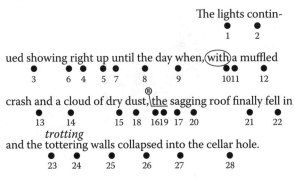

Figure 11.3
Eye movements and omission of *with*.

information he found in the text in favor of the independent clause + subordinate WH-clause syntax, beginning with a noun phrase (*a muffled crash*) he had predicted. When he reaches the end of the noun phrase, he repeats *the*, possibly as a placeholder while he gathers more text information, and then fixates the sagging seconds before moving on. It is at this point that it becomes obvious that the sentence as he read it is not syntactically acceptable; thus, he may have disconfirmed his prediction but makes no explicit correction of his omission of *with*.

As this example demonstrates, the analysis of the conjunction of eye movements and the oral reading record can provide copious information about how a reader navigates a text. However, a thorough EMMA exploration of the readings collected in this study is beyond the scope of this chapter, as is a detailed description of the theoretical foundation of the combination of eye movements and miscue analysis. Instead, the focus here is specifically whether visual explanations—such as failing to fixate a word or fixating it for an abnormally short time—play a part in the production of oral substitutions and omissions.

Equipment

Eye-movement data were collected with Applied Science Laboratories 4000SU and Model 504 eye trackers, which record pupil and corneal reflections with an infrared reflection source and are accurate to within 0.5°. In addition, the 4000SU utilizes a head tracker, and the Model 504 uses a remote pan-tilt camera, both of which negated the need for a chin rest or bite bar. The eye-movement data were captured and produced as a series of *x,y* coordinates. A video camera simultaneously recorded a cursor that reflects eye position superimposed on the text and the readers' oral reading.

Participants

The eye movements of 15 readers (11 male and 4 female university undergraduate students) who volunteered to participate were used in this study. All were effective readers with vision correctable to 20/20. In addition to practice materials designed to alleviate any trepidation or nervousness they might have felt, the participants read aloud a fictional narrative short enough to be read in its entirety, retold, and discussed in a short period of time. Following miscue analysis procedures, after reading the story aloud, each participant retold the story to ensure that basic levels of comprehension were met.

Results

In general, the results from an analysis of the eye-movement data that follow are typical of normal, adult reading. Across readers, an average of 67.36% (SD = 6.25%) of the words in the texts were fixated in this study. This percentage of fixations is consistent with the same measure found in early and contemporary eye-movement studies (e.g., Fisher & Shebilske, 1985; Judd & Buswell, 1922; Just & Carpenter, 1987; Paulson & Freeman, 2003; Paulson & Goodman, chapter 2, this volume; Rayner, 1997). Although, on average, almost one third of the words in the texts in this study were not fixated, the readers reported no comprehension problems and were all able to give complete and inclusive retellings of the readings. The average duration of each fixation across readers was 371.13 ms (SD = 61.28 ms), and 16.19% (SD = 5.66%) of fixations were regressions.

Because a lack of visual information, the oft-suspected cause of some oral reading miscues, manifests itself in eye movements as either failing to fixate a word or fixating for insufficient duration, instances of fixation percentages or fixation durations relative to substitutions and omissions that were lower than the averages reported could hold explanatory power. Results specific to substitutions and omissions follow, each with an example to illustrate the miscue/eye movement relationship, a brief narrative describing the results, and a discussion section. In the results for both substitutions and omissions, the eye movements that are reported took place before the miscue in question was produced, not after. Eye movements made after a miscue is produced could conceivably be part of a correction strategy as opposed to a cause of the miscue, and it is the latter phenomenon that is of interest in this chapter.

Eye Movements Relative to Substitutions

In Figure 11.4, the reader substituted *unusable* for *usable*, possibly predicting a continuation of the idea of a "rundown house" presented at the beginning of

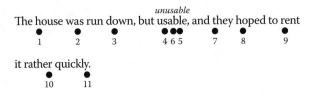

Figure 11.4
Substitution of *unusable.*

the sentence. The reader fixated 60% of the words in the sentence, and little is remarkable about his eye movements before and after his miscue in that there are no regressions or other eye-movement patterns that would indicate difficulty with the text. The word *usable*, however, received three fixations, including an intraword regression. In this instance, the reader hesitated briefly after reading aloud *down*, made the three fixations on *usable*, then said *but unusable*. It is tempting to think of the intraword regression as an implicit, nonverbal correction of the miscue, but the reader made all the fixations on the word before verbalizing it, so it cannot be a correction when there is nothing yet to correct. This reader actually fixated on the word that was then miscued and fixated for a long time—a phenomenon not unique in this study.

Differences between the percentage of all words fixated across the text and the percentage of substituted words fixated were not significant ($t = -1.2496$); in fact, instead of substituted words failing to be fixated, in these readings they tended to be more likely to be fixated than the other words in the text. Although 67.36% of all words in the text were fixated, 75.24% ($SD = 23.61\%$) of the substituted words were directly fixated. In other words, most words that were substituted were looked at before the oral substitution was produced. Note that these fixations on substituted words refer to the first time the miscued words are encountered, not to regressions or any other fixations that take place subsequent to a fixation after the word as part of a correction strategy. So, in these readings, most words that were substituted were actually looked at by the readers.

Although it is important that the words that were orally substituted were looked at by the readers, equally important is the amount of time the readers spent on those words; it could be argued that a smaller fixation duration on substituted words might not have provided the reader with enough time to accurately perceive the word. This was not the case; differences between the duration of fixations on substituted words and the duration of all fixations in the text were not significant ($t = -1.4211$). In fact, the mean duration of the fixations associated with substitutions tended to be almost 25% longer than the average duration of all fixations in these readings. This suggests not only that oral reading substitutions were not caused by a too-brief glance, but also that these readers were likely to look at them for a longer period of time than nonsubstituted words, although this was not a significant difference.

Traditional views of oral reading substitutions center around substitutions as caused by "a careless reader" (Ekwall, 1981, p. 26). Similarly, Dechant (1981) included carelessness and reading too rapidly as causes of substitutions, as well as "failure of pupil to scan the word thoroughly enough to identify the order of the letters and to be certain that the word is a particular word and not another" (p. 333). In addition, entire studies have been constructed around the premise that substituted words are not seen "correctly." For example, Nicholson, Pearson, and Dykstra's (1979) study, designed to emulate certain miscues, assumed that when readers make oral substitutions they have not seen the correct word and failed to see at all words that they omit. The researchers explained:

> It was assumed that in trying to understand a story, the unskilled reader is not only faced with insufficient text data (caused by failing to respond at all to certain words) but anomalous data as well (caused by responding with certain semantically inappropriate substitutions). (p. 341)

In general, the traditional explanations for the generic causes of substitutions are carelessness, reading too rapidly, and not using enough visual information. However, in this study there was no lack of visual information where these miscues were concerned; any difference in the number of words fixated or the durations of those fixations was not significant. Instead, the readers directly fixated a higher percentage of substituted words than the percentage of words fixated overall. In addition, instead of looking at substituted words for a short time, the average duration of fixations relative to substitutions tended to be longer than the average duration of all fixations. Contrary to intuition, substituted words in these readings are examined and examined thoroughly.

Eye Movements Relative to Omissions

Figure 11.5 shows that the reader omits the word *that*. The word *that* does not function as a necessary semantic or syntactic unit in this sentence. The reader fixated that, then, not satisfied with the syntactic construction, omitted the word in his oral reading and continued the rest of the sentence verbatim. Note also that the word *the* is not fixated, but it is verbalized. The

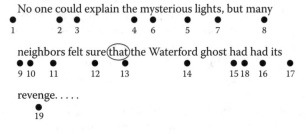

Figure 11.5
Omission of *that*.

fixation on the omitted word in this example is typical of other omissions in this study.

This reader's fixations brought the omitted word into foveal focus as a direct fixation, a pattern that was repeated for over half of the omitted words in the text; readers fixated 59.57% (SD = 37.73) of the words they orally omitted. As with the figures given for substitutions in foveal focus, these fixations on omitted words refer to the first time the miscued words are encountered, not to regressions or any other fixations that take place subsequent to a fixation after the word. Although the percentage of omissions that were directly fixated is lower than the percentage of all words directly fixated in the text, this is not a significant difference (t = 0.7889) and still amply demonstrates that a substantial number of omitted words were fixated. In addition, if fixations that are not directly on the omitted word but are close enough to bring it into foveal focus are considered, then 95.55% of the words that were omitted in these readings were at least partly in sharp focus.

As with the eye movements relative to oral substitutions, the duration of the fixations on words that were omitted was examined. Fixating an omitted word might not be interesting if those fixations were substantially shorter than the average fixation—it might seem as though it were only a fleeting glimpse. However, any difference in fixation duration was not significant (t = −0.4699); in fact, instead of shorter than the average fixation, fixations on omitted words in these readings tended to be longer. As with substituted words, omitted words were looked at for a considerable amount of time.

The omissions that these adult readers made were not made deliberately in an effort to avoid a difficult or unknown word; rather, they are nondeliberate omissions that reveal the reader's parallel, constructed text—in the case of omissions, a text that does not use the omitted word. The evidence for this is the fact that most of the omitted words were function words or short verbs, like *do, to, the, a, and, that,* and *of;* few would suggest that these adults, none of whom omitted lower frequency and "harder" words like *tuberculosis* and *untenantable,* were unable to read the word *the.* Goodman and Gollasch (1980) reported that nondeliberate omissions often involve words read correctly without hesitation elsewhere in the text. Thus, it is not the word itself that the reader rejects, but its use in the specific context in which it is found.

The traditional visual explanation of the cause of nondeliberate omissions is similar to that of substitution-type miscues, that readers are careless or reading too fast. For example, Spache (1964, p. 255) stated that "omissions of whole words, particularly among intermediate grade and older pupils, may indicate either excessive speed or a tendency to skip over unknown words." A. J. Harris and Sipay (1980, p. 216) argued that "omissions usually are caused by carelessness or inattention." However, differences in eye-movement measures—number of words fixated and the duration of those fixations—between omitted words and all the words in the text were not significant, as noted: Readers were as likely to fixate an omitted word as they were to fixate a word that was not omitted. In addition, in this study readers looked at more than half the words they orally omitted. In the case of omissions, it is especially useful to look at not only direct fixations, but also omitted words that were only in foveal focus because traditional explanations suggest that omitted words are not seen at all. For example, Nicholson et al.'s (1979) study viewed omissions as "insufficient text data" that were "caused by failing to respond *at all* to certain words" (p. 341; italics added). But, if the omitted word was in foveal focus, then it was physiologically seen, and 95.55% of omissions were in foveal focus (all others were in the parafovea). Thus, in these readings it is not a lack of visual data that causes the reader to omit the word; rather, the omission is the reader's response to that text item.

General Discussion

Figure 11.2 asks the intuitive question, Since approximately 20–40% of the words in a given text are not fixated/looked at, are those the words that are miscued by the reader? The results of this study indicate that the answer is no. Figure 11.6 illustrates one relationship between fixations and miscues. Note that the right-hand part of the chart, which signifies the proportion of miscues that were and were not fixated prior to producing the miscue,

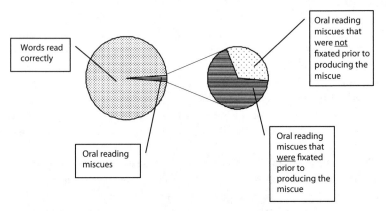

Figure 11.6
Relationship between fixations and miscues.

is similar to the pie chart in Figure 11.2, which illustrated the proportion of fixated words to nonfixated words overall. Miscued words are fixated at approximately the same rate as all other words in the text, a finding that has been replicated with a variety of ages and linguistic backgrounds (see Duckett, chapter 5, this volume; Ebe, chapter 6, this volume; Paulson & Freeman, 2003). The explanation for this relationship—how we can look at one word but see a different word and, conversely, not look at another word yet still see that word—is perceptual in nature.

Our eyes do not deliver concepts to our brain but provide a "diffuse and continual bombardment of electromagnetic radiation, minute waves of light energy that vary only in frequency, amplitude, and spatial and temporal patterning" (Smith, 1994, p. 69). Another, less-technical way to describe the data our eyes deliver to us is to say that "we are given tiny distorted upside-down images in the eyes" (Gregory, 1966, p. 7). The reason we do not perceive the world upside-down, much less in terms of electromagnetic radons, is because it is the brain, not the eyes, that constructs our visual world. The eyes merely deliver raw data to the brain, and the brain decides what needs attending. This, then, is perception—not what the eyes look at, but what the brain does with the visual information it receives. Thus, when the brain constructs perceptions it has to decide *what* to see, a process that the familiar Necker cube* illustrates in Figure 11.7.

Although the "o" seems to alternate from the front to the back face and vice-versa, the figure itself and the information the eye transmits to the brain have not been altered. This popular optical illusion is evidence of the brain constructing different perceptions of the same visual input. This example is a microcosm of what the brain is engaged in on a continuous basis, what may be called *hypothesis checking*. As Gregory (1966) argued, "… the senses … do not give us a picture of the world directly; rather they provide evidence for checking hypotheses about what lies before us. Indeed, we may say that a perceived object *is* a hypothesis, suggested and tested by sensory data" (pp. 11–12). The Necker cube provides no clues regarding which hypothesis (i.e., A. The circle is on the front face, or B. The circle is on the back face) is more acceptable, which is why we do not perceive one hypothesis as better than the other. For the most part, however, our brains construct hypotheses about the world

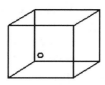

Figure 11.7
Necker cube.

---

* This example is after Gregory, 1966, p. 12.

that allow us to settle on a perception that has meaning. In a similar way, as readers search for meaning in a text, they are also engaged in a perceptual activity.

Depicting reading as a perceptual activity lends itself to understanding reading as a transactive process in which reading involves an interaction between the processing of graphic information and the readers' experiences and expectations they bring to the text (Harris & Hodges, 1995, p. 256). Goodman (1996) describes the cyclical nature of reading:

> We are constantly anticipating where a text is going, what will come next, what we will see, what structures we will encounter, and we make inferences from what we think we've seen and predicted. Our predictions are based on the information we've selected and sampled from the text, but they also guide the process of selecting and sampling. (pp. 112–113)

So, what readers find when they read depends on what they think they will find, which is informed by what they actually find. Smith (1994, p. 161) states that "the way readers look for meaning is not to consider all possibilities nor to make reckless guesses about just one, but rather to predict within the most likely range of alternatives." Expectations, predictions, and hypotheses are crucial to perceptions, both of the world in general and of text.

Although in this study some substituted or omitted words were not looked at, or looked at for a below-average duration, these differences were not significantly different from the fixation percentage and fixation duration averages of all words in the text. In other words, readers were as likely to fixate a word they orally substituted or omitted as they were to fixate a word they produced verbatim to the text. In fact, with the exception of the percentage of omitted words that were fixated, fixation percentages and duration averages for substituted and omitted words tended to be higher than average. Thus, the results of this study suggest that readers are likely to look directly at words they omit or substitute for an ample duration, which prompts the question, Why are thoroughly examined portions of text changed during the course of constructing a parallel text?

The answer may lie in the nature of the reading process itself. As this study demonstrated, readers nondeliberately deleted or changed text items that they fixated and thoroughly examined. This seems counterintuitive because if a prediction does not mesh with the input, it is usually easier to change the a priori prediction than to "change" the a posteriori input. Yet, in these readings most substituted and omitted text items are visually examined and then perceived differently—evidence of the transactive and constructive nature of reading. The Necker cube (Figure 11.7) may provide a limited analogy:

As with the Necker cube, readers have the ability to change the structure of the graphic information the eye sends the brain. And, just as readers try to understand the Necker cube, they also try to understand text. As they disregard a version of the Necker cube, so readers disregard an element of the text. But, although the Necker cube flits back and forth from one perception to another, readers' perception of the text item makes sense and satisfies their expectations, and they can move on. In this way, readers have the task of deciding, subconsciously, which aspects of the written text are to be used and which aspects are to be disregarded and may change the written text if it does not fit their meaning-centered predictions.

That these readers looked at the word they then omitted or substituted shows that the perceptual cycle is not short circuited and suggests that readers actively examine the text and search for meaning. Readers change the text instead of changing their minds because they can—reading is not passive, but active and constructive. The route to meaning is not in information transfer from text to reader but in a transactive construction of meaning between text and reader. It is to be expected that in the process of constructing a text there will be changes in the written text and in the reader (Rosenblatt, 1978). Portions of the text where observable changes—oral miscues—take place were fixated and examined by the reader, then changed, presumably because readers' predictions made more sense than the text item found in the written text. In making changes to the written text, readers exercise their implicit authority to disregard text items that do not make sense for text items that do make sense: They allow themselves to construct a meaningful text even if it is not graphically identical to the published text.

The basic premise of this chapter finds support in data generated by Grant Fairbanks in 1937. He recorded the eye movements of college freshmen reading aloud and combined the oral and visual records. As noted, the results of his study do not support visual explanations for the production of oral "errors" (Fairbanks's term). Fairbanks found that most words that readers orally substituted, omitted, changed, inserted, or repeated were within foveal focus and stated that "fixation is equally precise when an error is made as when it is not" (p. 96).

In general, this chapter is meant to provide impetus for further exploring the idea of reading as a perceptual process, but it also has pedagogical implications. For example, because the majority of omitted or substituted words in these readings are not only examined but also tended to be looked at for longer than average, the exhortation to the student to "slow down and look carefully at the text" loses its validity. Especially in today's educational atmosphere in which even college students are targeted by commercial curriculum producers as needing "accurate and orderly seeing" visual training to read better (Taylor Associates, 2000, p. 16), it may be important to think of this study as further evidence that reading, as Smith (1996, p. 30) reminds us, depends on what is "behind the eyes."

References

Anderson, I. H., & Swanson, D. E. (1937). Common factors in the eye-movements in silent and oral reading. *Psychological Monographs, 48*(3), 61–69.

Beebe, M. J. (1980). The effect of different types of substitution miscues on reading. *Reading Research Quarterly, 15*, 324–336.

Brown, J., Goodman, K. S., & Marek, A. M. (1996). *Studies in miscue analysis: An annotated bibliography.* Newark, DE: International Reading Association.

Dechant, E. (1981). *Diagnosis and remediation of reading disabilities.* Englewood Cliffs, NJ: Prentice-Hall.

Duckett, P. (2001). *First grade beginning readers' use of pictures and print as they read: A miscue analysis and eye movement study.* Unpublished doctoral dissertation, University of Arizona, Tucson.

Duckett, P. (2002). New insights: Eye fixations and the reading process. *Talking Points, 13*(2), 16–21.

Ekwall, E. E. (1981). *Locating and correcting reading difficulties* (3rd ed.). Columbus, OH: Merril.

Fairbanks, G. (1937). The relation between eye-movements and voice in the oral reading of good and poor silent readers. *Psychological Monographs, 48*(3), 78–107.

Fisher, D. F., & Shebilske, W. L. (1985). There is more that meets the eye than the eye mind assumption. In R. Groner, G. W. McConkie, & C. Menz (Eds.), *Eye movements and human information processing* (pp. 149–157). Amsterdam: Elsevier Science.

Freeman, A. E. (2001). *The eyes have it: Oral miscue and eye movement analysis of the reading of fourth grade Spanish/English bilinguals.* Unpublished doctoral dissertation, University of Arizona, Tucson.

Goodman, K. S. (1996). *On reading.* Portsmouth, NH: Heinemann.

Goodman, K. S., & Gollasch, F. V. (1980). Word omissions: Deliberate and non-deliberate. *Reading Research Quarterly, 16*, 6–31.

Goodman, K. S., & Goodman, Y. M. (1982). Learning about psycholinguistic processes by analyzing oral reading. In F. V. Gollasch (Ed.), *Language and literacy* (Vol. 1, pp. 149–168). Boston: Routledge and Kegan Paul.

Goodman, Y. M., & Goodman, K. S. (1994). To err is human: Learning about language processes by analyzing miscues. In R. B. Ruddell, M. R. Ruddell, & H. Singer (Eds.), *Theoretical models and processes of reading* (4th ed., pp. 104–123). Newark, DE: International Reading Association.

Goodman, Y. M., Watson, D. J., & Burke, C. L. (1987). *Reading miscue inventory.* Katonah, NY: Richard C. Owen.

Goodman, Y. M., Watson, D. J., & Burke, C. L. (2005). *Reading miscue inventory* (2nd ed.). Katonah, NY: Richard C. Owen.

Gregory, R. L. (1966). *Eye and brain.* New York: McGraw-Hill.

Harris, A. J., & Sipay, E. R. (1980). *How to increase reading ability* (7th ed.). New York: Longman.

Harris, T. L., & Hodges, R. E. (Eds.) (1995). *The literacy dictionary.* Newark, DE: International Reading Association.

Hogaboam, T. W. (1983). Reading patterns in eye movement data. In K. Rayner (Ed.), *Eye movements in reading: Perceptual and language processes* (pp. 309–332). New York: Academic Press.

Huey, E.B. (1968). *The psychology and pedagogy of reading.* Cambridge, MA: MIT Press. (Original work published 1908)

Judd, C. H., & Buswell, G. T. (1922). *Silent reading: A study of the various types.* Chicago: University of Chicago Press.

Just, M. A., & Carpenter, P. A. (1984). Using eye fixations to study reading comprehension. In D. E. Kieras & M. A. Just (Eds.), *New methods in reading comprehension research* (pp. 151–182). Hillsdale, NJ: Erlbaum.

Just, M. A., & Carpenter, P. A. (1987). *The psychology of reading and language comprehension.* Newton, MA: Allyn and Bacon.

Leu, D. J. (1982). Oral reading analysis: A critical review of research and application. *Reading Research Quarterly, 17,* 420–437.

Levin, H. (1979). *The eye-voice span.* Cambridge, MA: MIT Press.

Marek, A. M. (1996). Surviving reading instruction. In Y. M. Goodman & A. M. Marek (Eds.), *Retrospective miscue analysis* (pp. 71–86). Katonah, NY: Owen.

Nicholson, T., Pearson, P. D., & Dykstra, R. (1979). Effects of embedded anomalies and oral reading errors on children's understanding of stories. *Journal of Reading Behavior, 11*(4), 339–354.

Paulson, E. J. (2000). *Adult readers' eye movements during the production of oral miscues.* Unpublished doctoral dissertation, University of Arizona, Tucson.

Paulson, E. J. (2002). Are oral reading word omissions and substitutions caused by careless eye movements? *Reading Psychology, 23*(1), 45–66.

Paulson, E. J. (2005). Viewing eye movements during reading through the lens of chaos theory: How reading is like the weather. *Reading Research Quarterly, 40,* 338–358.

Paulson, E. J., & Freeman, A. E. (2003). *Insight from the eyes: The science of effective reading instruction.* Portsmouth, NH: Heinemann.

Paulson, E. J., & Goodman, K. S. (1999, January). Influential studies in eye-movement research. *Reading Online.* Retrieved January 9, 1999, from http://www.readingonline.org/research/eyemove.html

Rayner, K. (1997). Understanding eye movements in reading. *Scientific Studies of Reading, 1,* 317–339.

Rayner, K. (1998). Eye movements in reading and information processing: 20 years of research. *Psychological Bulletin, 124,* 372–422.

Rayner, K., & Pollatsek, A. (1987). Eye movements in reading: A tutorial review. In M. Coltheart (Ed.), *Attention and performance XII: The psychology of reading* (pp. 327–362). Hillsdale, NJ: Erlbaum.

Rayner, K., & Well, A. D. (1996). Effects of contextual constraint on eye movements in reading: A further examination. *Psychonomic Bulletin and Review, 3,* 504–509.

Rosenblatt, L. M. (1978). *The reader, the text, the poem: The transactional theory of the literary work.* Carbondale: Southern Illinois University Press.

Smith, F. (1994). *Understanding reading: A psycholinguistic analysis of reading and learning to read* (5th ed.). Hillsdale, NJ: Erlbaum.

Smith, F. (1996). *Reading without nonsense* (3rd ed.). New York: Teacher's College Press.

Spache, G. D. (1964). *Reading in the elementary school.* Boston: Allyn and Bacon.

Taylor Associates. (2000). *Reading plus 2000* [Reading program literature]. Huntington Station, NY: Author.

INTRODUCTION TO CHAPTER 12

*M*UCH HAS BEEN MADE in the research literature on reading concerning quantitative versus qualitative analysis. Alan Flurkey's research on reading flow demonstrates that this is a false dichotomy. The research on fluency, which he thoroughly demolishes, uses a simple quantitative measure, words per minute over a text, as a measure of fluency. *Fluency* has been defined in the research literature as reading rapidly and accurately and with a natural voice, but the measure of fluency was reduced to reading fast and accurately because measures of voice involve qualitative judgments. Then, the measurement of fluency was further reduced to just speed; that was justified because speed correlates with other quantitative measures of reading comprehension. But, the relationship of speed in reading to reading proficiency, which Flurkey defines as both effective in making sense of a text and efficient in doing so with the least amount of effort, is not simple.

As Flurkey says after carefully demonstrating the variability of reading rate in one effective reader:

> As has been shown in the analysis of this effective reader, the use of a single numerical index such as words per minute per text is not only inadequate at capturing the dynamic element of reading speed that has been described here, but also it obscures the underlying character of the reading process. Reading rate is not a characteristic, which is simple and static; on the contrary, it is the outward sign of one dimension of a dynamic and complex process.

Using a simple program available on any computer, Flurkey was able to use a quantitative measure, the speed over any subunit of a text—word, sentence, paragraph, section—to show that rate varies from unit to unit within any one reading of a text by a reader. Then, he went further and showed that more efficient readers—although they read faster—show even more variability in their rate of reading per paragraph or per sentence than less-efficient readers. Because he is using actual reading of individual readers reading the same text, his research is an example of scientific realism even though to this point his analysis is all quantitative.

But, then he asked the next question: Why is the rate so variable? Here, he examined the same oral reading of individual readers he used to measure rate using a qualitative measure, miscue analysis. He was able then to pinpoint how aspects of the reader's transactions with the text accounted for how they used time in their reading. He is able to offer a more complete metaphor than fluency: Reading flows over a text like a river over its bed; reading responds to the twists and turns of the text itself.

It was the transactional view of reading as meaning construction that led him to dispute the research on fluency in the first place, and it is the same theory that enables him to place his findings in the context of that theory and explain—using both quantitative and qualitative data—why rate varies as the reader constructs meaning. In doing so, he adds to our understanding of the structures and processes involved in making sense of reading.

One other aspect of Flurkey's important research is worth considering. Although no one has disputed his findings or his reconceptualization of fluency and flow in reading, there also has not been any observable move to adopt his fruitful methodology or to reexamine the use of fluency measures in reading research. This is a painful example of how paradigm influences progress in a field. His work is ignored because it does not fit a word recognition view of reading, and giving it the attention it deserves would require researchers to examine their own paradigm.

Ken Goodman

12

READING FLOW*

Alan D. Flurkey

*T*HIS CHAPTER SUMMARIZES A study of time-related aspects of the reading process. It shares the findings of a study of oral reading that builds on Goodman's model of the reading process (Goodman, 2003b) and a develops hydrological metaphor for concepts that link reading and time. The study of reading flow results in key inferences about how the reading process works. For example, the study of reading flow illustrates how readers *use* time. Readers use time when they need to reflect on the concepts they encounter or when they need to work out the linguistic structures that they are anticipating in the text—in other words, when readers take the time they need to ponder ideas or when they need to solve problems they encounter as they read. The study of reading flow provides illustrations of the tentative nature of reading (Goodman, 2003a).

Few things are as misunderstood as the relationship between reading and time. Parents and teachers voice concerns about choppy, halting oral reading—a source of concern about an indication of a reading problem. And, "fluent" oral reading is thought to be a positive indicator of a reader's skill. This "commonsense" view also has its share of proponents in some corners of the field of reading research. There are reading researchers who argue that *fluent reading* is defined as rapid and accurate (or "automatic") word identification. Furthermore, it is believed that automatic word recognition is a requisite of reading comprehension (Samuels, Schermer, & Reinking, 1992). Measurements of reading fluency are stock components of several

---

* This chapter is based on and updated from work published in "Time and Tide: The Dynamic Nature of Oral Reading," A. Flurkey, 2002, *Hofstra Horizons*, Spring, pp. 13–18, and in "Reading as Flow: A Linguistic Alternative to Fluency," A. Flurkey, 1998, Occasional Paper, Program in Language and Literacy No. 26, University of Arizona, Tucson.

widely used standardized assessments of reading ability. In the professional literature, book and journal space has been dedicated to discussions of reading fluency as a dimension of skilled reading (Rasinski, 1990), as a topic for theoretical analysis (Carver, 1990; Stayter & Allington, 1991), and in practical advice from researchers to teachers, as an end in itself (Pikulski & Chard, 2003; Rasinski, 2003; Zutell & Rasinski, 1991).

With that in mind, one might think that skilled, fluent readers who comprehend a text would orally read a text at a fairly consistent rate. But, is this commonsense view a fair description of what happens during reading? Illustrations of reading flow provide insights about the nature of reading and time that differ markedly from those that might follow from a word recognition view of reading. This chapter reports some findings from a study of six readers of various ages. The study investigated the nature of oral reading rate as readers read and retell whole, authentic narrative texts (Flurkey, 1997). The study was informed by a sociopsycholinguistic transactional view of reading (Goodman, 2003b). The findings suggest that this commonsense view of reading fluency is but a simplistic explanation that clouds understanding of a complex process.

Reading Is Dynamic

Applied psycholinguists like Kenneth Goodman and Frank Smith have urged us to view the personal and psychological aspects of literacy processes from the widest scope possible. Instead of focusing on how individuals respond to elements of written language flashed on a screen by a tachistoscopic projector, for example, applied psycholinguists have demonstrated that literacy activities are cultural and social practices as well as acts of individual use. As they explain how an *individual* processes written language, their observations address the social and cultural functions and purposes of written language as it is used in literacy events (Goodman, 1996; Smith, 1996).

Issues related to reading and time take on a different meaning when discussed from this perspective than they do in discussions about reading fluency as rapid word recognition. If comparison among readers is of interest, then it seems reasonable that any two readers will read at different speeds. Speed is influenced by a reader's particular purposes.* Different readers have

---

* The term *speed* is used here because it seems a better fit in a discussion about reading habits. The term *rate* is a statistical index used in measures of fluency commonly reported as words per minute.

different life experiences to bring to a text, and they may bring different linguistic resources to a literacy event. In short, no two individuals will read the same text at the same speed and they should not be expected to do so.

If a comparison is made between an individual's reading of one text with a reading of a different text, then it is also reasonable to expect differences. The same reader on a given day may bring different intentions, purposes, mood, interests, and background knowledge to different texts; a reading of *Popular Science* magazine in the waiting room of a dentist's office will be different from the reading of a novel at home or the reading of a professional journal at work (Rosenblatt, 1978).

This same reasoning can be applied to different readings of the same text. Take the example of a person who is interested in becoming her own contractor in building a custom home. She has gathered several books and articles from the library about varieties of plumbing materials. Suppose she has quickly read through some chapters and articles paying just enough attention to detail to get information on price, material availability, degree of required expertise, and specialized tools associated with each type of material in the construction of a water system and so on. Now, after this first quick reading, suppose this reader goes back to one or two articles that she has determined are particularly suited to the building circumstances she has in mind and reads them closely and more slowly to obtain the more detailed information she seeks. Of course, the opposite approach to this task can work just as well. In the real world, readers' shifting purposes require that they read the same text with different speeds at different times. Clearly, reading is dynamic: It is characterized by continuous change.

The phenomenon of continuous change should be expected if reading is regarded as tentative information processing (Gollasch, 1982; Goodman, 1982). In relating prediction to comprehension, Frank Smith (1994) writes the following:

> As we read, as we listen to someone talking, as we go through life, we are constantly asking questions, and if we are able to find answers to those questions, then we comprehend. ... There is a *flow* to comprehension with new questions constantly being generated from the answers that are sought. (p. 19; italics in the original text)

There is indeed a flow to comprehension. There is also a flow to comprehend*ing*. However, to obtain a more complete description of the relationship between reading and time, a description that documents how readers use strategies *as they are comprehending* text, a shift in focus to formulating a scientific description of the tentative nature of reading is required.

Reading Flow

Miscue markings on a typescript document a reader's efforts at negotiating the meaning of a text by providing a record of the unexpected responses (miscues) a reader produces during an oral reading of a whole, authentic text (Goodman, Watson, & Burke, 1987). An excerpt of a marked typescript (Figure 12.1) yields a wealth of information—not only about a reader, but also about the nature of the reading process itself. Each of a reader's unexpected responses (miscues) to a text tells us something of interest: the concern for meaning evident in the "double backing" of simple repetitions, self-corrections, or multiple attempts at producing a meaningful structure; the economy produced by omissions; the enrichment provided by meaningful insertions. Collectively as patterns, these miscues allow for inferences about a reader's concern for constructing meaning as the reader engages in reading—what Kenneth Goodman calls "comprehending" (Goodman, 2003a).

Patterns of miscues also allow us to infer insights about reading and time. Miscue analysis research has shown that when a text is familiar, mature readers proceed confidently and produce few repetitions or miscues that result in meaning loss (Goodman et al., 1987). But, when a text is unfamiliar or when a reader does not yet have mature control over the reading process, one observes that the reader produces frequent repetitions or proceeds more slowly when their predictions are not confirmed by the visual cues they expect to see. As a reader negotiates a particular text, it is common to hear the reader speed up and slow down as he or she constructs a meaning.

A common meaning for *flowing* is smoothness, but it can also mean to follow a course, the sense in which it is used here. If miscue markings on a typescript are paired with observations of a reader's speed, one gets a sense of a reader's dynamic response to a text—of speeding up and slowing down across a text. This is flow. Just as evaluating the quality of patterns of miscues yields insights into a reader's concern for constructing meaning, evaluating a reader's varying speed across a text provides a means of interpreting the efficiency with which readers employ the strategies of sampling, inferring, predicting, and confirming. Flow relates to the dynamic quality of reading speed.

The following example illustrates the concept of reading flow. The markings in Figure 12.1 document the miscues produced by a seventh-grade reader during a proficient reading of a folktale. By carefully looking at a miscue-marked excerpt of her reading, we can imagine the reading speed ebb and flow of her response to the text. The excerpt in Figure 12.1 is the 14th paragraph from the story "The Man Who Kept House" (1962).

Note that the reader's miscues show a high degree of concern for meaning. In Sentence 37 on Line 0316, the reader produces a complex miscue.

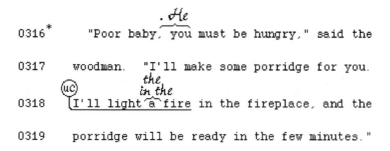

Figure 12.1
A miscue-marked typescript.

Her structural reorganization of the text transforms the woodman's quote (which is directed to the baby) into a quote in which the woodman seems to be thinking aloud to himself about his predicament. "'Poor baby. He must be hungry,' said the woodman." In Sentence 39 on Line 0318, the reader produces another complex miscue. This time, she produces what seems to be an incomplete prepositional phrase, *"I'll light in the —."* Then, she returns to the beginning of the sentence, but instead of producing the expected response *a,* she produces a determiner substitution in the form of a definite article (*the,* which performs the same grammatical function as the expected text) and continues reading. A detailed transcription of the reading would be: *"I'll light in the — I'll light the fire in the fireplace and the porridge will be ready in a few minutes."* Her repetition can be interpreted as a response to a prediction that was disconfirmed by the cues she sampled in the text. The subsequent production of the second miscue *the* suggests at least two interpretations:

1. That she possesses an understanding of the architecture of peasant dwellings or at least the pragmatics of food preparation. A woodman's house probably only has one fixture dedicated for cooking fires, hence the assignment of a definite article in place of an indefinite one.
2. That she possesses an understanding of the pragmatics of intentionality; the fire the woodman intends to light will indeed be the same one on which he will cook the porridge to feed the hungry baby.

Either way, the reader's miscues in this sequence show that she is comprehending what she reads.

So, after initially proceeding forward at the beginning of Line 0318, the reader stopped because she perceived a problem that required her to reconcile the wording and syntax that she had predicted and assigned with the wording and syntax that she was sampling. She then doubled back to the beginning of the sentence and produced a meaningful and fully acceptable structure before proceeding forward again. But, backing up takes time. If one could gauge her reading speed as she progressed across this section of the text, then a recording of the successive positions of the gauge's needle would look something like "fast, stop, slow, fast." That is reading flow. In this way, the concept of flow works together with miscue analysis to enhance an understanding of the reading process.

Water flowing in a river is a helpful metaphor for understanding reading flow. Imagine measuring the speed at which water travels on the surface at any point along a particular segment of a river's path. Now, imagine the range of physical circumstances in the riverbed that contributes to variations in the water's traveling speed along the river's course: changes in depth, submerged boulders, bottlenecks, and the like. If you were to follow the progress of a floating leaf as it travels down the river, then you would notice that as the banks of the river widen, the speed of the leaf decreases — almost stopping, perhaps. On the other hand, you would notice that the speed rapidly increases as the distance between the river's banks narrows and the leaf shoots through a narrow canyon. The leaf's speed would decrease rapidly as it approaches a bottleneck of the type that a logjam might create, and then it would increase rapidly over the stretch where the water flow finds an outlet. In fact, one can think of any variety of physical characteristics in a riverbed, one after another, that would be metaphorically illustrative in describing what happens as readers "navigate" a text.

The Text as a Riverbed

Goodman (1997) has suggested that the flow metaphor can be extended to include the text: "If reading is flow, then the reader is the river and the text is the riverbed." The extension of the flow metaphor to include the text is a useful one, to be sure. Here is how it might work. In a river, the change in flow that occurs when a channel descends so steeply that submerged objects in the riverbed disturb the river's surface is called a *rapids*. These submerged objects create unique patterns of flow in the water that courses over them. An example of one such pattern would be a surge that is formed when a channel is narrowly constrained by rocks that form the shoulders of a bottleneck. The water forms a chute that maintains its shape even as water continually flows through it. Another example of a pattern is a standing wave that remains in place even though different water molecules continually move through the rapids at any given time.

Here is a third example: When a volume of water exceeds the capacity of a channel to carry it, like the water before a bottleneck, an eddy is formed. Water in an eddy current moves contrary to the direction of the main current, especially in a circular motion. Like the standing wave, the pattern of flow that is an eddy current remains stationary even though molecules of water continue to flow past.

Goodman, Watson, and Burke's (1987) observations of text characteristics and miscues make a nice parallel to the discussion of riverbed features that result in patterns of reading flow:

> Readability means the ease or difficulty with which a reader constructs meaning. By using the same material over a period of time, it becomes obvious which miscues are caused by the complexity of the text. When a large number of readers regardless of background and ability miscue at the same point, the miscue can often be attributed to a feature or features of the text. (p. 39)

Enlisting miscue analysis to determine how text complexity contributes to the production of miscues is precisely what Altwerger and Goodman (1981) did. Using data gathered from many readers, Altwerger and Goodman analyzed sentences from three stories for the purpose of identifying aspects of text that contributed to high miscue rates. When miscue frequency was analyzed in terms of both the linguistic complexity of texts and in light of readers' transactions with text, several characteristics were determined to have a bearing on miscue frequency: lack of relevant prior context; unfamiliar or unusual use of terminology; weak syntax; unpredictable simple structures; unusual stylized syntax; complex syntax; or combinations of all of these elements.

In the river metaphor, using miscue analysis to determine which miscues are caused by the complexity of the text is akin to plotting the topographic contour of a riverbed to determine causes of patterns of water flow. If we examine a text by noting the occurrence of miscues produced by large numbers of readers in the same places in the text, then we can find out where the "eddies" and "standing waves" are. Likewise, we can use a reading flow analysis to identify text features associated with higher or lower rates even in the absence of the production of miscues. By using miscue analysis with reading flow analysis, we can combine our observations of readers' unexpected responses and readers' use of time to arrive at a more sophisticated determination of those text features that predictably contribute to visible patterns of reading flow.

Conceptualizing Reading as Flow

In this section I outline a methodology for measuring rate within a text along with some language that describes this different view. I demonstrate that it is through an alternative method of measuring reading rate that theoretical insights into reading fluency are revealed. Before I introduce this procedure, some points about reading and time and some assumptions about language require brief mention.

Reading and Time

Most researchers have implicitly characterized reading rate as a phenomenon that is stable and sustained throughout a text during an act of fluent reading:

> [Fluent reading is] generally smooth reading with some breaks, but word and structure difficulties are resolved quickly, usually through self-correction. ... Consistently conversational. (Zutell & Rasinski, 1991, p. 215)

> Cognitive psychologists who study reading conceive of reading fluency as the ability to recognize words rapidly and accurately. (Stanovich, 1991, p. 19)

> Reading successfully is a complex interaction of language, sensory perception, memory and motivation. To illustrate the role of fluency, it helps to characterize this multifaceted process as including *at least* two activities: (1) word recognition or decoding and (2) comprehension, or the construction of the meaning of text. In order for reading to proceed effectively, the reader cannot focus attention on both processes. Constructing meaning involves making inferences, responding critically, and so on, and it *always* requires attention. The nonfluent reader can alternate attention between the two processes; however, this makes reading a laborious, often punishing process. If attention is drained by decoding words, little or no capacity is available for the attention-demanding process of comprehending. Therefore, automaticity of decoding — a critical component of fluency — is essential for high levels of reading achievement. (Pikulski & Chard, 2003, p. 511)

The implication is that, for a competent reader, oral reading should be smooth, rapid enough to be considered "conversational," free from hesitations and miscalls, and free from indications that the reader is laboring under the task. Rate and prosodic pacing are treated as related aspects. And, although fluency advocates probably would not go so far as to suggest that rate is constant throughout a text, the issue does not get addressed. One notable exception is Carver (1990), who states unequivocally that "most individuals do have a constant reading rate [across texts], in standard words per minute, Wpm" (p. 437).

Procedure for Illustrating Reading Flow*

The procedure for illustrating reading flow is simple and straightforward. First, a text interval is chosen. An *interval* is the portion of printed text over which reading rate is calculated. Possible interval choices might be: whole text, text divided into equal thirds, paragraphs, sentences, clauses, words, or syllables.

Second, reading rate is calculated by dividing the number of printed words in the interval by the elapsed reading time in minutes. This index is expressed in words per minute (wpm).† The amount of time (duration) taken to read the text in the interval is determined by the following procedure:

- *First Interval*: The timing is started at the beginning of the first oral reading utterance, and it is stopped at the end of the last utterance as the final sound dissipates. *First utterance* is defined as the beginning of the first perceivable sound in a sound stream. *Last utterance* is defined as the last perceivable sound in a sound stream as the final sound dissipates. When finding the duration of an entire text, treat the entire text as a first (and only) interval.

- *Subsequent Intervals*: The timing is started at the end of the last utterance of the previous interval and is stopped at the end of the last utterance of the current interval. When determining the duration of each of several intervals, proceed in this fashion by going from the end of the last utterance in the previous interval to the end of the last utterance in the current interval until the last interval is reached.

For example, when determining the rate throughout successive paragraphs or sentences, follow this procedure (Figure 12.2). Timing proceeds from last utterance of previous interval to last utterance of current interval. This method produces seamless continuity.‡

---

* For a detailed description of this methodology, see Flurkey, 1997.

† Derived expressions of reading rate (correct words per minute and errors per minute) contain internal inconsistencies that inflate the estimations of counts of reading errors. Simple rate, on the other hand, requires no judgments to determine which responses count as errors.

‡ See Flurkey (1997) for a discussion of procedures for measuring the duration of intervals that contain repetitions that cross interval boundaries and other special circumstances.

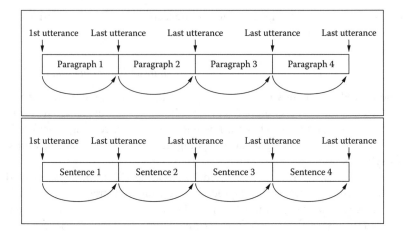

Figure 12.2
Procedure for timing intervals.

Locating Interval Boundaries

Patterns of reading flow can be determined by partitioning a whole text into sections (units of analysis) and then measuring the duration of an oral reading of each selected section and dividing the duration by the number of words in the section. The measurement of reading rate requires that one locate the boundaries between sections with a high degree of precision. However, perceiving boundaries between words in normal speech is challenging. The difficulty comes from the fact that individual phonemes are produced in a continuous sound stream. This phenomenon makes the boundaries that separate individual phonemes difficult to perceive because it sounds to the listener as if individual phonemes are run together. An example is the phrase "Once upon a time", which in a continuous stream sounds something like "Wunsupannahtime".

To solve this problem, computer software was used to capture sound, digitize the sample, and produce a graphic waveform. Once captured and displayed on a computer screen, any portion of the waveform can be played (and replayed several times if necessary). Once the phonemic boundaries of a word, sentence, or paragraph have been determined, one can use the computer software's "ruler" to determine the time elapsed between the boundaries. This is done by excerpting and measuring a particular sample of digitized sound in much the same way that one would cut a segment of string from a spool, stretch it next to a ruler, and measure its length. By determining the time elapsed between the boundaries, one can obtain a measurement of duration of a given segment of a sound stream with a precision of up to 1/100th of a second (0.01 s).

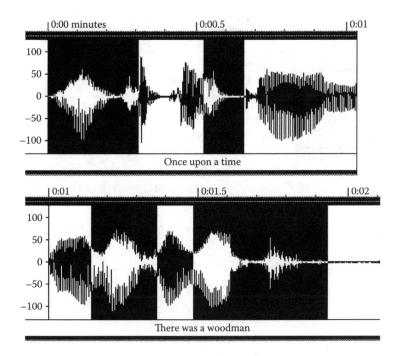

Figure 12.3
Digital voice waveform.

Figure 12.3 illustrates this procedure. The figure shows a waveform representing a digital sampling of a person reading the phrase "Once upon a time there was a woodman" at a brisk rate of 220 wpm. The waveform segments that represent individual words are highlighted in alternating black and white to illustrate word boundaries and digital representations of phonemes in the digitized sound stream. As such, this procedure can be used to help determine the boundaries that separate paragraphs, sentences, and words.

Using the Procedure to Analyze a Reading

The Entire Text as Interval By applying the interval-partitioning procedure with its precise methodology to the analysis of oral reading, it becomes clear that reading rate is not static or stable, but that it varies throughout a text in response to readers' transactions with text. To demonstrate how the procedure reveals the variability of reading rate *within* a text, an analysis of a reading of the entire text as a single interval must first be undertaken to allow for a comparison of the two views of reading rate. The following is a brief analysis

Table 12.1 Statistical Summary for Reader 1 With the Whole Text as the Interval

Whole Text

The Man Who Kept House

790 words @ 18 min., 11 sec.

Rate: 43 words per minute

Repetitions (all types): 145

Number of pauses: 17

(Pause = Lapse > 5 s)

Total duration of all pauses: 3 min., 37 sec.

Total number of miscues: 98

Miscues per hundred words (MPHW): 12.40

Meaning construction

No loss: 64%

Partial loss 31%   } 95%

Loss 5%

Grammatical relations

Strength 58%

Partial strength 6%

Overcorrection 17%   } 81%

Weakness 9%

of the oral reading of a story by a third grader (designated Reader 1 in this chapter). It should be noted that the reader is, at the least, an effective reader of this passage. She is effective because understands what she reads (Goodman, 1982; Goodman et al., 1987). The reader's retelling is thorough and complete. Further evidence of the reader's effectiveness is provided in Table 12.1 (note that the miscue analysis meaning construction index is 95%). A calculation of the reading rate with the whole text as a single interval and a summary of the quality of miscues are provided along with additional information that relates to the reader's reading rate throughout the entire text.

Note that Reader 1's reading rate of 43 wpm is far below that almost all fluency advocates would consider appropriate or acceptable for third graders. Carnine and Silbert (1979) suggest that a rate between 120 and 135 wpm would be appropriate for a reader at the third-grade level; Howell and Lorson-Howell (1990) propose a rate of 145 wpm or more for third graders. Even fluency advocates who might harbor misgivings about recommending a specific reading rate would probably agree that, based on the sheer number of repetitions (145) and excessive pause time (3 min., 37 sec. is nearly 20% of

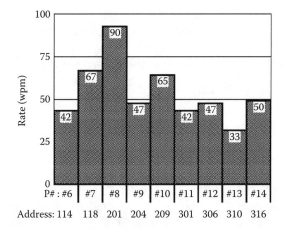

Figure 12.4
Successive reading rates across paragraph intervals.

the total reading time), this reading of the text is unacceptably disfluent.* But, such a contention would conflict with what is already known about this reader — that she is an effective reader. This is a conflict because the concept of reading fluency, which is predicated on theories of reading as rapid and accurate word recognition, stipulates that a reader who reads at such a low rate should lack the necessary free cognitive attention required to achieve the high degree of comprehension that Reader 1 has demonstrated as indicated by her retelling.

Analysis of Rate Throughout Paragraph Intervals When the analysis of rate is conducted on paragraphs within a text, an intriguing pattern appears. Figure 12.4 represents the juxtaposition of nine intervals where Reader 1's

---

* The identification of pauses is an important aspect of reading flow analysis. Because readers sometimes briefly hesitate when reading orally, a criterion is needed for distinguishing between brief lapses in oral production and longer lapses that are counted as pauses. The criterion that I have chosen is to designate lapses of 5 s or longer as *pauses*. Lapses of less than 5 s are not counted as pauses. I have chosen 5 s as a criterion because pauses of similar duration seem to signal that a reader has earnestly focused on a problem and is committed to search for a solution. In the professional literature, 5 s is also the maximum time that researchers in the word identification research tradition have waited for a response before offering a word prompt to a reader and considering the hesitation as an error (see Flurkey, 1997, p. 41, for a summary). In miscue analysis research, of course, the reader is not interrupted.

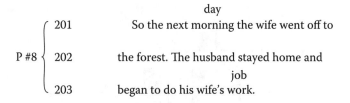

Figure 12.5
Marked typescript for Paragraph 8.

reading rate was measured throughout successive paragraphs taken from the middle of the text (Paragraphs 6 to 14).

Not only is there a variation of the reading rate throughout successive paragraphs, but also the variation in speed of paragraph reading from the mean rate for the entire text (43 wpm) is clearly visible. In this example, notice that the reading rate throughout paragraphs is neither constant nor stable: Paragraph 13, read the slowest, was read at a rate that was 25% slower than the mean rate for the entire text; Paragraph 8 (Figure 12.5), the fastest, was read over twice as fast as the entire text (209% of the mean rate for the entire text). It is also important to note that, as illustrated in Figure 12.5, Paragraph 8 contains two high-quality substitution miscues that have little graphic similarity and no sound similarity to the text: *day* for *morning* and *job* for *work*.

Another point about Reader 1's reading bears mentioning: If this reader's rate throughout paragraph intervals had not been calculated, then one might not be aware that the reader is indeed capable of reading at a rate that is significantly higher than the 43-wpm mean. The reader is not simply a slow reader of this text, an insight that is in square opposition to commonsense assumptions that reading is a "word-by-word" enterprise. In this analysis, the reader's pacing is dynamic and responsive to what is "happening" in various parts of the text. Furthermore, as Figure 12.4 suggests (and Figures 12.5–12.7 demonstrate), Reader 1 is efficient as well as effective over some sections of the text. That is, she is able to understand the text successfully while sampling the fewest cues necessary.

Analysis of Rate Throughout Sentence Intervals   As shown in Figure 12.4, Paragraph 13 was identified as the paragraph that was read at the slowest rate of the nine successive paragraphs that were measured. An analysis of the rate at which each sentence was read within that paragraph reveals more intriguing observations. One might be tempted to guess that the entire paragraph was problematic for Reader 1, and that each of the sentences was read relatively

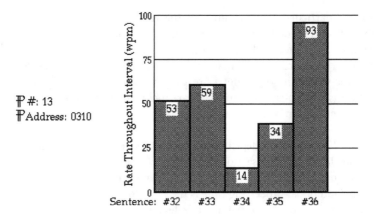

℗ #: 13
℗ Address: 0310

Figure 12.6
Successive reading rates across sentence intervals.

slowly. But, a graph of the reading rate of successive sentences reveals just the opposite.

Figure 12.6 shows that the sentences in Paragraph 13, which was read at the rate of 33 wpm, contain wide variations of reading rate. In fact, the general "contour"* of the data (the stair-stepping or undulating up-and-down shape to the juxtaposed rectangles) looks similar to the contour of successive paragraph intervals in Figure 12.4. By changing the interval at which reading speed is measured, from the whole text, to a paragraph, to sentences within the paragraph, it becomes evident that there are sentences in which the reader reads much faster than the 33-wpm mean for the entire paragraph. For example, Sentence 36 is read at a rate that is 282% of the 33-wpm mean (nearly three times as fast), whereas Sentence 34 is read at a rate that is less than half the mean for the paragraph (42% of the mean). Similar results emerge when comparing the rate throughout sentences with the mean rate for the entire text. Sentence 36 was read at 216% of the mean for the entire text (43 wpm), and Sentence 34 was read at a rate that was only 32% of the mean for the text.

Just as was the case for representing rate across paragraphs (Figure 12.4), the representation of rate throughout sentences shows a wide range of variability. To find the factors that contribute to this variability, one must look beyond a simple numerical representation of juxtaposed intervals; one must look at the marked miscue typescript to obtain a sense of how the reader's transaction

---

* A *contour* is the curve mapped by the tops of each of the columns.

with this particular text accounts for the variability observed. Qualitative information is needed to make the quantitative information meaningful.

Figure 12.7, which includes information on both speed and reader miscues, is a rich source of information that illustrates the factors that contribute to the variability of Reader 1's reading rate. Note that when the pauses, repetitions, and substitution miscues are included on the typescript, creditable inferences can be made about the reasons for variability in the reader's reading speed.

Figure 12.7 couples a depiction of reading strategies with reading rate to illustrate the reader's transaction with the text. Observe that when she perceives a conceptual or linguistic "problem," the reader engages in additional processing. The additional processing time is the result of her production of pauses, repetitions, or both. The variability of rate that Reader 1 displays is related to the efficiency with which she employs reading strategies. The production of pauses or repetitions results in a lower reading rate for a given sentence.

Continuous Change in Reading Rate

For much of the reading research community, *fluent reading* is characterized as word identification that is rapid and accurate. The alternate view offered here describes reading as a process of meaning construction: the reader constructs personal meaning by transacting with written text.

Traditional beliefs about reading fluency hold that fluent readers accurately and rapidly identify words, and that slow, labored, and inaccurate oral reading does not proceed at a sufficient rate required to maintain comprehension. Furthermore, according to this view, a simple index of reading fluency can be determined by calculating a reader's reading rate over an entire text (expressed as words per minute: total words in the text divided by the time taken to read aloud).

However, as has been shown in the analysis of this effective reader, the use of a single numerical index such as words per minute per text is not only inadequate at capturing the dynamic element of reading speed that has been described here, but also it obscures the underlying character of the reading process. Reading rate is not a characteristic, which is simple and static; on the contrary, it is the outward sign of one dimension of a dynamic and complex process. And, instead of simply using reading rate as synonymous for a static measure of words read per minute, it is more helpful to think of reading rate as the variable rate of processing text as measured by record of oral output.

The use of rate to analyze oral reading of a whole text adds an unexplored dimension to miscue analysis. When simultaneously displayed with

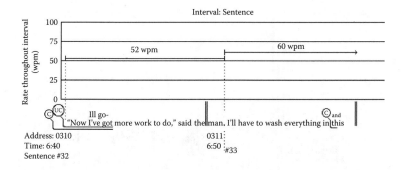

Interval: Sentence

Address: 0310
Time: 6:40
Sentence #32

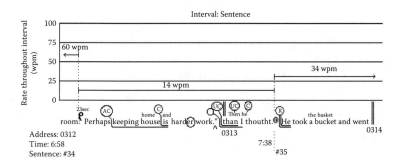

Interval: Sentence

Address: 0312
Time: 6:58
Sentence: #34

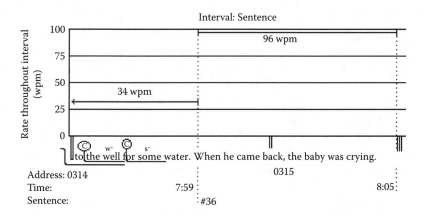

Interval: Sentence

Address: 0314
Time:
Sentence:

Figure 12.7
Sentence interval rate and reading strategy use.

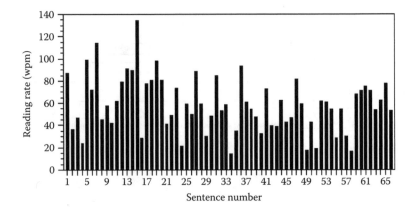

Figure 12.8
Reading rate for successive sentences across entire
text for effective reading (Reader 1).

a miscue-marked typescript, a rate interval analysis provides an understanding of how the contour of a reader's pattern of rate is an indication of
the effective and efficient employment of reading strategies* (Figure 12.8).

Reading Rate Compared for Proficient and Nonproficient Readings

When the reading rates for individual sentences in a text are juxtaposed, a
'stepped' contour is evident (Figure 12.8). Figure 12.9 shows the reading flow
analysis of two readers reading the folktale "The Man Who Kept House."
The figure shows a comparison of the reading flow pattern of a proficient
reading (by Reader 6) to that of an effective but nonproficient reading (by
Reader 1).†‡ These patterns show a striking similarity in that both display
the up-and-down stepped contour. Furthermore, when the patterns of variability are compared between the proficient reading (right graph) and the
nonproficient reading (left graph), there appears to be a greater variability of
sentence reading rate observed in the proficient reading.

---

* A reading of a text is *effective* when the reader is successful at constructing a personal
  meaning. The term *efficient* means reading while using the fewest print cues necessary.
† The term proficient means that a reader is both effective and efficient when reading a particular text.
‡ It is important to differentiate the term *reader* from *reading*. All readers can be efficient
  readers of some texts. Likewise, mature readers may struggle over texts with high concept loads, unfamiliar content, or complex syntax.

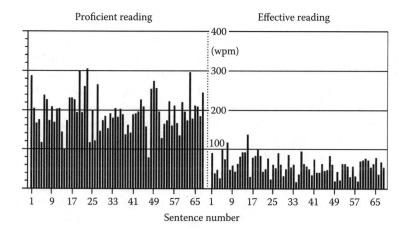

Figure 12.9
**Comparison of rates for proficient and effective readings
for successive sentences. Across entire text: "The Man Who
Kept House." Proficient reading rate = 181 wpm over entire
text. Effective reading rate = 43 wpm over entire text.**

This stepped contour evident in Figure 12.8 is typical of all 12 readers
for whom data were collected, and the observation that there appears to be
greater variability of reading rate in the more proficient reading is a finding
that is typical of the readings that have been analyzed. This last observation is an important one because it reveals the nature of reading when a
reader possesses mature control over the employment of reading strategies.
A theory of reading as automatic word identification lends itself to the suggestion that a reader who is highly skilled at word recognition would present
a "flatter" contour. However, reading flow data show that proficient readings
display *greater* rate variability.

Using Reading Flow to Describe Flexibility of Strategy Use in Reading

Research is about finding patterns—finding relationships in places where
such things were not previously suspected. Miscue analysis is concerned
with uncovering patterns of miscues that demonstrate a reader's tendency
for producing an abundance of high-quality or low-quality miscues or for
overcorrecting. Reading flow analysis provides a way to document how and
why reading flows. This information can be used to provide a useful summary of an individual reader's pattern of reading flow.

Profiling Reading Flow With Frequency Polygons

Analyses of reading flow can provide a unique graphic summary—a "fingerprint" of a specific oral reading. This is done by constructing a frequency polygon* from a reader's sentence rates for all of the sentences collected during a miscue analysis reading sample for a single story. The construction of a frequency polygon requires the sorting of sentence rates for each sentence in a text into "bins" of a specified rate range. The result is a frequency distribution that is unique to each reading and that, along with a few summary statistics, provides quantitative information about the range and amount of sentence rate variability or dispersion.†

The observation mentioned in the preceding discussion—that the more proficient readings display greater sentence rate variability—is evident in the analysis of all of the readers for whom data are available. Figures 12.10a–12.10f display the sentence rate distributions for readings of "The Man Who Kept House" by six readers. The retellings for all of the readings were satisfactory and complete, indicating all of the readers comprehended the story. The proficiency of the readings ranges from less proficient on the left to more proficient on the right. One gets a sense of each reader's mean sentence rate and standard deviation in relation to the others' by displaying all six polygons in the same chart (Figure 12.11).

Using Reading Flow Analysis as an Index of Flexibility

The frequency polygons in Figures 12.10a–12.10f and 12.11 show that more proficient readings (Figures 12.10d, 12.10e, and 12.10f) display greater sentence rate variability. Frequency polygons also provide a useful way of conceptualizing readers' employment of reading strategies.

Table 12.2 shows that several key features vary together. Mean sentence reading rate varies with standard deviation, showing that readings with faster average sentence rates also display greater variability. The total number of repetitions and total pause time decrease as standard deviation increases. Thus, the pattern that emerges from the data in Figure 12.10a–12.10f and Figure 12.11 is that more efficient readings are associated with higher reading rates and greater variability.

---

* The tips of the frequency polygons in Figures 12.10 and 12.11 have been rounded to give a more curve-like appearance.

† Three statistics are used to summarize the dispersions of sentence rates: X_s = the mean sentence reading rate, σ = the standard deviation, and R = the range of sentence reading rates where range is calculated as the maximum rate minus the minimum rate plus 1 (Max − Min + 1).

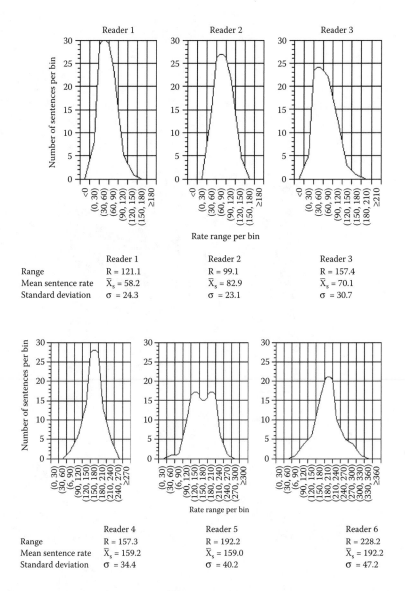

Figure 12.10
Frequency polygons for six readers.

Table 12.2 Comparison of Efficiency-Related Features for Readings of "The Man Who Kept House"

Reader	R1	R2	R3	R4	R5	R6
Total repetitions	148	39	77	25	23	14
Total pause time (s)	337.1	19.8	218.8	11.1	7.72	2.9
Mean sentence rate X_s (wpm)	58.2	82.9	70.1	159.2	159.0	192.2
Standard deviation σ	24.3	23.1	30.7	34.4	40.2	47.2

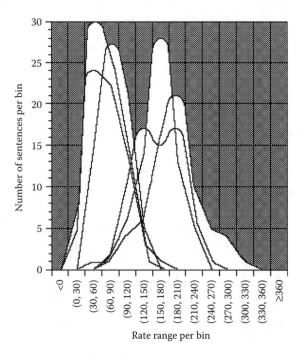

Figure 12.11
Display of frequency polygons of all six readers.

The presence of a wider range and greater variability for the proficient reading runs counter to what one might expect if reading was best described as a process of rapid and accurate word identification. If that was the case, then it would be reasonable to expect that less, not more, variability would accompany greater skill in identifying words, resulting in higher mean sentence rates. But, that does not happen. Instead, variability increases as readings become more proficient. The question is, Why? To use the language of topography: *Why are the peaks higher and the valleys lower, and why are both the peaks and valleys set in a higher average elevation?*

The pattern to the data suggests that more proficient readings are characterized by greater flexibility in the employment of reading strategies. In other words, what makes readers proficient is not only that they are faster and produce fewer repetitions and pauses, but also that they are more flexible. Readers who display mature control over use of the reading process when transacting with a particular text are able to efficiently and flexibly control their use of the reading strategies of sampling, predicting, inferring, and confirming. When readers produce proficient readings, they display greater facility in speeding up when they can and slowing down when needed. Their control enables them to do whatever they deem necessary to identify and solve problems as they construct meaning. That is why the sentence rate distributions for the more proficient readings have a "wider spread." Given these insights about reading flow and strategy use, standard deviation can be thought of as a statistical measure that communicates the degree of flexibility of strategy use—an index of flexibility.

Reading Flow and Schema Processes

Although I have provided a method for visualizing the variability of reading rate—the how part of reading flow, I have not provided a theoretical explanation for the tentativeness that results in rate variability. The concept of schema proves most helpful here insofar as it is used to help explain the generation of miscues. In drawing from the theoretical framework for schema provided by Piaget (1977), Goodman and Goodman (2003) define *schema* as "an organized cognitive structure of related knowledge, ideas, emotions and action that has been internalized and that guides and controls a person's subsequent use of information and response to experience" (p. 237). Goodman and Goodman state that humans possess schemata for all aspects of the human experience: linguistic schemata (rules) for producing and comprehending language and conceptual schemata for ideas, concepts, and knowledge of the world. Furthermore, humans also develop overarching schemata for the creation of new schemata and the modification of existing ones. Because language and thought are inextricably linked, linguistic and conceptual schemata are at work simultaneously.

This discussion of schema processes can be used to explain the nature of oral reading miscues by making a distinction between schema-driven miscues and schema-forming miscues (Goodman & Goodman, 2003, p. 238). The Piagetian concepts of assimilation and accommodation are relevant here (Piaget,

1977). Goodman and Goodman make use of these concepts to describe the distinction between the two types of miscues in the following way:

> A schema-forming miscue may be seen as a struggle toward accommodation, while a schema-driven miscue shows assimilation at work. Further, the effect of the miscue on subsequent language processing or intent may result in a disequilibrium, which may lead to reprocessing — that is, self-correction. Schemata may need to be abandoned, modified, or reformed as miscues are corrected. ... A schema-forming miscue is likely to involve new information, either linguistic or conceptual, which may not be easily assimilated.
>
> A schema-driven miscue may involve either old (given) information or new information in a predictable context. Furthermore, the schema, as well as the information, may be old or new. ... A schema-driven miscue is one that results from the use of existing schemata to produce or comprehend language. (pp. 238–239)

Here is another way to think about schema processes. Schema formation results from the employment of processing operations that readers perform when they need to disambiguate a message — schema formation is a process of disambiguation. Miscue structures that result from schema-driven processes occur when readers' linguistic and conceptual knowledge come together in such a way that their predictions direct their sampling strategies to shape perception and override the text.

Substitutions, omissions, insertions, and similar miscues that do not result in meaning loss are typically found in the production of schema-driven structures. The following is an example of a structure containing schema-driven miscues:

```
"You don't know what hard work is! You (should) try
                                        chopping
cutting wood!"
```

In this example, the reader is constructing a personal meaning in such a way that his uses of sampling and prediction strategies enable him to override the text — observed as: "You try chopping wood!"

Schema formation, on the other hand, is not easily visible because it is often the result of ongoing processes. Bearing that in mind, one example of when the formation of new schema (or the modification of existing schema) indeed makes itself visible is when readers produce partially acceptable miscues that may or may not be reconciled through efforts at correction. In such circumstances, either linguistic or conceptual schema (or both) are formed or modified. In the following example, the reader is clearly predicting an alternate structure other than that observed in the text. The result is the production of a schema-forming structure:

```
0204        He began to make some butter.  As he put

0205        the cream into the churn, he said,  "This is
                          ©         at  a-
0206        not going to be hard work.  All I have to do
```

In Lines 0206 and 0207 before repeating to self-correct, the reader says, "This is not going to be hard at a___." Judging from the reader's intonation, it is likely that she had initially assigned an alternate syntax and wording to the end of the sentence, one that would have resulted in the structure, "This is not going to be hard at all." This production would have been entirely acceptable and would have resulted in a complex schema-driven miscue, but something troubled the reader. Perhaps she was unsettled by the prospect of ending one sentence with "all" and beginning the next with the same word: "This is not going to be hard at all. All I have to do … ." Through additional text sampling, she may have noticed that there are not two *all*s in the text. So, instead of continuing through the text, the reader stopped, backtracked, and produced the expected response, "hard work." This is an example of linguistic schema formation because, although the reader initially substituted one structure, circumstances required an accommodation (in the form of additional sampling and a reassignment of syntax and wording) to reconcile her construction with the text that followed.

This conceptual framework for schema formation and use as articulated by Goodman and Goodman (2003) is relevant to the construction of a model of reading flow. Flow and schema processes are concepts that are linked. Readers' constructions and modifications of schemata are in continuous transaction with their employment of cognitive strategies. This transaction accounts for flow. From a reading flow standpoint, the key difference between the production of schema-driven and schema-forming structures is that *productions that involve schema formation require comparatively more thinking and processing time than productions that are schema-driven.*

Reading Flow and Schema Processes in an Effective (But Not Efficient) Reading

To illustrate this principle, the principle that schema formation requires more time, a comparison is made between sentences that were read by Reader 1 at the highest rates (Table 12.3) with sentences read at the lowest

Table 12.3   Sentences Read at Highest Rates (Descending Order) During Effective Reading (Reader 1)

Sentence rate (wpm)	134.3	113.9	98.7	97.7	93.3	91.4	89.5
Sentence number in text	15	7	5	19	36	13	14
Number of miscues in sentence	1	1	0	0	0	1	1
Sentence-level meaning loss (semantic acceptability)	Partial loss[a]	No loss	No loss	No loss	No loss	No loss	No loss

[a] This sentence would have been entirely semantically acceptable except for the production of a nonword in the following sentence.

Table 12.4   Sentences Read at Lowest Rates (Descending Order) During Effective Reading (Reader 1)

Sentence rate (wpm)	18.8	17.2	16.3	14.7
Sentence number in text	51	49	58	34
Number of miscues in sentence	1	5	3	6
Resultant sentence-level meaning loss	Partial change	Loss	Loss	Loss

rate (Table 12.4). In both cases, Reader 1 produced these sentences during the effective but nonproficient reading.

Table 12.3 shows that, of the fastest seven sentences produced during an effective reading of "The Man Who Kept House," four sentences (57%) contain miscues, including the first two sentences read at the highest rates (134.3 and 113.9 wpm). Based on this small sampling of evidence, one might argue that the production of miscues actually assists the reader in reading faster. These four sentences containing miscues are displayed in Figure 12.12.*

So, of the seven fastest sentences, four sentences contain miscues. Of those sentences that contain miscues, all four are produced as schema-driven,

---

* In a marked typescript, sentences are numbered in order from the first sentence to the last in a text. In Figures 12.12–12.15, the sentence number in the text is indicated by a number inscribed in a circle. The sentence number is located at the beginning of the sentence to which it refers. The line address, the series of four numbers located at the left of each line, indicates where in the text the line can be found. The first two numbers of a line address refer to the page in the text where the line can be found. The last two numbers refer to the location of the line on the page. For example, a line address of 0411 indicates that the line of text can be found on page 4 (04), line 11 from the top of the page, or line 11 on page 4.

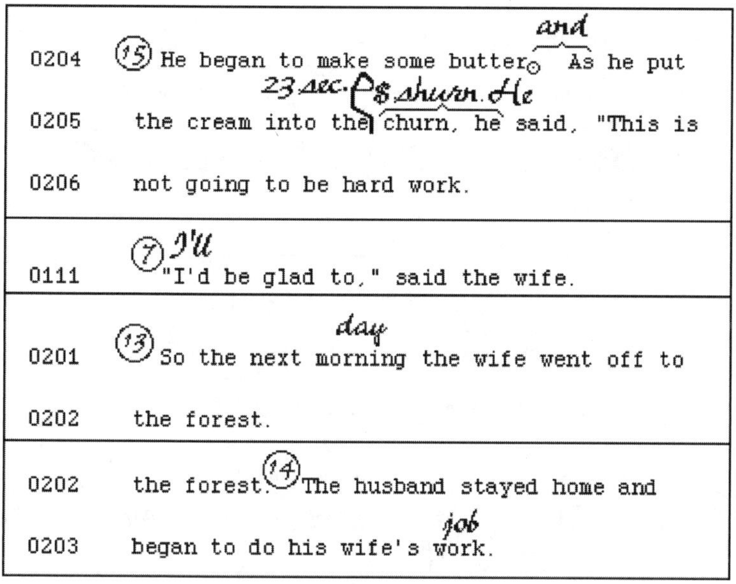

Figure 12.12
**Highest-rate (wpm) sentences that contain
miscues: effective reading (Reader 1).**

miscue-bearing structures insofar as the reader's perceptions have overridden the text.

Now, what about the other extreme? Table 12.4 displays data pertaining to the four sentences that were produced at the lowest rate during the same reading. To understand why these sentences are produced at such low rates, an inspection of the typescript is warranted. Figure 12.13 displays the typescript for the four sentences produced at the lowest rates.

The typescript markings in Figure 12.13 show that each of these sentences is characterized by multiple repetitions and long pauses—evidence of schema formation in each. Of course, just as a high rate does not guarantee sentence acceptability (as Sentence 15 in Table 12.3 shows), it is also true that a low reading rate is not necessarily associated with sentence unacceptability, as Sentence 51 in Table 12.4 shows. Sentence 51 is syntactically and semantically acceptable with partial meaning change. Because reading is a complex act, the relationship between acceptability and reading rate is likely to reflect this complexity. (Indeed, it suggests itself as a topic for future study.)

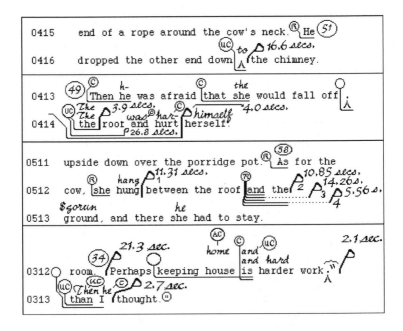

Figure 12.13
**Lowest-rate (wpm) sentences that contain
miscues: effective reading (Reader 1).**

Reading Flow and Schema Processes in a Proficient Reading

The preceding section's paragraphs have been devoted to a discussion of the relationship between schema processes and reading rate — but for an effective reading only. The next analysis focuses on schema use during the proficient reading.

Not surprisingly, the principles illustrated in the excerpts of Reader 1's effective reading of "The Man Who Kept House" (Figures 12.12 and 12.13 and Tables 12.3 and 12.4) are upheld by the data collected during Reader 6's proficient reading of the same text. Namely, the production of schema-driven structures requires less processing and thinking time than the production of schema-forming structures. Table 12.5 shows the statistics for the four sentences read at the highest rate during the proficient reading produced by Reader 6.

Observe that although all four sentences are syntactically and semantically acceptable (no meaning loss), the sentence read at the second highest rate (Sentence 63) contains a schema-driven miscue. Figure 12.14 shows the marked typescript for Sentence 63. The data in Table 12.5 and Figure 12.14

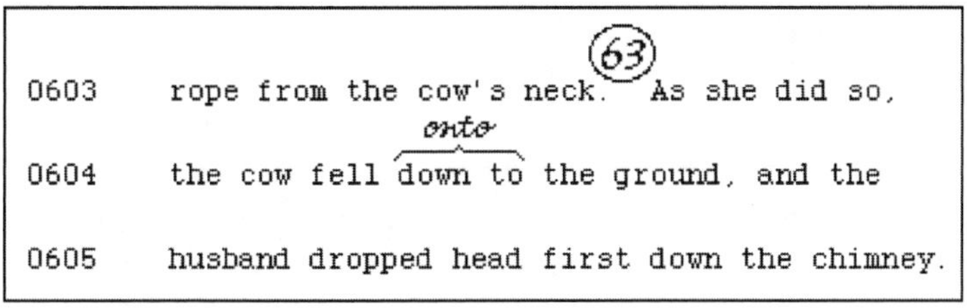

```
0603    rope from the cow's neck.  As she did so,
                                 (63)
                         onto
0604    the cow fell down to the ground, and the

0605    husband dropped head first down the chimney.
```

Figure 12.14
Highest-rate (wpm) sentence that contains a
miscue: proficient reading (Reader 6).

support the argument that schema-driven miscues are involved in highly efficient sentence productions for proficient reading as well as those in effective reading in Table 12.3.

The data from the proficient reading is also supportive of the principle that schema formation requires thinking and processing time. Table 12.6 provides a summary of the data for the four sentences read at the lowest rates during the proficient reading. The data in Table 12.6 show that all four of the sentences are syntactically and semantically acceptable, and the only sentence that contains miscues was the one read at the second-to-the-lowest rate (Sentence 14). To understand why these sentences were produced at such low rates requires an inspection of the marked typescript (Figure 12.15).

The typescript markings in Figure 12.15 show that these sentences are characterized by tentative or purposeful, slow articulation; multiple instances of

Table 12.5 Sentences Read at Highest Rates (Descending Order) During Proficient Reading (Reader 6)

Sentence rate (wpm)	309.2	291.4	282.7	281.6
Sentence number in text	23	63	20	1
Number of miscues in sentence	0	1	0	0
Resultant sentence-level meaning loss	No loss	No loss	No loss	No loss

Table 12.6 Sentences Read at Lowest Rates (Descending Order) During Proficient Reading (Reader 6)

Sentence rate (wpm)	113.4	111.0	96.1	74.1
Sentence number in text	24	5	14	47
Number of miscues in sentence	0	0	3	0
Resultant sentence-level meaning loss	No loss	No loss	No loss	No loss

0301	㉔ ⌐ 3.0 *secs.* ⌐In his hurry, the woodman had left the
0302	door open behind him.
0108	*extra long juncture—* ⑤ *sounds tentative* "Hard work!" said the husband. "You don't /
0109	*(1.9 secs.)* know what hard work is! You should try
0202	the forest. ⑭ The husband stayed home and
0203	© *doing* ⑤ *wife works* *(laughs)* began to do his wife's work.
0410	㊼ ⌐ 4.0 *secs.* → "Oh, yeah. O.k." on the roof. You'll find something to eat
0411	up there. "

Figure 12.15
**Lowest-rate (wpm) sentences that contain
miscues: proficient reading (Reader 6).**

repetitions; or long pauses. In each case, there is evidence of schema formation. In Sentence 24, the reader pauses for 3 s before reading the phrase, "In
his hurry." This suggests that formation or modification of linguistic schema
occurred for this reader at this point in the text. In fact, there is evidence that
most readers, regardless of proficiency, are troubled by the wording of the
phrase, "In his hurry" (Goodman et al., 1987). The data in this study support
this inference because, of the six different readers studied, five produced pauses,
multiple repetitions, or nonword substitutions for the expected text "hurry"
immediately before or during the reading of the phrase, "In his hurry."*

In Sentence 5, the reader does not pause in excess of 2 s, repeat, or produce
miscues. But, she does sound tentative: The word productions are elongated,
and there is a noticeably long juncture (1.9 s) before the sentence.†

---

* Miscue analysis research has documented the phenomenon in which large numbers of
readers produce miscues in the same areas of a particular text (see Altwerger & Goodman, 1981). The "text-as-riverbed" metaphor is developed in Flurkey, 1997.

† The elasticity of word productions as a feature of tentativeness reading is introduced
in Flurkey, 1997. The concepts of tentative-efficient and tentative prosodic modes of
sentence rate dispersion are introduced in chapter 6.

Sentence 14 was the only one of the four lowest-rated sentences that contained miscues. The reader predicted an alternative verb structure, *doing* for *to do*. Even though this production is syntactically and semantically acceptable, and probably represents a construction that is more familiar to the reader, she corrects it nonetheless — an overcorrection in miscue analysis terminology. This event is followed by the complex miscue of *wife works* for *wife's works*. The miscue is also corrected. Although either event may be the result of accommodation of linguistic schema, it may be true of neither. But, if not for reasons of accommodation, then why else might the reader have bothered to self-correct? Interestingly, it is likely that these miscues and repetitions are both evidence of activity of an overarching schema — the rule that says "read-aloud text has to make sense to the audience" — a feature of oral reading. Then again, perhaps the repetitions are the result of the simultaneous operation of all of these processes. One thing can be documented with certainty, however. Because of the low rate of production and two repetitions of all 68 sentences, Sentence 14 was produced with the least efficiency.

Sentence 47 was produced at the lowest rate. Like Sentence 24, this section of the text also frequently causes readers trouble (Goodman et al., 1987). But, unlike Sentence 24, the additional processing time is probably the result of conceptual (as opposed to linguistic) schema accommodation. In this reading, the reader pauses for 4.0 s and then says, "Oh, yeah. O.K." to herself before beginning the sentence. A reasonable interpretation of this event is that this reader was wondering why the man in the story would put a cow on his roof to forage. Then, perhaps by studying the illustration or simply by "figuring it out" for herself, she apparently realizes that the roof is on a sod house and is, itself, covered with sod — grass for the cow to eat. After making this accommodation to her ongoing story schema and her house schema (processes that require thinking time), she continues reading.

In this section, I stated that schema formation results from the employment of processing operations that readers perform when they need to disambiguate a message. In other words, schema formation is a process of disambiguation. This process occurs in oral discourse as well, but there is a distinct difference. In conversations, a listener has the option of performing operations to disambiguate a message by asking the speaker for clarification. With written language, because it is inconvenient or implausible for a reader to make inquiries to the author to obtain clarification, the alternative is for the reader to engage in additional processing of the printed text. That is another way to conceptualize "why reading flows." Reading flows because it can.

Implications: Reading Flow and a Theory of Instruction

The instructional goals that this type of research speak to most clearly are those that support efficient reading. The result of this research supports a curriculum in which extensive and intensive reading for authentic purposes is integral. The results also support instructional strategy lessons that focus on meaning-centered reading, like retrospective miscue analysis (RMA)* and related strategy lessons that focus on comprehension. An instructional application of this research lies in documenting changes in readers' control over the reading process.

It is equally important to state which types of instruction this study does not support. A widely cited instructional activity aimed at training readers to become more fluent is the method of repeated readings (Chomsky, 1976; Samuels, 1979; Samuels et al., 1992). This approach encourages readers to focus on improving surface aspects of reading performances without requiring readers to focus on understanding what they read. The implicit logic behind this activity is that reading competence is raised through improving the quality of a reading performance: We can make readers better if we can teach them to do the things that good oral readers do.

Another widespread instructional practice aimed at improving readers with fluency is the practice of cueing students by supplying them with text words when they hesitate, attempt to repeat, or pause during oral reading. This practice is troublesome insofar as I have argued that readers use this time to engage in additional reflection and processing. The marked type-scripts in Figures 12.16 and 12.17 illustrate this point. The data are taken from RMA sessions with fourth-grade readers.

In the top example of Figure 12.16, it is clear from the configuration of repetitions that the reader is using the text as his teacher. His opportunity to read for meaning and his use of repetitions to provide additional sampling allow him to become more successful at reading for meaning as he produces the expected responses to four miscues in this single excerpt. Note that the reader produces the expected response for "horribly" and "cute" in Line 1602 after producing semantically unacceptable miscues involving these words in the previous two lines.

In the lower example in Figure 12.16, the reader's long repetition is a measure of his concern for meaning. His focus on meaning allows him to take the

---

* RMA (retrospective miscue analysis) is structured language study engagement that involves readers in the study of the reading process through the examination of the tape-recorded miscues that these readers produce during an oral reading (Goodman & Marek, 1996).

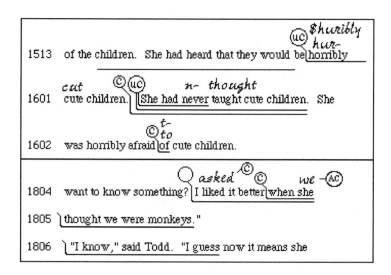

Figure 12.16
Use of repetitions.

initiative to go back two lines in the text to work out a problem resulting from an unreconciled prediction (*asked/liked*). Because the reader is free to make repetitions, he is also free to make sense for himself. Once the reader becomes accustomed to exercising this strategy, he then has opportunities to improve his control in the future by using less effort to confirm his predictions.

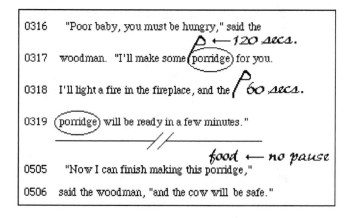

Figure 12.17
Use of pauses.

Figure 12.17 makes a point about pauses. In his reading of "The Man Who Kept House," this reader is troubled by the expected response *porridge*. In Lines 0317 and 0319, he produces lengthy pauses, then decides to omit the expected response, and he keeps reading. Then, on the next occurrence in the story on Line 0512, he produces *food*, a semantically and syntactically acceptable substitution miscue, without pausing. Furthermore, he produces the same substitution of *food* for *porridge* in each of the three remaining occasions in which the word is encountered in the story— again, each time without pausing. A week later, during the RMA session that focused on this particular reading, James was asked why he paused. He responded simply: "I was thinking." When asked what he thought a pronunciation of the word might be, he responded: "I thought it was porridge, but I wasn't sure."

Use of Pauses

A pedagogical technique aimed at raising readers' competence by focusing on and attempting to ameliorate aspects of performance is unhelpful and potentially damaging. Interventions of this sort deny readers the very things they require to improve their reading: experience in exercising strategies that allow them to formulate the questions they need to pose to successfully understand what they are reading. It is strangely incongruous that although support abounds in the literature on reading instruction for the benefits of "wait time" (the practice of teacher waiting after posing a question to give students time to formulate an answer), the practice of supplying readers with words denies them the time they need to answer their own questions.

The results of the study recounted in this chapter do not support the practice of supplying the next word or discouraging readers from backtracking because reading has been shown to be a thinking process of tentativeness and uncertainty reduction. As such, it indicates that strategy lessons that focus on meaning will be most helpful.

Conclusion

Applications of the Study of Reading Flow: Other Research Directions

Further investigations need to be conducted with a variety of texts and more readers who display varying degrees of proficiency, possess a variety of background experiences, speak a variety of dialects of English, speak languages other than English, and read nonalphabetic written languages. The point of further investigations would be to determine the breadth of the reading and time relationships as they have been identified in this chapter.

A variety of topics can be explored using the procedures I have developed. For example, text difficulty can be studied by analyzing the responses of several readers to a particular set of texts. Another intriguing question concerns the robustness of reading flow patterns: Is it generally true that proficient readers produce more widely distributed sentence rates (what I call *strategy employment flexibility*) than nonproficient readers? Study of a larger sample of readers of varying proficiency reading a small number of texts would be necessary to answer this question. Another related question involves examining how patterns of flow change as the same reader reads texts of different degrees of difficulty. And, is there a difference in patterns of flow in different sections of a text? For example, is reading generally faster or slower in the first third of a text when a reader is "settling in"? A third area of exploration—using case studies—involves documenting changes in flexibility of strategy employment across texts and time as a reader becomes more proficient.

Several highly focused studies would help to clarify the nature of flexibility of strategy employment. For example, one could investigate the latency period between production of partially acceptable miscues and subsequent correction for proficient and nonproficient readings. Word and sentence juncture studies can also be done in this line of inquiry.

Reading flow analysis also can be combined with the technology used in eye-movement studies to provide a comprehensive map of how readers visually and perceptually navigate a text (see the following chapters in this volume: Duckett, chapter 5; Ebe, chapter 6; Paulson, chapter 11).

Summary of Findings

The variability of reading rate in connected text and other reading and time relationships are aspects of reading that have received little attention in reading research literature. Indeed, a significant portion of this chapter is devoted to the development of a methodology that enables the documentation of reading flow. Using this methodology, it has been demonstrated that a hydrological metaphor is helpful in conceptualizing the variability of reading rate. This conceptualization has enabled me to document that reading rate variability is present in effective readings as well as in readings that are proficient (effective and efficient). Furthermore, the proficient readings that were studied showed evidence of greater variability than those readings that were merely efficient.

In constructing the theoretical framework that was necessary to interpret the data gathered with the procedure for documenting reading flow, Kenneth Goodman's sociopsycholinguistic transactional theory of reading has been extended. This theory has allowed for an explanation of reading flow in terms of schema processes and the tentative nature of language processing. In doing so, Goodman's theory provides a foundation for an explanation for the greater rate variability produced by proficient readers as a function of the reader's flexibility in cognitive strategy employment. The flexibility of cognitive strategy use, as illustrated in frequency polygons constructed from readers' sentence rate distributions, provides support for a sociopsycholinguistic transactional model of reading.

References

Altwerger, B., & Goodman, K. (1981). *Studying text difficulty through miscue analysis*. Tucson, AZ: University of Arizona, College of Education, Division of Language, Reading and Culture.

Carnine, D., & Silbert, J. (1979). *Direct instruction reading*. Columbus, OH: Charles E. Merrill.

Carver, R. P. (1990). *Reading rate*. San Diego, CA: Academic Press.

Chomsky, C. (1976). After decoding: What? *Language Arts 53* (March): 288–296.

Flurkey, A. (1997). *Reading as flow: A linguistic alternative to fluency*. Unpublished doctoral dissertation, University of Arizona, Tucson.

Flurkey, A. (1998). *Reading as flow: A linguistic alternative to fluency* (Occasional paper, Program in Language and Literacy, No. 26). Tucson: University of Arizona.

Flurkey, A. (2002). Time and tide: The dynamic nature of oral reading. *Hofstra Horizons* (Spring 2002): 13–18.

Gollasch, F. V. (Ed.). (1982). *Language and literacy: The selected writings of Kenneth S. Goodman* (Vol.1). Boston: Routledge and Keegan Paul.

Goodman, K. S. (1982). The reading process: Theory and practice. In F. V. Gollasch (Ed.), Language and literacy: *The selected writings of Kenneth S. Goodman* (Vol. 1, pp. 19–31). Boston: Routledge and Keegan Paul.

Goodman, K. S. (1996). *On reading*. Toronto: Scholastic.

Goodman, K. (1997). How miscue analysis and retrospective miscue analysis help us understand reading. In *The 1997 Dean's Forum for the Advancement of Knowledge and Practice in Education*. Tucson: University of Arizona.

Goodman, K. (2003a). Miscues: Windows on the reading process. In A. Flurkey & J. Xu (Eds.), *On the revolution of reading: The selected writings of Kenneth S. Goodman on the reading process* (pp. 107–116). Portsmouth, NH: Heinemann.

Goodman, K. (2003b). Reading, writing and written texts: A transactional socio-psycholinguistic view. In A. Flurkey & J. Xu (Eds.), *On the revolution of reading: The selected writings of Kenneth S. Goodman on the reading process* (pp. 3–45). Portsmouth, NH: Heinemann.

Goodman, Y., & Goodman, K. (2003). To err is human: Learning about language processes by analyzing miscues. In A. Flurkey & J. Xu (Eds.), *Revolution in reading: The selected writings of Kenneth S. Goodman on the reading process* (pp. 222-245). Portsmouth, NH: Heinemann.

Goodman, Y., & Marek, A. (Eds.). (1996). *Retrospective miscue analysis: Revaluing readers and reading.* Katonah, NY: Richard C. Owen.

Goodman, Y., Watson, D., & Burke, C. (1987). *Reading miscue inventory: Alternative procedures.* Katonah, NY: Richard C. Owen.

Howell, K., & Lorsen-Howell, A. (1990). Fluency in the classroom. *Teaching Exceptional Children 22* (3): 20–23.

The man who kept house. (1962). In J. McInnes (Ed.), *Magic and make-believe* (pp. 282–287). Toronto: Nelson.

Piaget, J. (1977). *The development of thought: The equilibration of cognitive structures.* New York: Viking.

Pikulski, J., & Chard, D. (2003). Fluency: Bridge between decoding and reading comprehension. *The Reading Teacher, 58,* 510–519.

Rasinski, T. V. (1990). Investigating measures of reading fluency. *Educational Research Quarterly, 14*(3), 37–44.

Rasinski, T. V. (2003). *The fluent reader.* New York: Scholastic.

Rosenblatt, L. M. (1978). *The reader, the text, the poem: The transactional theory of the literary work.* Carbondale, IL: Southern Illinois University Press.

Samuels, S. J. (1979). The method of repeated readings. *The Reading Teacher 32* (4): 403–408.

Samuels, S. J., Schermer, N., & Reinking. (1992). Reading fluency: Techniques for making decoding automatic. In S. J. Samuels & A. E. Farstrup (Eds.), *What research has to say about reading instruction* (pp. 124–144). Newark, DE: International Reading Association.

Smith, F. (1994). Understanding reading: *A psycholinguistic analysis of reading and learning to read* (5th ed.). Hillsdale, NJ: Erlbaum.

Smith, F. (1996). *Reading without nonsense* (3rd ed.). New York: Teachers College Press.

Stanovich, K. (1991). Discrepancy definitions of reading disability: Has intelligence led us astray? *Reading Research Quarterly 27* (1): 7–29.

Stayter, F., & Allington, R. (1991). Fluency and the understanding of texts. *Theory Into Practice, 30*, 143–148.

Zutell, J., & Rasinski, T. (1991). Training teachers to attend to their students' oral reading fluency. *Theory Into Practice, 30*, 211–217.

INDEX

P

R